Media, Messages, and Men

New Perspectives in Communication

Media, Messages, and Men

New Perspectives in Communication

by
John C. Merrill
and
Ralph L. Lowenstein
(University of Missouri, Columbia)

DAVID McKAY COMPANY, Inc., NEW YORK

Media, Messages, and Men

To our Journalism 300 Students,
who have helped us crystallize
many of these ideas and opinions

LIBRARY OF CONGRESS CATALOG CARD NUMBER: 77–155260
MANUFACTURED IN THE UNITED STATES OF AMERICA

Table of Contents

Introduction

This is not a typical "survey of journalism" or introductory textbook in mass communications. At least we hope it is not that. We have tried to provide a distinctive kind of book, one which should at least be a beginning in the direction of involving the reader in thoughtful consideration of the basic issues in journalism (and communication generally) as they relate to individual men and to society.

Rather than attempting to survey the whole, multifaceted field of mass communication and submerging the reader beneath a mountain of facts and dates, we have tried to delve into a number of problem areas and issues that we believe will serve as a stimulus to serious thinking, discussion, and further reading by the student. Instead of producing a "fact-oriented" book and engaging in the routine task of informational "bead-stringing" so often found in books of broad scope, we have sought to make this an "idea-oriented" book—one that we believe will have a special appeal in today's academic atmosphere where students are concerned with issues and imbued with a healthy desire to challenge sacred cows, debunk traditional and unanalyzed clichés, and get directly to the core questions and first principles.

Therefore, the reader expecting to find on these pages an exposition of journalistic *technique*—how to write headlines, editorials, etc.—or a restatement of historical highlights, media statistics, and the like will be disappointed. Innumerable books and directories are available to provide such data. This book, rather than providing such a broad substantive overview, is designed to provide some catalytic observations about issues and problem areas related to the mass media. These are issues and problems that are increasingly being discussed by all segments of our society; they are no longer simply intellectual subjects to be considered by journalists and mass media people at professional meetings or in professional and academic journals. They are now, as they always should have been, *public* issues and problems.

For several years each of the authors has taught a large section of a required course every semester called "Mass Media and Society" at the University of Missouri School of Journalism. We have found that the juniors, seniors, and graduate students enrolled (some 500 a year) are intrigued and challenged by a course oriented in the same way as we have tried to fashion this book. Since most curricula of journalism schools and departments give overriding stress to practical, professional, or techniques courses such as reporting, editing, and feature writing, we feel that an "idea" course such as this is essential somewhere in a journalism student's education. Increasingly, similar courses are making their appearance in journalism curricula—on the undergraduate and graduate levels—and we feel this book will be useful in these courses.

We have, to a large extent, based this book on lectures given in our "Mass Media and Society" course and on many discussions with students about the course. Since the book deals with the broad problems of communication and society and overlaps with concerns of many academic fields (e.g., sociology, psychology, and philosophy), it is certainly possible that it might be valuable as collateral reading in several nonjournalism courses. Practicing journalists and even laymen might even find it interesting.

At any rate we have tried to provide an eclectic book, a heuristic book—a volume that will invite the reader to think and to argue, to read further about the various issues and problems facing modern journalism and society. The reader will, certainly, accumulate some factual information from these pages, but the book's main purpose is to serve as a catalyst to thought and discussion. Footnotes are kept to a minimum since the book is largely an attempt to provide fresh insights and theoretical concepts. However, we have provided at the end of the book an annotated bibliography of a few carefully chosen books related to the subjects discussed in these pages; these books are suggested for the student's further reading if he feels so inclined to obtain contrary viewpoints, deeper histori-cal perspective, or a more substantial body of facts.

For those readers who might like to know which of the authors wrote which of the chapters, this guide is provided: *Merrill*—Chapters 1, 7, 9, 11, 12, 14, 15 and 16; *Lowenstein*—Chapters 2, 3, 4, 5, 6, 8, 10, 13, and 17.

Certainly the authors realize that not all students and professors—and certainly not all media practitioners—will agree with many of our view-points, opinions, and ideas. We welcome such disagreement. We are not trying to gain proselytes for our concepts; we are attempting to get people concerned with issues and problems related to mass communication and society. If we are able to stimulate discussion, thinking, argument, and further reading by what we say in these pages, we shall have our reward.

J.C.M. and R.L.L.

Part I

Media: A New Look
at Changing Roles

1.

The Process of Communication

THE 1960S, AND EVEN MORE THE 1970S, MAY WELL BE considered the Age of Communication. Everyone appears to be concerned about the communicative act, about understanding and misunderstanding, about human involvement and human response. Talk and printed words proliferate on the subject of language, symbols, signs—on the whole matter of a person speaking to another person, people speaking to people, and institutionalized persons speaking to specialized and mass audiences. Language about language, communication about communication—*metalanguage* and *metacommunication*—is in vogue.

It is understandable that concern about communication is growing. Certainly communication has been, is, and will be, a fundamental—essential—process in human activity and society, since in social living men must share, at least to some degree, their desires, knowledge, experiences, and thoughts. It is only because of communication that societies exist, we are told. But in spite of all the benefits we might list for communication, it would be well for us to consider the possibility of having too much communication, that moderation in all things, including communication, is the most rational position. Surely no per-

3

son—at least in an "advanced" nation—can believe we are moderate in our communication activities.

As crises escalate throughout the world, as population and pollution explode everywhere, we find an interesting accompanying phenomenon: an escalation of rhetoric and an explosion of spoken, electronic, and printed messages.

The Communication Explosion

Everybody is talking. Increasing thousands of persons are writing. Messages are flooding in upon us from all sides in tidal waves. A "concern" with communication has increased messages in geometric proportions since the late 1950s, the dams of verbal restraint have burst, and the entire social and intellectual environment may well be undergoing a communication pollution that will threaten our whole social fabric with chaos and frustration and disrupt the functioning of our interpersonal civilizing ecology. The more communication we get, the less it is taken seriously. In a sense we are having a period of communication inflation where messages become "cheaper" (of less value) as they become more numerous.

Many readers will perhaps think these words too harsh or pessimistic. It may be that they are, but increasingly we are made aware of the tremendous verbal pollutants stretching endlessly before our eyes and droning ever more loudly in our ears. Fortunately for us and our sanity we are able to screen out most of these messages; we are able to select and reject with our amazing perceptive mechanisms; we are able to "tune out" much of the communication content that daily inundates us.

The greater the number of messages, the greater the bulk of trivia and destructive material that fights for our attention. Undoubtedly in it all there is also an increase in total quality, but this seems to become obscured in the repetitious, jargonized gush of pap and prattle. No wonder there is a "credibility gap." What do we believe? Which of the many viewpoints, versions, is the correct one? Does the mushrooming of information really help us to live better lives, react more humanely toward other persons, understand better the world around us, grow less frustrated?

Little wonder more and more sensitive persons are largely detaching themselves from the world of communication. Having too much information, too much knowledge, may well be a dangerous thing. Ignorance perhaps is really bliss, and a kind of "ostrich complex" may prove the sanest stance for a human being to take today. Of course, it is impossible for a person to escape entirely the pervasive impact of communication. For, as the national populations explode throughout the world, the additional millions are talking and writing—thrusting their opinions and ideas on one another with growing intensity. Physically we cannot escape the communication explosion; we must learn to live with it, and if our psychological shelters are not constructed quickly and well, we and our children will certainly suffer serious and lasting damage from the intellectually and emotionally debilitating fallout.

The Nature of Communication

What has been said above will not find favor with many modern students of, and apologists for, communication. And their number is large. It is the "in" thing to see communication not only as *social cement* but to view it as the hope for a troubled world. If we could only communicate with one another, we could solve many of our problems, go a long way toward eliminating friction, and usher in a new day where understanding has replaced misunderstanding; and we are told that this understanding would result in social harmony, interpersonal brotherhood, and peace. If there are persons who have such faith in communication, and there are many, we should take a closer look at this miraculous process of communication that offers us such hope.

The term "communication" comes from the Latin *communis* (common) or *communicare* (to establish a community or a commonness, or to share). At least it is clear that the term implies a sharing, a meeting of minds, a bringing about of a common set of symbols in the minds of the participants—in short, an understanding. Communication, then, as a process, is a two-way street; messages flow both ways, resulting in a participating procedure, in shared responses. It should be reiterated here that we are considering communication as a *process*, not as a synonym for "message." One may speak of *a communication* in the way he speaks of a message. In that sense there may be a communication without there being a receiver of the message. But when we speak of communication (a process), there must be both sender (communicator) and receiver (communicatee).

Communication is basically a social process. Not only with a spoken and written language do we communicate, but also with a wide variety of actions (kinesic communication), with smiles, frowns, gestures, nods, handshakes, shrugs, embraces, pushes, blows, etc. Actions do, indeed, speak louder than (or as loud as) words in interpersonal communication, as well as in communication between nations. In addition to gesture, tactile, and action "language," we also communicate in innumerable subtle ways such as modes of dress and social formalities. We constantly create misunderstandings with our nonverbal "language" as well as with our verbal language. As Edward T. Hall says in *The Silent Language*, an excellent discourse on nonverbal communication, tremendous distortions exist among men trying to communicate with each other. "The job of achieving understanding and insight into the mental processes of others," Dr. Hall says, "is much more difficult and the situation more serious than most of us care to admit."

Students of communication look at the communication process in different ways. Colin Cherry in his *On Human Communication* has called communication essentially a "relationship" formed by what he refers to as the "transmission of stimuli and the evocation of responses." Probably the most common way to look systematically at the communication process is to resort to the well-known paradigm by Harold Lasswell: *Who says what, in which channel, to whom, with what effect?* So we can say that in every communication situation there is a *source* generating a *message* that is transmitted through a *channel* to an *audience*. And, then, theoretically there is some kind of response on the part of the audience. José Aranguren, a highly respected Spanish philosopher and student of communication, has said that communication may be defined as any transmission of information by: a. the emission, b. the conduction and c. the reception of d. a message. Most writers on communication would probably add an e. to Aranguren's paradigm: the response by the receiver.

However, in theory a situation may be envisioned where a speaker speaks and there is no audience; this would be the case of a message destined nowhere outside the speaker. Of course, the speaker may not know this. The *response* in this case would take place within the speaker himself. Actually this is a very real possibility in communication; most of us "talk to ourselves" more often than we care to admit. Taking into consideration all the many ways to look at the communication process, it is probably safe to say that the communication always requires four factors—source, message, channel, and destination. When the source (communicator) has translated his mental message into symbolic stimuli (message), he channels it to the destination (communicatee) in some manner (medium or channel). If these stimuli (message) "get through" and are understood by the destination (communicatee is able to decode it), then the communication process is concluded. Most likely, if the communicatee does respond to the message overtly, his response will actually be the first step in another communicative process, he becoming now the communicator and his "response" being the new "stimulus" or message directed toward somebody else.

Many communication scholars are insistent that really we do not communicate "messages"; rather we physically transmit only signals or signs—visible, audible, or tactile. But, as Colin Cherry points out, the mere transmission and reception of a physical signal does not bring about communication. It stimulates the "message" *in* the recipient who perceives it; in other words the signal has the potential for triggering or selecting responses in the recipient. Messages, then, are really no more than "triggering" mechanisms; they actually have no *content*. As Cherry has said, the information content of a message is nothing really more than the property or *potential* of the signals to elicit a response in the receiver.

In the process of communication there are participants, interacting. The *encoder* (formulator of the message) either sends the message himself or relays it to another to send (the communicator). Most often the encoder and the communicator are one and the same person. The message is sent to a person who translates the symbols of the message into his own meaning context; this receiver-translator is called the *decoder* of the message. He can also be called the communicatee, the receiver, the recipient, the receptor, the audience, or the destination. The communicatee or receiver of the message, upon getting the message, then reacts or responds, and when he does this *overtly* he becomes the encoder (communicator) of a message which goes back to the original communicator or to someone else. In other words, the decoder becomes the encoder of a new message, a return-message usually. This return-message, sent by a receiver back to the sender, is usually referred to as "feedback." This feedback or response may be immediate or delayed in reaching the original sender of the message. In some circumstances, the original sender may "sense" or "infer" a kind of response on the part of the receiver when really there is no empirical manifestation. This type of feedback is sometimes called *inferential feedback;* it is certainly not highly reliable.

Immediate feedback occurs in small-group dialogue or in person-to-person communication where a conversation necessitates a give and take. It may occur in any communication situation where a speaker may be interrupted in the process of his talk by a question or a comment.

Delayed feedback occurs in various kinds of situations, but most often it is thought of as having to do with *mass* communication, where, for instance, a newspaper reader might write a letter to the editor about something he read in the paper, or a television viewer might phone a station about some remark he has just heard or about a program that he watched the day before.

Mass communication delayed feedback, of course, is highly selective and the communicator only gets an insight into how a very minuscule portion of his audience feels about his message. In addition, this delayed feedback usually comes in so slowly that the communicator is unable to use it to revamp his message. It is also quite likely that those members of a mass audience who provide feedback are *atypical* members of the audience; therefore, the communicator cannot assume very much on the basis of their delayed feedback. On the other hand, in small-group, face-to-face communication where immediate feedback is possible, the communicator can see immediately (simultaneously with his message) how he is doing, how he is being understood, and if need be he can revamp his message or can repeat all or portions of it until misunderstandings have been eliminated. Immediate feedback basically answers this question for the communicator: "How am I doing?" Delayed feedback answers the question: "How have I done?"

Types of Communication

Communication can be classified in many ways. One way is to talk of *intra*personal and *inter*personal communication. *Intra*personal communication, of course, simply means the process that goes on *within* a single person whereby he thinks and reacts to his own thinking. The study of this kind of communication is mainly a concern of the psychologist and neurologist and does not interest us in this book except as the process of thinking interests all of us. *Inter*personal communication, the process of communication going on between or among persons, however, is of paramount importance to anyone concerned with man as a social being.

The journalist especially needs to understand this interpersonal process, for it is the world in which he works every day.

He is constantly concerned with the various aspects of interpersonal communication—from the time he seeks to get information from his source through an interview or from an event through observation until he encodes his message for the transmission via a mass medium. Mass communication is a kind of interpersonal communication. Since the mass communicator (an institutionalized person) is endeavoring to communicate with a mass audience, he finds himself in a most difficult and often frustrating situation. Before looking more closely at mass communication, however, let us consider a typology for classifying interpersonal communication generally.

Four main types of interpersonal communication exist: 1. person to person, face to face, 2. small group, face to face, 3. large group, crowd, and 4. mass.

The first of these is the most personal, the most informal and unstructured, and the relationship between the two participants (or the very few participants) who are in immediate proximity is one in which a very great degree of dialogue and empathy can take place, where immediate feedback or reaction is a normal unconscious part of the communication situation. Theoretically, all other factors being equal, this person-to-person communication situation has the best chance for success of the four types.

The second type, the small group, is what Aranguren has called a *microgroup* situation. Examples would be the conference, the discussion group, the forum or round-table discussion, the board meeting, or the seminar. Ample opportunity is provided for the participants to talk and respond but the whole thing is more formal, better structured, more institutionalized than is the person-to-person situation.

The third type of communication situation is the "mass" rally or "crowd-oriented" gathering, which Aranguren calls a *macrogroup*. Members of this situation can, and do, react with one another or with some others in largely an emotional manner. Here, by and large, everyone is a part of the audience, a receiver, a communicatee. One person, or a very few persons, do the primary message sending. Here, for example, might be a Hitler addressing a vast audience in the stadium at Nuremberg, a Billy Graham preaching to an overflow crowd in Madison Square Garden, or a "rock" music group performing before thousands of young people on a hillside. In this kind of situation there is the potential for a kind of "infectious exaltation," a sort of mass hysteria or "collective hypnosis" which will affect thought and action.

The fourth type of communication is mass communication. The media or channels of mass communication are often referred to as "artificial channels" since they have been set up to act *as* (or *for*) *persons;* they are, in effect, institutionalized channels and are generally considered to be newspapers and magazines, radio, television, films, and cheap books. These mass communications media (to be discussed more fully in the next chapter) have an advantage over large gatherings: they rule out pathological crowd phenomena, collective hysteria and loss of self-control. Audience members, in other words, usually react *individually* to messages from mass media.

Mass Communication

The mass (or institutionalized) communicator is much like the bird hunter who fires his shotgun into a clump of trees which he knows contains a large number of different types of birds. He aims at no one bird in any one tree. He does not even see the individual trees or the individual birds. He simply blasts away in a scatter fashion having faith that he will have some success. And, of course, he will—but to a limited degree. Many birds in the tree cluster will not be hit at all, by any of the pellets. Others will be hit solidly with many pellets, and others will receive only glancing shots having little or no effect on them. The hunter may have a fairly good idea as to what kinds of birds are in the tree cluster but he is not sure, nor does he know the proportions of types. He knows that his blast (the mass communicator's message) is capable of achieving its purpose if it hits enough birds with the proper impact to bring about his purpose.

The mass communicator, like the hunter, knows nothing very helpful about the mass audience. He knows that it is large, unseen, that it is composed of members who are unknown to him and to one another, that it is scattered in an uneven pattern, that it is impersonal, and that it is heterogeneous. He knows that his message being sent simultaneously into this mass audience will reach some, and not others, of the audience. He knows also, however, that his message will reach other members of the audience *second hand* (the bird-hunter analogy breaks down here) through opinion leaders and *conveyer persons*. He knows that, probably, his message will be distorted as it diffuses through various stages of conveyer persons. And what is more frustrating to him, he will never really know *how* his message was understood by the mass audience or portions of it. All he can assume is that it reached *some* persons who selectively perceived it in many different ways.

When we talk about "mass communication," we immediately get into semantic trouble. We understand it to some extent, but not completely. For instance, we say that a mass communicator is an institutionalized person: a person representing a disseminating medium such as a newspaper, a television station, or a magazine. Or we think of the institution *itself* as communicating *to* (seldom *with*) the mass audience. The complication really begins, however, when we begin thinking about the mass audience itself. Sociologists tell us that it is large, anonymous, heterogeneous, ever changing, and scattered. They tell us more, but that is the gist of their definition. So we know that the mass audience is large. But how large? We do not really know. We know that it is anonymous. And by that we assume that its members are unknown to one another and to the mass communicator. We know that it is heterogeneous. By that we assume that its members are diverse—of different sexes, ages, educational levels, religions, races, and on and on. And we know that the mass audience is dynamic and scattered. By this we assume audience members are tuning in and out and they are not in one geographical location; they do not form a group. They cannot be addressed by the communicator in one place, in a face-to-face situation.

Now, after saying all this, we still are not quite satisfied. There are still unanswered questions, but generally such a definition suffices; it gives us a generalized idea of what a mass is, although it is very fuzzy around the edges. It certainly is meaningful enough to indicate quite clearly how very difficult it would be to communicate with it. How does the mass communicator make his decisions about what this mass audience wants? How does he know how well he has done with his messages? How does he know when he should change (or stop) his messages? Mainly *by intuition*. Of course, many mass communicators have access to surveys, polls, and selective-delayed feedback that give them some "feeling" about their audience, but generally they communicate intuitively or egoistically. They sense, on the basis of their own likes and dislikes, what at least many in the mass audience will want. In effect, they project their own biases on the mass audience. Contrary to many high-sounding rationales for message determinism by mass communicators, the day-to-day decisions are made in a self-projective, existential manner. And it is probably about as good a way as you can handle messages going to this amorphous, ever-changing, almost mystical entity (or nonentity) called a mass audience.

Barriers to Communication

Effective communication implies communication where an understanding is established, where the message elicits in the receiver the response desired by the sender. In effective communication the message "gets through" to the communicatee and his meaning is very similar to that of the communicator. It is extremely difficult to achieve effective communication; in fact, many students of communication say it is really impos-

sible. But, at least we can say that there are cases where participants come to something that must pass for understanding—a
similar sharing of meaning. Many barriers exist to disrupt or
frustrate communication. Probably the two most important are
often referred to as "noises." They are: 1. mechanical noise,
and 2. semantic noise. And they are at work in every type of
communication situation.

Mechanical noise. This is often referred to as physical or
channel noise. It is in most respects what laymen think of as
"noise," at least when related to the electronic media of mass
communication or to oral interpersonal communication. For
example, mechanical noise that would disrupt communication
would be static on radio, "snow" or other screen distortion on
television, hums in public-address systems, coughing or laughing
by members of an audience. In the print media, examples of
mechanical noise would be poor printing that results in illegibil-
ity, lines of type missing or upside down, torn pages, missing
paragraphs or story continuations to other pages, or muddy or
wet pages.

Semantic noise. This is, in a sense, not really a noise at all.
It is an interference with the message brought on by "meaning"
discordance or breakdown. Semantic noise filters into a message
through the language used. The more confusion there is among
the participants in the communication situation over the
"meaning" of terms and concepts, the more semantic noise
there is in the message. Semantic noise results in misunderstanding. The participants, in effect, interpret the language of the
message in different ways; therefore, they have differing meanings in their minds. They may have received the message very
clearly, mechanically or phonetically—physically it got through
loud and clear—but due to meaning difficulties (semantic noise)
their communication has broken down.

What are some of the other barriers that tend to hinder or

disrupt effective communication? Here are a few:

Divergent backgrounds of the participants

Differences in education, formal and informal

Differences in interest in the message

Differences in IQ

Differences in language levels and usages

Lack of mutual respect among participants

Differences in such factors as age, sex, race, and class

Mental and/or physical stress at time of communication

Environmental conditions at time of communication

Little or no chance for "feedback" or interaction

Little or no "experiential overlap"—few, if any, common experiences

Lack of skill on part of communicator (poor writer or speaker)

Lack of skill on part of communicatee (poor reader or listener)

Lack of information in message ("empty" message)

Message Entropy

All of these hindrances or barriers to effective communication, and many others which are not mentioned, tend to frustrate, to dissipate, to diminish, to complicate—in short, to change—the messages during the process of transmission. Often this frustration of communication, this change brought about on the message by a multiplicity of barriers, is referred to by communications scholars as *entropy*. Used somewhat differently than it is in the context of engineering or physics, entropy in a more "journalistic" sense relates to the natural tendency of a message to dissipate, fly apart, change, lose information or proper emphasis during the complex communication process.

This is, of course, related to the more precise use of the term by mathematicians and physicists, for as Norbert Wiener has said, there is a tendency everywhere toward disintegration, toward disorganization—an inclination to run down. Entropy might be considered a "measure of disorder," the concept stemming from the Second Law of Thermodynamics which says in essence that systems can only proceed to a state of increased disorder. This, then, can be adapted to communication in a journalistic sense. Just as Wiener sees overall society plagued with increasing confusion and disorientation (entropy), we can look at journalism or simply at one message ("story") and see a similar kind of entropy. Always in journalism there is a breaking down of reality, a tendency toward disorganization and disorientation, a loss of, or change in, primary or basic information, a trend toward informational anarchy.

To give a simple example: a newspaper reporter goes out to "cover" an automobile accident. He arrives on the scene *after the fact*. He begins selecting data related to the accident; he talks with certain persons; he observes certain signs of the accident; he makes certain references. In short, he selects or abstracts a very few aspects of the accident from the *real* accident and proceeds to put these in his notes. The actual accident, with its billions of simultaneous stimuli produced as the accident was taking place, has now been reduced to a few hastily selected impressions in the reporter's mind and notebook. The process of entropy—of loss of information from the message— has begun.

Next, the reporter returns to his typewriter to write "the story" from his notes and mental impressions. Selecting again from his memory and scribbled notes, he types out a story which is again a bare skeleton of even his superficial "stimuli-world" collected at the scene of the accident. Then his story goes to copyreaders or editors who further tamper with the information, changing it in some way and very often deleting portions of it. The message changes further, loses additional information. Then the story is sent to the typesetters who often distort the story further in some way. And, if the story, after being set in type, is too long for the space available, it will be shortened until it fits. So the story loses more information. At last the story of the accident is printed in the newspaper, hopefully with no lines missing or out of place.

Now we have the story of the automobile accident translated to some three or four inches of type in a narrow column, competing for readership with dozens of other "stories." The reader will finally add to the process of entropy by further selecting portions of the story to perceive—if he bothers to see the story at all. In other words what finally filters into the consciousness of the reader is only a small part of the printed story, which was a small part of the reporter's total perception, which was only a small part of the actual event. So we have an example of message entropy related to a journalistic situation. No wonder many persons are concerned about "communication gaps" and "credibility gaps." These gaps are intrinsic in the very process of communication, and the mass media simply project them on a mass screen.

2.

The Elements of Mass Media Channels

MASS MEDIA RESEARCHERS TEND TO CONCENTRATE UPON THE people and messages involved in the communication process, often giving short shrift to the study of *channels* of mass communication. Perhaps this is because the humans (communicators and audiences) provide a challenge for the complex tools of behavioral science, and because many of the messages lend themselves to precise measurement by content analysis. The channels themselves appear too familiar to warrant much more from the researcher than some sort of communication census—number, locations, ownerships, circulations.

The channel is too basic to the study of mass communication to be so ignored. Marshall McLuhan has declared that "the medium is the message." If he has done no more than force those involved in communication to take a closer look at the media—the physical media—he has done an important service. Perhaps the medium is not the message.* But the medium often *shapes* the message and sometimes influences the event

*McLuhan has also referred to the medium as the "massage" and the "mess-age."

that forms the basis of the message. It always affects the communicator and the audience.

The chart on the following page is an attempt to take a second look at the physical and economic characteristics of the media from a slightly different perspective. These elements of mass media channels are certainly not newly invented ones. They are qualities that are familiar to everyone, but they are arranged in a pattern that allows us to compare the media to each other and gain new insights into the effect of the channel on the event, the communicator, the message, and the audience.

Elements of Reproduction

In the pre-mass-communication period, the ordinary individual depended upon other men to record, interpret, and transmit messages for him, usually in a very personal way. The era of mass communication arrived when men were able to develop machinery of reproduction that could either substitute for the personal communicator or multiply his messages. The era of mass communication began with Gutenberg's development of movable type in the fifteenth century, and it continues today with the perfection of computers and satellite transmission. Man has just now completed the task of popularizing machinery that can utilize all the elements of reproduction. He stands only on the threshold, however, of sophisticating his machinery for maximum fidelity and multiplication of the original message.

The five elements of reproduction are: 1. *verbal symbols*, the use of ideographs or the phonetic alphabet to reproduce the spoken language, 2. *picture symbols*, the use of woodcuts, engravings, and similar devices (including photoelectric cells) to depict the original event, 3. *color*, processes utilized to highlight verbal symbols or give lifelike hues to picture symbols, 4. *sound*, the reproduction or transmission of the original voices, music, noises, etc., and 5. *motion*, the reproduction or transmission of animation.

Elements of Mass Media Channels

Print Media → Books, Magazines, Newspapers

Sound Media → Radio, Recordings

Motion Media → Movies, Television

	Books	Magazines	Newspapers	Radio	Recordings	Movies	Television
elements of REPRODUCTION	Verbal Symbols Picture Symbols Color	Verbal Symbols Picture Symbols Color	Verbal Symbols Picture Symbols Color	Sound	Sound	Verbal Symbols Picture Symbols Color Sound Motion	Verbal Symbols Picture Symbols Color Sound Motion
elements of CIRCULATION	Portability Reviewability	Portability Reviewability	Portability Reviewability	Portability Simultaneity	Reviewability		Simultaneity
elements of FEEDBACK	Verbal Non-Verbal	Verbal Non-Verbal	Verbal Non-Verbal	Verbal Non-Verbal	Verbal Non-Verbal	Verbal Non-Verbal	Verbal Non-Verbal
elements of SUPPORT (U.S.)	Single Sales	Single Sales Subscriptions Advertising	Single Sales Subscriptions Advertising	Advertising	Single Sales	Single Sales	Advertising

The print media (books, magazines, and newspapers) have utilized the three elements of reproduction to which they have been limited since the earliest days of printing. The Gutenberg Bible, for example, used color to highlight initial letters, and some books of the same era were color illustrated (illuminated). The challenge through the centuries has been to improve the fidelity of these elements through better designed letters and reproduction processes, and to design machinery that would speed up the printing process itself.

Theoretically, the motion media should be superior to the print and sound media, since movies and television can utilize all five basic elements of reproduction. Verbal symbols, for example, can be reproduced on film, and certainly television is, in a sense, a radio, since it can transmit sound in the same way as radio. In fact, if the screen went "black," the television set could substitute for a radio set, and if a page of print were flashed on the TV screen, the screen could substitute for a newspaper.

Though motion media symbolize perhaps the ultimate in gathering together all the elements of reproduction, they lack certain elements in other categories and some of their advantages are potential rather than actual.

Elements of Circulation

Given a literate (in the case of print media) and moderately affluent audience, three basic elements are necessary to achieve maximum circulation: 1. *portability*, the ability of the medium to reach members of the audience, wherever they may be, 2. *reviewability*, the ability of the message to be received and/or reviewed at the audience's convenience, and 3. *simultaneity*, the ability of the medium to deliver the message to the audience at the instant the message originates.

Obviously, portability and reviewability are relative terms, while simultaneity is an absolute term. For example, radio has achieved real portability through the development of the transistorized and battery-operated set; some record players and television sets are transistorized and battery-operated, also, and thus have achieved "portability," but such equipment is not in common usage. Most sets are bulky (when compared to a newspaper or a transistor radio) and umbilically dependent on an external power supply.

Only radio and television have achieved simultaneity. Through these media, the listener or viewer can make instantaneous contact with an event or message. With the other media, there is always a time lag, newspapers experiencing the shortest and books and motion pictures perhaps the longest. It should be noted, however, that paperback book publishers can, when the need arises, deliver a product to the newsstands and booksellers within a week after receiving the raw copy. The ability of radio and television to "circulate" a message immediately has all but eliminated the tradition of newspaper "extras."

Reviewability, too, is a relative term in that one could review a radio program if he chose to record it, and technology has now placed electronic recording of television programs almost within the grasp of the affluent American. Since the first practice, however, is too awkward to be practical, and the latter technology is not yet commonly and economically available, we could say that these two media are not reviewable.

Reviewability also implies "previewability," the quality of permitting the audience to know what they will find inside the total message presentation. Books, magazines, and newspapers accomplish this with tables of contents, indexes, and headlines. Recordings use the dust jacket for this purpose, and some television news shows give hints of the various messages to be presented by locating the correspondents who will appear on the program.

Since movies do not achieve any of the three elements of circulation, there would seem to be an implication that movies do not "circulate" at all. This, of course, is not true. What the blank space in the chart implies is that movies have the most severe circulation handicaps. The product of all the other channels can be consumed by the audience without the aid of a middleman; the product of motion picture studios is a film that is of no benefit to the average viewer until it is projected by someone else. Projection equipment achieves a low degree of portability. People must come *to* the projector under normal conditions* and even then a special darkened room must be provided—or the film must be shown at night. The film is not easily reviewable by the viewer. He must sit through the entire film again to review any part of the message. And in most cases he must pay a second time in order to review it a second time. Finally, it usually takes longer to record, edit, and distribute a professionally produced motion picture than the messages distributed by any other medium. It should be added, however, that the motion picture industry has been able to improve circulation by grafting its product onto the medium of television.

Elements of Feedback

The channel is a major determinant in the flow of feedback from the audience. A medium that encourages feedback is likely to adjust more rapidly to audience needs and involve its audience more in the process of mass communication. Conversely, a channel that restricts feedback is likely to lag behind audience tastes. Worse, such a medium contributes to audience (and society's) frustration.

Each medium receives two kinds of feedback, *verbal* and *nonverbal*. To say that all media feedback is of the same quality and quantity, however, would be far from the truth. These are relative terms. Verbal feedback for books, recordings, and movies might consist of reviews by critics and direct suggestions by distributors. For television, it could mean reviews, actual criticism from viewers in the form of letters and telephone calls, or comments from the sponsors who support the program. For

---

*In developing countries, or rural and isolated areas of modern countries (e.g., Russian Siberia), "portable" projection equipment is brought into villages on a regular basis to provide visual entertainment, education, and information.

radio, it would consist primarily of telephone calls to local stations; for magazines, most verbal feedback would be in letters to the editor; for newspapers, there could be a barrage of letters and phone calls to editors of various departments (including the circulation department).

In considering verbal feedback, we must consider two subfactors, *proximity* and *participation*. It is simpler and more convenient for a reader to transmit feedback to a local newspaper (it is closer) than to a national magazine. It is simpler to complain to a television station about locally originated programs than about network programs. The latter complaint necessitates an intermediary for transmission—or the expense of a long-distance call, or the consumption of time in writing a letter.

As far as participation is concerned, it is more satisfying to write a letter to a local newspaper or a national magazine because the reader then has some hopes that his feedback message will be shared with other readers. His chances of getting his letter into the newspaper are, of course, best, because he faces less competition for more space. By the same token, however, one could say that such a letter writer, while increasing his chances of sharing his opinions with the newspaper's audience, settles for a more limited audience than that of a national magazine.

These subfactors of participation and proximity are extremely important ones because they concern the frustration level of the audience itself. A medium that carries noncontroversial material need worry little about feedback. But a medium that proposes to transmit controversy—and depends upon a sustaining audience for its economic existence—must absolutely open up the reverse channels of feedback or risk frustrating its audience to the point of alienation.

Book publishers generally do not face this problem from the mass audience because they do not depend upon a sustaining audience for continuance of their service, but rather upon single sales. But radio and television do depend upon a sustaining audience. Radio has created "open line" or "party line" programs at the local level to open the channels for feedback. The very nature of television has made this more difficult, although some local stations have produced "talk back" programs in which station representatives answer mailed and telephoned questions and complaints about programming. At least one network news program with a "magazine" format innovated in this area by "printing" (on the television screen) excerpts from letters sent in by viewers.

Each medium also receives some form of nonverbal feedback. This would consist primarily of sales in the case of print media, recordings, and movies; it consists of audience size in the case of radio and television. In short, the audience can register its preferences by buying, subscribing, listening, or viewing. It can register its dislikes by cancelling a subscription or turning off a set. Nonverbal feedback is perhaps far more important than verbal feedback, because verbal feedback is usually only the tip of the iceberg of audience reaction. With books, recordings, and movies, all of which depend upon single sales for a wide variety of offerings, their audience's purchases and admissions are the most important barometer of nonverbal reaction. Newspapers and magazines watch subscription and sales carefully, but gain additional feedback through readership studies. Radio and television must depend upon rating services.

An increasing number of critics, both in and out of government, are now pointing out that feedback is important for the welfare of society itself. The media, they say, must not only permit feedback, but encourage it, and especially encourage the sort of feedback that can be shared with other members of the audience. Feedback thus serves as a safety valve for the frustrations of society and as a means for minority groups to express their views in the mass media that we all consume.

Elements of Support

There are four basic elements of support: *single sales*, *subscriptions*, *advertising*, and *subsidy*. In the United States, subsidy by government and nongovernment organizations is an insignificant factor of support for the mass media. In developing countries, Communist-bloc nations, and countries with both varied and vigorous political parties, this element would become far more important.* The kind and variety of support affect the content of the medium, i.e., "He who pays the piper calls the tune." Books, recordings, and movies, while relatively unaffected by their audiences' verbal feedback (as opposed to critics' feedback), receive almost immediate audience reaction to a product or type of product. The verdict of single sales is swift and often merciless. And since the sometimes mercurial reaction of audiences can be measured more quickly by single sales, even magazines that depend on subscriptions for the great bulk of their circulation give more weight to single sales for gauging current audience satisfaction with the publication—and so do advertisers.

One could hypothesize that those media having an even balance of income from single sales, subscriptions, and advertising would have distinct advantages over those media that do not. The support from the audience would then provide about two-thirds of the income of the medium, and this income would be produced by thousands of sources (members of the audience). In such a situation, single sales would be a finely tuned barometer of audience reaction, subscriptions would provide long-term financial stability, and advertising would enable the medium to provide better programming at a cheaper price.

Such a situation, of course, is Utopian. Books and recordings sell at a relatively high price, since they depend upon single sales only. The risk is high for each book or record because the audience awaiting each message is rather unpredictable. The same situation holds for movies, although at least one part of the channel (the local distributor) introduces advertising

---

*The subsidy in such cases is often outright payments. But it may take more subtle forms: government advertising, government purchases of bulk copies of the publication, or government subsidy of programming.

at the local level and subsidizes the operation by selling refreshments.*

Popular magazines and newspapers in the United States are largely supported by advertising income, and the loss or gain of advertising lineage can alter the profit status of a publication much more rapidly than single sales and subscriptions. Radio and television are wholly supported by advertising, forcing these media to react more quickly to the exigencies of advertising than to their own good judgment about the needs of the audience and society.

Advertising's impact on media, then, is a result primarily of its concentrated power. It provides more money from fewer people. Unlike the audience, it does not buy the message; it adds to the message, it interrupts the message—and sometimes it alters the message. It has a power not only for bad, but also for great good. The entire question of advertising will be considered in more detail in Chapter 6 of this section.

Additional Elements

Although the elements of reproduction, circulation, feedback, and support are the major elements determining media characteristics, there are additional factors that also affect the efficiency and effect of each medium: 1. number of channels within a medium, 2. expense of operation, 3. complexity of distribution, 4. frequency of publication, and 5. flexibility of channel.

Number of Channels. Print media, recordings, and movies theoretically can proliferate to infinity. In fact, their numbers are limited by factors of competition and audience saturation. There is a limited spectrum of frequencies for both radio and

---

*The movie-going habit is so pronounced in Israel (which did not establish general television on a regular basis until 1969) that an equivalent to the Audit Bureau of Circulations actually measures movie audiences for purposes of setting advertising rates at major movie houses.

television, and this initially invited government intervention as a "traffic cop" to assign and patrol frequencies. It also justified later intervention by the government to force the limited number of licensees to act in the public "convenience and necessity." However, technology and affluence are constantly expanding the spectrums of radio and television, e.g., frequency modulation (FM), shortwave, ultra high frequency (UHF), and cable television (CATV), to name a few. The channels of television will be opened even wider in the future by communication satellites and "cassette TV" (also known as electronic video recordings).

Expense of Operation. Wide fluctuations in cost occur within each medium. Television is a highly expensive medium to establish and operate. Letterpress (hot type) newspaper operations are expensive; offset presses (cold type) are less expensive; and a publisher can sometimes "rent" a newspaper channel for a very low price indeed. Underground presses operate on a shoestring by doing all their layouts and pasteups themselves, then simply taking the finished pages to an offset job press for publication. However, many magazine and book publishers do the same thing, though in a somewhat grander and more sophisticated style. Centralized presses handling many different publications utilize equipment at greater efficiency and reduce publication costs. Networks already "rent" cable and line facilities from the telephone companies, and sometimes they share the costs of "pool" equipment and operators for special events.

Complexity of Distribution. The more middlemen, the more complex the process of distribution for each medium. Book publishers have to deal with a tangle of salesmen, distributors, book clubs, and retail outlets. Magazines must consider address changes, the Teamsters, and mail schedules, among other things. Newspapers, if they are lucky, have fewer problems with the Teamsters and the mails, but more with the paperboy who throws the paper into the proverbial puddle—or forgets to throw it at all. Radio and television have no middlemen (only a few middle machines) in the distribution process, although local stations frequently do not buy, and thus do not retransmit, the entire package of programs offered by the networks. The complexity of distribution can result in a control just as severe as a limitation on the number of channels. If it is too difficult to get a magazine or book to a retail outlet in a small town, for example, the publication will never be delivered there at all.

Frequency of Publication. The first newspaper in the American colonies, *Publick Occurrences Both Forreign and Domestick*, pledged to publish "once a moneth (or if any Glut of Occurrences happen, oftener)." Today, magazines and newspapers are committed to regular publication, and radio and television to regular broadcasting. Leo Rosten referred to two deadly "curses" of the mass media: they are "committed to periodic and unalterable publication," and a "gargantuan amount of space" and time "*has* to be filled."* The more frequently a medium publishes or broadcasts, the more likely it is to transmit news and present it briefly. Conversely, the less frequently a medium publishes, the more likely it is to transmit interpretation and present it in detail. We move on a continuum from books (lengthy interpretation) to magazines (short interpretation) to newspapers (lengthy news) to television (brief news) to radio (headlines). These are oversimplifications, of course. There is sometimes news in books and often interpretation in radio.

Flexibility of Channel. Print media can adjust their sizes to accommodate differing quantities of information and advertising. A Saturday afternoon newspaper is usually extremely thin, a Sunday paper normally quite fat. Unfortunately, advertising content is usually the key to size, not the amount or importance of the news. Radio and television are cursed and

---

*Leo Rosten, "The Intellectual and the Mass Media," *Daedalus* (Spring 1960), p. 335.

imprisoned by time. They must operate a certain number of hours each day, and they have to fill up the hours. And when there is a "Glut of Occurrences" they cannot expand into another frequency or stretch the viewing hours during which they operate. To present such material, they must encroach upon other time already allotted to entertainment or advertising. When they feel the need for more revenue, they tend to add more commercials rather than simply increasing the price of a commercial minute, and to do this they must reduce the amount of time previously assigned to entertainment and information. In emergencies, when the electronic media must present breaking news, they must preempt commercially sponsored time, at great financial cost to the networks and local stations. In borderline cases—such as the Senate Foreign Relations Committee hearings on Vietnam in 1966—network executives are torn between public service and corporate loss. The decision is not always easy to make, especially when the financial loss to the networks can extend into the millions of dollars.

Emphasis in the Different Media

Although it is not an "element" as such, some note must be taken of the emphasis in each medium. Certainly the physical advantages and limitations largely determine whether emphasis is on the news, interpretation, or entertainment. Of all seven media, only newspapers emphasize news above interpretation and entertainment. Television has become the preeminent entertainment medium, and both movies and recordings are including much more interpretation in their fare than they once did. Magazines and books have both moved in the direction of offering more interpretation than they did in the past, and less pure entertainment, especially in the form of fiction.

How to Exploit the Elements

Enumerating the elements of mass-media channels and describing them should provide more than an academic exercise.

There is practical value in stopping and taking a hard look at the media with which we deal each day. Audiences are far more aware of what they *don't* like than they are of what they *would* like. It is up to media executives to anticipate audience needs and analyze their own competitive disadvantages, finding solutions if possible.

There are some areas, naturally, in which handicaps cannot be overcome. The print media cannot incorporate sound and motion, for example, under any foreseeable circumstances. But books and newspapers can utilize color to better advantage than they have in the past. It is interesting to note that books, even when they use illustrations, rarely use color illustrations. And newspapers are decades behind magazines in developing techniques for handling color adequately. Advertisers have learned to use color strikingly in newspapers through introduction of preprinted newsprint rolls. Few, if any, newspapers have ever tried the same techniques for the regular news sections of the paper. This would be expensive at first and perhaps too slow for practicality, but innovation in this area of color would be interesting.

A more practical aspect of circulation (and competition) generally being neglected by newspapers and television is the entire element of reviewability and "previewability." Once, when newspapers were four pages or eight pages in size, it took no great effort to read through those pages and at least scan each story. In any case, it was difficult to miss a story. Today, when some urban dailies are regularly producing a newspaper with more than one hundred pages, it is sometimes difficult to *find* a story. Many newspapers already run a simple index on page one, indicating where special sections and certain regular features can be found. *The New York Times* does better. It runs a complete index of all major stories, by categories. It helps the reader further by attempting to gather all related stories, either according to geography or special interest, on the same and succeeding pages. There are few newspapers that have copied the *Times* in this. As newspapers get larger, stories will be even harder to find, and there are many readers who do not want to spend long periods of time scanning and discarding hundreds of headlines in hopes of finding material in which they have a special interest. Newspapers must do a better job of categorizing the news—*and* advertising—and indexing them for readers. They must especially make the vast variety of news they present each day really "previewable."

Television generally does a sad job of "previewing" its own program schedule. *TV Guide* has built its gigantic circulation on the inability of newspapers and television to offer adequate indexes of the daily television fare and content. Television, of course, has definite handicaps in this area. But it is within the realm of possibility for the medium to better satisfy viewer curiosity, and perhaps win larger audiences. At one point during each evening—perhaps just before the prime-time period begins—each network could devote two to five minutes to simply posting on the screen a printed schedule for the rest of the day's (and perhaps next morning's) performances. The schedule could include main headlines and special news features to appear on the network news program, the regular programs for the evening with basic plots or guest stars, and a listing of guests for the evening talk program and next morning's talk program. As CATV operations expand, one entire channel probably should be given over to a programming index for viewers.

Newspapers and radio stations are permitting more verbal feedback generally than they did a few years ago. But there are some newspapers and radio stations that have not yet learned that "action line" and "letters" columns, and intelligently guided "open line" programs, are not only circulation builders but society builders, as well.

3.

The Progression of
Media Development

MASS MEDIA HAVE ALWAYS BEEN IN A PROCESS OF DYNAMIC change, although the progression has been far more visible in some countries than in others. This dynamism—multiplied in the latter half of the twentieth century by technological developments that have allowed mass media to permeate the whole of society—has tended to disguise the fact that there is a clearly defined growth pattern to the mass media in each society.

This pattern of media progression can be called the Elite-Popular-Specialized (EPS) curve: media in any nation grow from *elitist* to *popular* to *specialized*. In the elitist stage, the media appeal to and are consumed by opinion leaders, primarily. In the popular stage, media appeal to and are consumed by the masses of a nation's population, primarily. In the specialized stage, the media appeal to and are consumed by fragmented, specialized segments of the total population. We will define this EPS pattern more carefully later. But it must be noted that there are many countries that do not fall clearly into one stage of this pattern. It is frequently possible for different kinds of media to be in different stages of the EPS pattern within the same country.

33

ELITE-POPULAR-SPECIALIZED (EPS) CURVE
OF MEDIA PROGRESSION

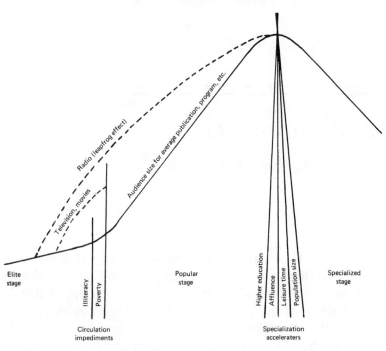

The Elitist Stage

Illiteracy and poverty are daily facts of life in most nations of the world. In such countries, only the elite are literate, and only the elite have the money to obtain the messages from all media. In an underdeveloped country, the average man—even were he literate—could not afford to purchase a daily newspaper regularly, nor could he buy magazines and books. Even for the illiterate, a radio and television set are expenditures not to be taken lightly, with television especially being out of the reach of the average man.

The two rings of this set of handcuffs—*illiteracy* and *poverty*— also serve to restrict large geographical segments of a nonaffluent nation. The urban areas of such a nation may have all the mass media accessible to them; the vast rural areas have none, with the possible exception of radio. Newspapers need roads and literate customers in order to circulate outside of urban areas. Television receivers and motion picture projectors must have sources of electric power; otherwise, with present technology, they are unable to operate in rural villages.

It follows that elitist media have a general content quite a bit different from those media in other stages of the EPS curve. Their material is aimed primarily at informing, but even the entertainment content is set at a higher cultural level. Income from circulation is higher than income from advertising, and the media themselves are relatively expensive to obtain.

Most of the nations of Africa and Asia fall within this stage of media development. In a typical African country, for example, there are only a few newspapers, and their readership is restricted to the elite. There may be no magazines, and such books as exist are imported from other countries. The audience for the print media is an urban, as well as an elite, audience. Television transmitters may not reach far beyond the urban areas; radio has reaching power, but limited "receiving" power, and the nature of radio programming beamed into the rural areas is didactic.

India is an example of a nation whose media fall almost completely in the elitist stage. Although the second largest nation in the world, the country suffers the severe handicaps of poverty and illiteracy. The media, reflecting this, are aimed at the urban elite. A surprisingly large number of newspapers are published in English—the elitist language of the country—and these are also the circulation leaders in most urban centers.* India has only about one radio receiver for every 100 persons in the population (the U. S. has more than 100 radio receivers per 100 population), and radio programming directed at the rural

---

*An exception is the *Malayala Manorama*, printed in the Malayalam language, with a circulation of 260,000. But the state in which it is published, Kerala, has a literacy rate of 90 percent, compared to India's average literacy of 24 percent.

areas has a heavy content of education and agricultural information.

The Popular Stage

Once a nation breaks through the barriers of poverty and illiteracy, its media move into the popular stage. Circulations begin to rise as the media are able to reach larger and larger groups of citizens who are able to read (in the case of print media) and afford mass media. During this stage, we see the dominance of the "mass-mass" media, those films, programs, and publications which appeal to a huge, heterogeneous audience. The contents of the mass media, in short, are designed to appeal to the great majority of the population. The "lowest common denominator" principle, which means that content is geared for the least sophisticated portion of the potential audience, is a successful tool in the popular stage, because most of the potential audience is not very far removed from the lowest common denominator. Of course, there are also specialized publications and programs available in this stage of media development, but these could be said to be vestiges of the elitist stage and elitist mentality in the country, rather than a deliberate attempt to reach a highly fragmented audience.

The media in most of the developed countries of Europe and North America are squarely in this stage of the EPS curve, and so, too, are those of Japan, Israel, Australia, and New Zealand, as well as the media located in the large urban areas of many other countries throughout the world.

It must be noted here that the inexpensive transistor radio has permitted radio stations in fairly primitive countries to *leapfrog* across the barriers of illiteracy and poverty into the popular stage. Radio appeals to the masses in those countries, and indeed reaches the masses. In such countries, radio programming is more didactic and has a lower common denominator than the content of the print media, which essentially remain in the elite category. Motion pictures and television are also able to leapfrog across the barrier of illiteracy, but at the present time are still affected by the poverty barrier. Movie houses, equipment, and admissions are still costly in underdeveloped countries, and no cheap, battery-operated television set has yet appeared to put it in the same class as the transistor radio.

The Specialized Stage

A fully developed country with a wide range of popular media is ready to move into the specialized stage—the third and final stage of the EPS curve—when four factors coalesce: higher education, affluence, leisure time, and population size. Like the transition from the elite to the popular stage, the evolution from popular to specialized is gradual, perhaps so imperceptible that many communicators themselves do not realize they have been left behind by a new audience quite different from the mass audience of the popular stage. A closer look at the four coalescing factors will explain why the audience is interested in more specialized media.

Higher Education. As people specialize professionally and/or intellectually, they have different intellectual and cultural tastes and interests. Elementary and high-school education is largely uniform throughout a nation. When a sizable proportion of the population goes on to university education, individuals leave the homogeneous education path and begin to follow new trails. Specialized literary, scientific, and professional interests are cultivated and developed. These new, individualized interests are not restricted to those who go on to the university. Urban and industrial societies demand job specialization, and those who specialize have a particular interest in publications that offer them an opportunity to hear from and communicate with other persons with the same job specializations.

Affluence. Specialized media can only be obtained by a population able to afford a variety of media; therefore, there is a need for the population to have a high standard of living before this stage can be reached. This means that the average family must be able to afford not only a variety of media (one television set, one radio, one newspaper, and one or two magazines), they must also be able to afford a variety of specialized units within each medium (several radios and television sets, and multiple numbers of publications). Specialized media appeal to a fragmented audience, and this implies a fragmented family, as well, because individual members of the family have different entertainment and intellectual interests. Children, for example, are not interested in television programs that appeal to their parents; wives frequently are not interested in the programs that attract their husbands.

Leisure Time. This factor is closely related to affluence, but it emphasizes that the population needs more than simply the money to buy the products of specialized media. It must have the free time away from work to pursue activities such as travel, hobbies, sports, and other special interests that whet the appetite for specialized media relating to these interests. And the audience must, obviously, have the leisure time in which to consume the greater variety of media products now available.

Population Size. A population must be large enough to support minimum circulations for media. A country with a small population can support publications and broadcasting with a wide appeal; it cannot support those with a very narrow appeal. The audience of any media unit must be large enough to justify the expense of production and distribution, whether income is derived from advertising or subscriptions. Preliminary studies indicate that a country must have a minimum population of about ten million or fifteen million before it can enter the specialized stage.

Some specialized media do exist in small nations, of course, but the communication scene is dominated by popular publications and programs. Theoretically, massive government subsidies could provide specialized programs and publications for a small nation that has otherwise achieved the other three factors characterizing the specialized stage. In fact, however, the cost would be prohibitive, and there are other avenues by which most such nations can obtain specialized media. This will be discussed later.

Only one country—the United States—has so far reached the point where the four factors coalesce, and the U. S. even now is on the point of plunging into the specialized stage of the EPS curve. "Mass-mass" publications are on the wane; popular programming in the electronic media has peaked. This could appear to be an exaggerated statement until one takes a closer look at the individual media.

Books have been in the specialization stage longer than any other medium. With the huge population of the United States as a market, book publishers have been able to attract a substantial number of buyers from among select audiences—children, hobbyists, educational specialists, etc. The era of a massive best seller, such as *Gone With the Wind*, has itself gone with the wind. The "mass-mass" magazines themselves are breathing their last, even as this book is being written. There are only two "mass-mass" magazines remaining in the U. S., *Life* and *Look*, and both are in trouble. They must by their very nature be too general for this era of specialization, a fact that advertisers noted before the publishers. Newspapers, recordings, radio, and motion pictures now seek out specialized audiences to a far greater extent than they did two decades ago. Only television has not yet made the full leap into the specialized stage. It is still a nonspecialized, "mass-mass" medium, gearing its programming, for the most part, to a heterogeneous audience.

Media may achieve specialization in one of two ways: by *unit specialization*, meaning that the entire publication or programming day appeals to a specific audience; or by *internal specialization*, meaning that parts of the publication or parts of the programming day appeal to different audiences.

The *Reader's Digest*, for example, is usually considered a "mass-mass" magazine, simply because it has the largest circulation of any periodical in the United States. But the *Reader's Digest*, though its "total audience" is heterogeneous, is able to appeal to specialized audiences within this group by offering a variety of articles on widely different subjects. It therefore achieves "internal specialization," in a far more effective manner than *Life* and *Look*, which also depend on a heterogeneous audience.

Ethnic stations and classical music stations in urban areas are examples of "unit specialization." The *Financial Times* of England and the *Wall Street Journal* of the U. S. are other examples of "unit specialization." More typically, the average daily newspaper in America is an example of "internal specialization." Since it is usually the only game in town, it must appeal to a heterogeneous audience; however, it runs specialized contents such as stock market reports, recipe pages, political columns, doctor's advice, and horoscopes in order to appeal to special tastes within the audience. For similar reasons, where there are only a few radio stations in a small city, the stations will attempt to appeal as a "unit" to a heterogeneous audience, but at the same time they will attempt to pick out specific audiences by offering a variety of specialized programs.

Television also utilizes "internal specialization," but to a lesser extent than any other medium in the United States. Specialized programs are mostly confined to the daytime hours, and even then the audience appeal is very broad—children, housewives, sports enthusiasts. Evening (or prime-time) programming is still directed toward an all-inclusive audience. Since television is affected by the coalescing of affluence, higher education, leisure time, and population size in the same manner as other media, it is logical to ask why it has been slower in moving into the specialized stage of media development in the United States. The answer is that television has been retarded by the relative expense of receivers, the great cost of programming, and the limited number of channels available in each area. As a result of the last two factors, American audiences have been dependent upon a few national networks for most of their programming choice. Ultra high frequency channels and cable television are now beginning to chip away at the dominance of the networks, and the outcome is likely to be television that is characterized by the same "unit specialization" and "internal specialization" that we already see in the radio medium in the United States.

As a country moves completely into the specialization stage, there is a withering away of the mass media as we know them today. "Mass" media cannot exist without a mass audience. Specialized tastes and abundant channels in every medium must result in an end to the age of the mass audience. Taking its place will be highly fragmented, "specialized" audiences.

Technological Language Theory

What happens to those fully developed nations in which the factors of affluence, higher education, and leisure time have coalesced, but in which there is a population smaller than ten million—or in which there are multiple languages, none of which is spoken by more than ten million persons? Most such nations become "borrowers" of the specialized media of other nations, a fact that has important implications for international communication.

The ability to "borrow" assumes that the entire country or significantly large groups within the country have a familiarity with one of the four "technological languages"—English, French, German, and Russian. Thus, a country like Switzerland could easily consume the specialized media of Germany and France (and, to a remarkable degree, those from English-speaking countries, as well), the French-speaking portion of Belgium "borrows" the media in France, New Zealand "borrows" from other English-speaking countries, etc.

This indicates that fully developed, but small population nations that are not in the mainstream of a "technological language" must make a conscious effort as a matter of national priority to adopt or develop a second language (English, French,

German, or Russian) or otherwise risk creating an ever-widening technology gap between themselves and the major modern nations of the world.*

There is evidence that some advanced nations are already making this effort. One indicator is the international distribution of news magazines, which can be considered specialized publications. Small nations are unable to provide enough subscribers to warrant establishment of a first-rate news magazine with international coverage; they therefore become "borrowers" of such publications from other countries. The table on the following page lists all those countries that have one or more subscribers per thousand of population to *Time* magazine.

It is perhaps not surprising that most of the non-English-speaking countries appearing on the list are nations with a relatively high per capita income, with a primary language unique to their own country, and with an educational program that encourages the study of English even during the years of elementary school. Exceptions to one or more of these factors are Singapore, which is isolated from Mainland China, its natural language link; Switzerland, whose multilanguage, cosmopolitan population probably subscribes to *Der Spiegel* and *L'Express* (German and French news magazines, respectively) in greater numbers than they subscribe to *Time*; and Lebanon, which stands apart from the rest of the Arab world in literacy, per capita income, and religious composition.

Similar studies would probably show that these same nations are very heavy borrowers of specialized English-language publications in fields such as medicine, science, the humanities, and social sciences. Small nations not in the mainstream of technological languages must demand that students seeking a university education first have a familiarity with a mainstream language. Their libraries are filled with books and research

---

*An interesting discussion of the serious disadvantages resulting from small population size can be found in Donald B. Keesing, "Small Population as a Political Handicap to National Development," *Political Science Quarterly* (March 1969), pp. 50-60.

World Distribution of Time Magazine

	Circulation (per 1,000)	Principal Languages	Population (in millions)	Per Capita Income
United States	20.0	English	199.8	$3,412
Canada	19.7	English French	20.8	3,004
New Zealand	10.5	English	2.8	1,930
Australia	6.4	English	12.2	1,840
Ireland	5.3	English	2.9	850
Israel	*4.8*	*Hebrew Arabic*	*2.8*	*1,016*
Singapore	*2.4*	*Chinese Malay*	*2.0*	*533*
Panama & Canal Zone	2.1	English Spanish	1.4	568
Switzerland	*1.7*	*German French Italian*	*6.1*	*2,062*
Liberia	1.6	English	1.2	225
Jamaica	1.5	English	1.9	460
Lebanon	*1.3*	*Arabic*	*2.4*	*480*
Netherlands	*1.3*	*Dutch*	*12.8*	*1,449*
Norway	*1.3*	*Norwegian*	*3.8*	*1,453*
Sweden	*1.2*	*Swedish*	*7.9*	*2,860*
South Africa	1.1	English Afrikaans	19.2	550
United Kingdom	1.0	English	55.3	1,358
Denmark	*1.0*	*Danish*	*4.9*	*1,652*

Sources: Circulation figures listed in *Time* advertisements in *Advertising Age* (Feb. 24, 1969); population and per capita income are 1968 statistics, listed in *The New York Times Encyclopedic Almanac 1970* (New York: The New York Times, 1969).

papers in a language or languages other than the one spoken as a primary language in the country. A nation of less than ten million population is simply incapable of producing up-to-date textbooks for courses that will enroll perhaps less than one hundred students a semester. If they are to offer higher education worthy of the name, they by necessity become borrowers from other countries, and their students must be prepared to do much of their research and reading in this second language.*

The need to know a second language in such countries also extends to those who would seek out specialized information or entertainment (movies, books, recordings) of any kind, because a small nation usually will be unable to satisfy such appetites unless it is done at a prohibitive cost.

Vast numbers of people live in countries of large population size, but where one or more of the remaining three factors necessary for the specialized stage are absent. In these countries, the elite—especially the scientific elite—usually learn a technological language and become individual borrowers from a lending nation offering specialized media. Unfortunately, this does not permit the underdeveloped nation to leapfrog into the specialized stage, nor does it do much to narrow the technology gap. However, it would seem that a conscious effort by such nations to impose the study of a second language during the earliest years of schooling would be a basic move to seek a short cut toward the goal of national development.

Obviously, there is the danger of language "imperialism." Some countries, for nationalistic reasons, artificially discourage the use of a technological language. Nations engaging in this sort of false pride are doing a severe disservice to their own citizens by robbing them of the basic tool for technological advancement.

---

*Hebrew and, to a far lesser degree, Arabic are the primary languages of Israel, which has the highest readership of *Time* of any non-English-speaking country. However, the study of English as a secondary language is mandatory, beginning in the fifth grade of elementary school. An Israeli who completes high school will have had eight mandatory years of English. No student who cannot show a high proficiency in this language is admitted to an Israeli university.

4.

The Print Media: A World View

THERE IS A GENERAL FEELING AMONG COMMUNICATORS THAT the course of print media was relatively placid until the post-World War II years, when the electronic revolution caused a tidal wave that menaced the entire print industry. In fact, however, the print industry has been in the middle of a constant revolution of techniques and tastes since Gutenberg developed movable type in the fifteenth century. Up until that time, the transmission of words had been limited by the output of scribes and controlled by the establishment for whom the scribes worked. Mechanical words, however, multiplied both ideas and literacy, and were the most important weapons in the assaults on the Church in the sixteenth and seventeenth centuries, and on the State in the eighteenth, nineteenth, and twentieth centuries.

The print industry itself, far from maintaining the status quo that one associates with metallic presses, matrices, and type, has undergone rapid changes in looks and appeal. It has not only spawned its own inventions—the steam-driven press, the Linotype, the halftone engraving—but quickly assimilated the inventions of others—the telegraph, telephone, computer, and satellites, to name only a few—and each time the products of the print industry have changed. The halftone, toward the end of the nineteenth century, offered as startling a new vision of the world as did the television set in the middle of the twentieth century. It enabled the print industry to become a picture medium as well as a word medium. It gave the illiterates and marginal literates greater access to information than they had ever had before, and served as a steppingstone toward the goal of full literacy.

Technical developments, then, have altered the looks of the print media and refocused their appeal. But the philosophy of the press has undergone significant changes, too, as a result of stresses exerted by dynamic men and dynamic audiences. Urbanization and rising levels of literacy in the United States forced print media to evolve from a colonial press to a penny press to a specialized press. Similar historical changes have occurred in other modern countries.

This is not to say that print media have been unaffected by television. But it does emphasize that there had been significant traumas caused by developments inside and outside the press before the invention of the cathode tube. Even in the twentieth century, tabloid journalism left its imprint on newspaper personality, and the widening popularity of radio forced the newspaper to relinquish a few of its traditional roles.

The worldwide effect of television on print media is difficult to assess. In many developing countries television, along with radio, has simply filled a communications void. In the more developed nations television has had a more profound effect on radio than it has had on the print media. Everywhere, publishers have feared that television would skim off their advertising revenues. But this has actually occurred only where the print media—magazines, primarily—had already lost the audience that advertisers wanted to reach. Otherwise, advertisers have expanded their budgets to purchase television commercials in addition to print media ads. Daily newspaper income from advertising in the United States, for example, has shown a steady rise in almost every year since World War II.

Television has seized a good portion of the audience (and advertising) of picture-oriented and general-audience-oriented magazines in the U. S. Television replaced them as a "mass-mass medium" and such magazines are perhaps nearing their end. But television has also created the need for new magazines devoted to television schedules and criticism,* and it has made the newspaper a necessity in some homes if only for the reason that the paper provides a schedule of the daily television fare.

Despite their inability to compete successfully with television for the public's time, the print media have still been able to retain the public's interest. Television has not caused a dissolution of the print industry, as some had feared. The number of daily and weekly newspapers in the United States has remained relatively stable since World War II (approximately 1,750 and 10,000, respectively), the production of books has increased (approximately 30,000 titles a year, currently), and magazine births far exceed magazine deaths.

There are obvious reasons for the steady popularity of print media: the world literacy pool gets larger each year, more people are able to afford books and periodicals, and more people find books and periodicals a necessity in obtaining and maintaining professional competence.

Advantages of Print Media

Beyond this, however, print media have innate advantages over radio and television. These advantages accrue despite the overwhelming popularity of the electronic media and their abil-

---

*The second largest circulation magazine in the U.S. is *TV Guide*, which includes a variety of television comment and criticism, as well as program listings. It is the authors' opinion that relatively large sales of *TV Guide* and similar publications in a community indicate that local newspapers are paying too little attention to an activity in which the average American is involved for more than four hours every day.

ity to attract the "mass-mass audience." The outstanding advantage of print media is *reviewability*. This factor was discussed in some detail in Chapter 2. The print media do not exist in "time" in the same manner as sound and motion media. They may be previewed, scanned, or reviewed at the convenience of the reader. One word, one chapter, one picture, or one advertisement can be examined and analyzed at the reader's leisure. The permanence of the written word and the accessibility of words on paper offer advantages that sound and motion media can never equal, even with the arrival of the age of electronic video recording.

There are a number of other factors that are in reality spin-offs from this reviewability factor. They are:

Media Choice. The consumer of print media shops in a supermarket of ideas, entertainment, information, and advertisements. In a free country, the selection available to him is virtually unlimited. The number of brands, their size and price may range toward the infinite as far as the human grasp is concerned.* The consumer of sound and motion media shops in the old corner grocery store. The selection available is finite; he must choose between a number of major brands (sometimes only one brand) in standard sizes and prices. The exotic and gourmet delights are usually not on the shelf.

Message Choice. We speak of "selective perception" as the unconscious act of picking out information that we prefer to read or see—usually information that reinforces our own beliefs—and ignoring information in the same source that goes against our preconceived notions or beliefs. "Message choice" is the characteristic of print media that permits us to make the *conscious* selection, for whatever motive that is within us. Headlines, chapter headings, and illustrations permit us to pick out, in a very convenient manner, information that we find interesting or useful. We spend a good deal of our newspaper reading

---

*The United States alone produces 20,000 magazine titles.

time, for example, simply culling through headlines, quickly discarding stories and advertisements that we do not want to read, and fixing upon those that are more attractive to us. Obviously, we also discard whole bundles of information that we *should* read—information that would be "good for us." But there is pleasure in this choice; we are rarely offended by information that we don't read. On the other hand, electronic media (which offer only limited "media choice") provide *no* "message choice." "Selective perception," of course, is working with a full head of steam, but even so the information that we find useless—or worse, offensive—is still pouring out in an unbroken stream that we can hardly avoid. Some broadcast managers have said that members of the audience can correct this situation by simply switching off the set. However, this is inconvenient for listeners or viewers, and can better be described as "abstention" rather than "choice."

"Message choice" implies that the reader has the option to separate and choose. There are many people in our society who would rather not know about war, poverty, or dissent. From the point of view of society, the fact that radio and television feed them this information, whether or not they want it, is advantageous. From the point of view of the individual, it is disadvantageous. There is wasted time and traumatic shock in being fed information and commercials that one finds useless and even unwanted. This obviously leads to audience frustration and dissatisfaction.

World Trends

The major world trend in the print media is toward monopoly ownership. In the United States, more newspapers each year are purchased by chains, or, as the proprietors themselves prefer to call them, "newspaper groups." Reflecting this trend at a higher level is the expansion of "media conglomerates," huge corporations engaged in multimedia ownership, including books, magazines, newspapers, movies, radio, and television.

The trend toward monopoly is also apparent in other modern, developed countries throughout the world, where, if the government is not already the sole owner of media, the large, privately owned "national" newspapers are tending to swallow those of smaller circulation.

Big business is a fact of life in the developed countries of the world. It is perhaps natural that this be reflected in the communications industry as well. Where newspapers are concerned, the increased competition from other media, especially television, has accelerated this trend toward fewer units owned by fewer corporations. The "party papers" long ago disappeared from the scene in the United States. Now they are beginning to lose the fight for survival in Western Europe, as well. Rising production costs, a failure to attract advertising because of limited circulations, and an inability to compete with the improved products and flexible editorial opinions of independent newspapers are some of the causes for the disappearance of party papers. In some Scandinavian countries, indirect government subsidies are prolonging the lives of party papers. But the fact seems to remain: where the people have a free choice between party newspapers and independently owned papers, the latter emerge victorious.

This will to survive in the face of tougher competition from other newspapers and other media has forced some of the most traditionally minded newspapers to alter their characters. Dependent more and more on advertising to compensate for rising labor and production costs, the "quality" newspapers are coming down from their pedestals and seeking a broader audience. Newspapers would thus seem to be moving counter to the "specialization" trend. On the contrary, they are becoming even more specialized, but it is an "internal specialization." The paper as a unit appeals to a more heterogeneous audience; individual parts of the paper appeal to specialized segments of the audience.

The trend toward monopoly ownership of the print media is not without both advantages and disadvantages. Concentrated ownership offers the press an increased amount of economic efficiency, and therefore adds to the economic stability of press units within the group. But it also reduces variety of criticism. This creates a dichotomy: the need for the press to be economically strong and independent, on the one hand; the need for the press to offer the ultimate amount of critical variety, on the other. The public is faced with an entirely different situation from that of concentrated ownership in industry. Monopolistic ownership of soap, for example, reduces the choice of the consumer—but it still gives him the product he seeks. Monopolistic ownership of the press threatens to remove from a democratic society the product itself—variety of criticism.

Fortunately, the trend toward concentrated ownership of newspapers in many Western countries has been accompanied by new means and new methods of communication, which have themselves supplemented the decreasing supply of criticism from the older media. News magazines and other specialized magazines have proved to be new sources of criticism. The electronic media, though highly restricted in the area of direct editorializing in many countries, have provided documentaries and commentaries which are, in effect, a source of political and social criticism. Paperbacks are still another source of popular criticism. American newspapers, realizing their responsibility for providing a variety of criticism, now present more syndicated political columnists than ever before.

But there is evidence that while these sources have contributed supplementary criticism of national government, they have not been able to adequately supplement the reduced variety of criticism on the local and regional levels.

Some critics have seen in group and conglomerate ownerships the potential power to mold public opinion on a vast scale. Others say that a more likely danger is that they will wield no power at all—that, becoming vulnerable to attack by government as a monopoly, they will recognize themselves as a public utility and assume a position of neutrality on political affairs, especially in those cities where their enterprises face no print opposition. In fact, there is already a move by the public and government toward regulating print media as public utilities, in much the same way that electronic media are already regulated. Press laws, press councils, and press subsidies in nations outside the United States are part of this particular mosaic. In the U.S., the major step in this direction came in the early 1940s when the courts ruled that the Associated Press was clothed with the public interest and therefore had to make its service available to virtually any newspaper that wanted it. The most recent efforts toward regulating print media as public utilities in the U.S. are: 1. a law that exempts certain newspapers from normal monopoly restrictions, on the grounds that a "combined operating agreement" between a failing newspaper and a strong one preserves pluralism of information and opinion, 2. regulations limiting multimedia ownership, also designed to preserve pluralism, 3. recommendations for local and national press councils to judge press responsibility, and 4. suggestions that the "fairness doctrine" be extended to newspapers, based on the argument that the First Amendment implies that each citizen has a right of access to the press.*

Jet Publications

One often considers the modern age in terms of the wonders of message communication, from the wireless to the communication satellite, without considering the new changes in the transmission of correspondents and publications themselves. Jet aircraft travel has made it possible for a large newspaper, magazine, or news syndicate to place its best correspondents in almost any spot in the world in a matter of hours. This means of transportation has inaugurated the age of "mobile bureaus." It has reduced reliance on the major international news services and permitted publications to offer a more individualized product to their readers.

---

*See Jerome A. Barron, "Access to the Press—A New First Amendment Right," *Harvard Law Review* (June 1967), pp. 1641-78.

Beyond this, however, jet transportation now encourages elite newspapers to spread their messages beyond their native countries; it has given meaningful international communication an immediacy never before achieved. The Journalism Library at the University of Missouri, for example, receives within a few days of publication the *Guardian, Le Monde, Pravda, An-Nahar* (of Beirut), and the *Jerusalem Post*. A subscriber in New York can receive European and Middle Eastern newspapers the day following publication; *The New York Times* can be purchased at some European newsstands on the day of publication. The major news magazines (*Time, Newsweek, U.S. News & World Report, Der Spiegel,* and *L'Express*) are delivered to subscribers all over the world at approximately the same time as subscribers within the country of publication receive them, and there are many other weekly publications that could be added to this list.

The influence of these jet publications goes far beyond that of international broadcasts, primarily because, with the exception of *Pravda*, they are privately owned and therefore more credible, they are purchased and therefore desired, and they are "reviewable" and therefore able to compete successfully with the media in the countries where they are distributed.

Understanding Media Characteristics

The vital statistics of every nation's press system are available in various sources. These statistics would include the number of morning and afternoon dailies, the number of weeklies, the types of magazines available, total number of book titles published each year, annual newsprint production and consumption, names and number of news agencies, etc. It is more interesting, however, to *understand* the nature of a country's print media by looking at these statistics in the light of three major factors: 1. population, 2. geography, and 3. politico-economic system.

Population. One must consider this factor in terms of population size, urbanization, languages spoken, education, and affluence. A large, literate population, highly urbanized and speaking one major language (Japan fits all these characteristics) has a high potential for large circulation "quality" newspapers and specialized magazines. A lower degree of literacy, more people living in villages, and a multiplicity of languages (India, for example) obviously reduces the potential for print media, even with a large population. A highly literate, but small population (Finland) may be able to support quality newspapers, but not specialized magazines or a great variety of book titles. If an urbanized, literate population is divided into language groups, the circulation potential for mass magazines and newspapers is reduced greatly, sometimes affecting both quality and specialization. Belgium, for example, is divided into two major groups, fragmenting a population of ten million into essentially a population of four and a half million French-speaking Belgians and five and a half million Flemish-speaking Belgians. Although many Belgians are bilingual, it is safe to say that most are more comfortable in one language than in another, and prefer—for political, cultural, and religious reasons, as well—publications printed in that language. Neither the French-language nor the Flemish-language Belgian publications are noted for outstanding quality or large circulations. One reason for this is the availability of quality publications from nearby France and Holland. But what about tiny Finland and Israel, whose major languages are unique to their own countries? Or compare the Swedish-speaking minority in Finland, who may subscribe to Swedish publications, to the Arabic-speaking minority in Israel, who are unable to obtain current periodicals from surrounding Arab countries.

Factors such as these help to explain why a country has few specialized magazines, why it may borrow heavily from the publications of other countries, or why it must subsidize its own publications and perhaps encourage the learning of a "second language" so its educated citizens may be able to consume the specialized publications of larger countries.

Geography. The size of a country, the physical barriers to overland communication, and the location of major cities are important elements for understanding aspects of the country's print media. The smaller a country and the fewer its physical barriers, the more likely it is to have strong "national" dailies that circulate throughout the country.* Large cities separated from each other by significant distances are able to nurture strong newspapers, since competition is kept to a minimum. Norway, for example, is not a large country. However, the physical barriers of mountains, a serrated coastline, and winter snows have served to reduce the circulation territory of Oslo newspapers and strengthen the provincial press. Mexico City, a center of population, culture, and the arts, could be expected to dominate the daily newspaper picture in Mexico. But the mountain chain running north and south through the length of the country forms an imposing barrier to east-west overland communication; therefore, the provincial press in the western half of Mexico is extremely vigorous.

Politico-economic system. Newspapers, especially, bear a close relationship to the politico-economic system in which they exist. It may appear quite obvious that the most independent newspapers are found in the most democratic countries. Less obvious, however, is the incidence of cooperatively owned papers in socialistic countries, newspaper chains in capitalistic nations, party-owned papers in multiparty systems, powerful religious newspapers in theocratic states, etc. England was a traditionally private-enterprise economy into which socialism made heavy inroads; in addition, vestiges of the class system remain in the country. It is not pure coincidence that the most influential "popular" newspaper, the *Daily Mirror*, is a "Labor"

---

*There are exceptions to this, especially where governments can exert control to subsidize papers or regulate circulation. Russia is a huge country, yet *Pravda* and *Izvestia* are "national" papers, published simultaneously at different plants throughout the nation.

daily, while the unofficial voice of the Tories is the "quality" daily, *The Times* of London. Communist countries can be expected to have state-owned newspapers with strong central direction.* In the "guided democracies" of the emerging African nations, the newspapers are also frequently "guided"—directly, if they are owned by government, and by more subtle means if they are owned by private corporations.

The number of variables lying within these three major factors alone (and certainly there are other factors, such as culture and tradition, to name only two) weave different print media patterns in every country. But taking only one country, the United States, as an example, we can understand how they offer important insights into media characteristics.

The United States

Population

Size:	200 million
Urbanization:	More than 70 percent
Languages:	English
Education:	Literacy, 97.8%; approximately 50 percent of high-school graduates go on to university education.
Affluence:	Per capita income, about $3,500

Geography

Size:	3.6 million square miles
Physical Barriers:	None of significance; overland communication excellent; Alaska and Hawaii not contiguous to mainland
Major Cities:	Scattered throughout country, with largest population centers in eastern U.S. and along West Coast.
Neighbors:	Canada (English, French); Mexico (Spanish)

Politico-economic

Political System:	Representative democracy with traditional two-party government
Economic System:	Free enterprise, with private ownership dominating

---

*In this, as in many other aspects of communist affairs, Yugoslavia is somewhat of an anomaly. Newspapers there are cooperative enterprises, more dependent on advertising and less responsible to central government than dailies in other Eastern-bloc nations.

Magazines

With the exception of China, the United States has the largest population in the world literate in a single language. This, along with the affluence and educational level of the population, has provided an optimum audience for specialized publications. Advertiser interest in pinpointing their customers, the ability of the average American to buy an assortment of publications, and the disparity of reader tastes due to varying educational experiences and leisure-time pursuits have caused a sharp trend toward specialized publications.

At the beginning of the 1970s, there were only two "mass-mass magazines" (*Life* and *Look*) remaining in the United States. Both had their highest circulations in history, largely due to vigorous subscription campaigns. But both were in deep trouble due to their inability to be all things to all people. Advertisers, realizing this, were beginning to abandon ship, and the two magazines were producing a thinner product, since advertising accounts for about two-thirds of a mass magazine's income.

The two magazines with the highest circulations in the U.S. (*TV Guide* and *Reader's Digest*) were already specialized. *TV Guide* is an example of "unit specialization," the entire publication appealing to an audience with a common interest, while *Reader's Digest* represents "internal specialization," a publication offering a wide variety of articles from which a heterogeneous audience can select items of particular interest. "Mass-mass magazines," of general interest, are likely to be found in a country of small population, or where the population has a common educational background, or where the average family can buy only a few publications. In the 1970s, not one of these factors exists in the United States, and so the age of the "mass-mass magazine" appears to be at an end.

Books

Because of the same elements of population size, education, and affluence, the U.S. produces more than thirty thousand different book titles each year. The vast literate population provides sizable audiences for a wide array of specialized books. The sharpest increase during recent years has been posted by university textbooks, reflecting the fact that more than fifty percent of all high-school graduates enter colleges and universities. University students are also large consumers of paperbound "trade books," frequently assigned in university courses as supplements to textbooks or (in increasing numbers) instead of textbooks. The reduced cost of paperbacks has made them competitive, in many cases, with magazines.

Other nations—both English speaking and non-English speaking—have become "borrowers" of America's specialized book production. For example, a small or medium-sized nation cannot affort to print textbooks for advanced university courses that enroll fewer than several hundred students a year. This is particularly true of textbooks in science, technology, medicine, and management, which become quickly dated. Such countries must "borrow" textbooks from a larger country, usually the United States. Students in those countries therefore must have a fluency in English. As a result of this acquired fluency in English (for educational purposes) they become potential consumers of other English-language trade books. In the last three years of the 1960s, export sales of American books tripled, rising from about $50 million a year in 1967 to more that $150 million a year in 1969.

Newspapers

The impressive statistics about the newspaper industry in the U.S. are handy for any student of communications. This passage will approach those statistics from the back door, going first to the important data about America itself to see if the data explain *why* the newspaper industry exists in its present form.

Population size. This is the least significant factor affecting the present form of the newspaper industry. In 1909 the U.S. had only about 90 million people, but approximately

2,600 daily papers (compared to about 1,750 today). Population growth, with more people entering the nation's literacy pool each year, does explain, however, why total newspaper circulations have increased each year despite the inroads of competing media.

Urbanization. Part of the urbanization pattern in the U.S. is "suburbanization," middle-class urbanites moving to their own homes in the suburbs. This accounts for the growth in weekly community papers. The proximity of suburbanites to large cities also accounts for the desire of metropolitan dailies (and their retail advertisers) to appeal to this audience in preference to the less affluent city dwellers.

Languages. Although the Spanish-language press has grown because of recent immigration from Mexico, Puerto Rico, and Cuba, it is insignificant when compared to total newspaper ciruclations. Any foreign-language press has been temporal in the U.S. because of the domination of the English language and culture. For the same reason, the non-English-language periodical press of other countries makes virtually no inroads in domestic circulation; the general American reader is unfamiliar with any language other than English.

Education. The relatively advanced education of the average American accounts for a weak tabloid press and the absence of sensationalism in American daily, weekly, and Sunday newspapers. There is no equivalent to *Bild Zeitung*, a sensational daily in West Germany, or *The People*, a sensational Sunday paper in England, both of which have massive circulations. In the 1920s, the United States saw a brief outburst of tabloid sex and scandal. Although some critics of American culture refuse to recognize it, the average American is now more educated and more sophisticated than his European cousins. He is therefore a poor audience for sensational copy.*

---

*The New York *Daily News*, the most sensational of American daily tabloids, has a conservative news approach in comparison to the "popular press" of Europe.

Affluence. Although Americans have a larger average disposable income (income remaining after the purchase of necessities) than the citizens of any other country in the world, they buy fewer newspapers per capita than the Swiss, English, Danes, Swedes, and Japanese. Indirectly, this is partly a result of American affluence. Americans have the money to spend and the means of getting to large department, grocery, and specialty stores in the central city and shopping centers. The stores must reach them by retail advertising in newspapers. Such advertising provides the largest part of an average paper's income. Retail advertisers are reluctant to buy space in competing papers with overlapping circulation. They prefer the newspaper with the largest circulation, thus speeding up the process of "natural selection" among papers. The average American therefore buys fewer newspapers because he has fewer from which to choose. (Only about a dozen cities in the U.S. now have "head-on competition" between two morning papers or between two afternoon papers.) This far oversimplifies the reason for newspaper monopoly in America. Geography, economics, and politics also play a role in this phenomenon, as we will see shortly. But it does suggest that at a certain level of newspaper development within a nation affluence becomes a negative, rather than a positive, factor.

Geographical size. The sheer size of the country explains why there is no "national" newspaper in America. Although facsimile transmission theoretically could permit a newspaper to publish simultaneously in different parts of the country, such a newspaper would have to print news of regional interest and perform a demonstrably better job of covering national and international news in order to compete with established local newspapers. *The New York Times*'s unsuccessful effort in the 1960s to maintain a West Coast edition indicates that it is as yet unfeasible for an American newspaper to go "national." The *Wall Street Journal* is the nearest thing to a national newspaper, but it is actually a specialized publication appealing to a select audience. The *National Observer*, produced by the same parent company, is a "national" weekly, but from the point of view of content bears more similarity to a news magazine than to a daily newspaper. The geographical size of the U.S. also explains why morning dailies account for only seventeen percent of the total number of daily papers, yet produce forty percent of the daily circulation. Metropolitan morning newspapers are able to travel between midnight and dawn to surrounding areas and arrive at the breakfast table with news as fresh as that in a local product. Metropolitan afternoon papers are unable to offer the same service to regional customers; their deadlines must be earlier or their deliveries later than local competitors. Because of the distance factor, small-town papers find it easier to compete with metropolitan afternoon newspapers than metropolitan morning papers. If a town has only one newspaper, it is therefore most likely to be an afternoon paper.

Physical barriers. Since overland communication is excellent throughout the U.S., this is not a factor affecting the nature of American papers.

Major cities. The fairly even distribution of large cities throughout the U.S. has caused the evolution of regional newspapers, metropolitan dailies (usually morning papers) that aim editions at surrounding areas. Such editions emphasize stories of statewide and regional interest. In a sense, these perform the function of a "national" newspaper for more limited regional areas. Small town and community dailies and weeklies are satellites within the gravitational field of these papers.

Neighboring countries. To a minor extent, Americans of Mexican descent are "borrowers" of Spanish-language newspapers published in the larger border cities of Mexico. This situation does not exist on the Canadian border, since there are no French-speaking communities of significant size on the American side.

Politico-economic system. A two-party system in a country as large in area and population as the United States implies that within each party there are heterogeneous groups with conflicting regional and ideological interests. This is especially true when there is negligible difference in the philosophies of the two parties, especially concerning the economic structure of the country. American newspapers reflect this politico-economic situation in the following ways: 1. newspapers are generally uncommitted to a specific political party; because of their private enterprise nature, however, they tend toward conservatism in political and economic outlook, 2. reflecting the all-inclusiveness of political parties, newspapers generally admit competing ideas and opinions into their syndicated columns and letters sections in order to attract a wide spectrum of readers; this also reduces the demand for competing papers, and 3. believing in minimal restrictions to business competition, the private enterprise system is receptive to chains, conglomerates, and limited monopolies; newspaper groups control about sixty percent of daily and Sunday circulation, while fewer than seventy cities have two or more dailies with separate ownerships.

This survey should demonstrate that the nature of a country's population, geography, and politico-economic system goes a long way toward explaining the characteristics of its press. Although all three factors exert nearly equal influence on the structure of the press in the United States, this may not be so in the case of other countries. In the Soviet Union, for example, central authority is powerful enough to emphasize the politico-economic factor, thus diminishing the influence of geography and population. In some developing countries, the factors of geography and population might well overshadow the influence of the policito-economic system.

5.

Electronic Revolution and the News

THE ELECTRONIC REVOLUTION IS A SUCCESSOR TO THE PRINT revolution. However, four hundred years elapsed between the development of movable type and the print media's attainment of *message saturation*—the ability to distribute a single message to a total mass audience. Even at the end of this four-hundred-year period, the Penny Press could achieve only a low degree of message saturation because of limitations on production, distribution, affluence, and literacy.

In the electronic revolution, a relatively short time elapsed between the invention of radio and television and their attainment of a high degree of message saturation. The electronic media did not have to reproduce a separate message for each member of the audience (everyone could read the same "electronic" newspaper), and distribution was a minor problem since transmission was dependent largely on the air. The nature of the audience was also different. At the beginning of the electronic revolution, part of the audience was affluent enough to quickly avail themselves of the sets for receiving the message. With the development of the transistor radio, the nonaffluent could receive the message, also. Radio, then, is within the reach of all;

television is on the threshold. And since literacy has never been a key to access to the electronic media, the revolution has had, and is having, vast impact on politics and culture throughout the world. In the words of Gamal Abdel Nasser, the late president of the United Arab Republic:

> It is true that most of our people are still illiterate. But politically that counts for far less than it did 20 years ago.
>
> Literacy and intelligence are not the same thing. Radio has changed everything. Once the villages had no knowledge of what was happening in the capital. Government was run by small coteries of people who did not need to take account of the reactions of the people who never saw a newspaper or could not read if they did.
>
> Today people in the most remote villages hear of what is happening everywhere and form their opinions. Leaders cannot govern as they once did. We live in a new world.*

The electronic revolution is not without its ironies and dichotomies. On the one hand it has the power to teach; radio and television can permeate a whole society, and reach the young even in their first moments of awareness. On the other hand, the electronic media may perpetuate illiteracy by making it possible to receive meaningful communications without knowing how to read. "Communication" is the highest order of priority in an underdeveloped country. "Education" is the highest order of priority in a developing country. Thus, this leap-frogging of literacy at one level of development may deprive the population of the necessary skills for attaining a higher level of development.

The electronic media also have great potential as multipliers of democracy. At the same time, they exist as powerful instruments for authoritarian control. Modern revolutionaries understand that if they would overthrow a government they must first control the radio and television stations. In some

---

*Quoted in Daniel Lerner, "Communication Systems and Social Systems: A Statistical Exploration in History and Policy," *Behavioral Science* (October 1957), p. 274.

countries the stations and their transmitters are guarded like Fort Knox.

In order to deal with the problems of electronic media, one must first keep in mind two broad propositions that deeply affect them: 1. Radio and television are highly susceptible to government control; 2. Radio and television are basically entertainment media.

Government Control

Outside the Western Hemisphere, radio and television were usually established as government or "public" owned instruments. In some cases, government attempted to assure the independence of the two media by setting up separate corporations to administer them. In other cases, government control was absolute and the media functioned directly as an arm of the government.

In the Western Hemisphere, with the exception of Canada,* radio and television stations were privately owned. But this did not mean that they were free of government control. To prevent chaos, frequencies and channels had to be assigned by government. In the United States, the Radio Act of 1927 provided a system for allocation of frequencies, and included a provision that stations must serve the "public interest, convenience, and necessity." This licensing process initially led to the "franchise" concept of electronic media, which implies that the station owner has virtually a permanent lease on a frequency in the absence of *negative* conduct. This has evolved over the years until now owners of the electronic media in the United States are recognized as "fiduciaries."† Under this concept, the station owner holds only temporary title to his frequency; in order to renew his license he must show that he has acted *positively* in the public interest.

---

*Privately owned radio and television stations exist side by side with the publicly owned Canadian Broadcasting Corporation's radio and TV networks.

†In legal terminology, a "fiduciary" is a person to whom property is entrusted to hold, control, or manage for another.

Two cases in 1969 confirmed that the courts in the United States now support the "fiduciary" principle. In one case involving a Jackson, Mississippi, television station, Warren Burger—later to become chief justice of the U.S. Supreme Court—ruled:

> The infinite potential of broadcasting to influence American life renders somewhat irrelevant the semantics of whether broadcasting is or is not to be described as a public utility. By whatever name or classification, broadcasters are temporary permittees—fiduciaries—of a great public resource, and they must meet the highest standards which are embraced in the public interest concept.

In the second case, one involving a Red Lion, Pennsylvania, radio station, Justice Byron White wrote for a Supreme Court majority:

> As far as the First Amendment is concerned, those who are licensed stand no better than those to whom licenses are refused. . . there is nothing in the First Amendment which prevents the government from requiring a licensee to share his frequency with others and to conduct himself as a proxy or fiduciary with obligations to present those views and voices which are representative of his community and which would otherwise, by necessity, be barred from the airwaves.
>
> It is the purpose of the First Amendment to preserve an uninhibited marketplace of ideas, in which truth will ultimately prevail, rather than to countenance monopolization of that market, whether it be by the government itself or by a private licensee. It is the right of the public to receive suitable access to social, political, esthetic, moral, and other ideas and experiences . . . .

Electronic media, then, even when operating under private ownership, are more bridled than print media because of government regulations to prevent "negative" conduct, and government surveillance to assure "positive" conduct.

Entertainment Emphasis

Because of their special appeal to the eye and the ear, television and radio are primarily entertainment media. "All news" radio stations exist, of course, but, taken as a whole, the overwhelming portion of broadcast programming is given over to entertainment, not information, shows. Radio Cairo is the most influential station in the Arab world not simply because Egypt is the largest country or has the most to say. Its influence rests on its ability to present the top entertainment stars in the Arab Middle East. Egyptian information broadcasts directed to neighboring countries thereby gain a captive audience.

In democratic countries, the entertainment function is so dominant that it tends to smother the information and education potential of the medium. This dominant role of entertainment is not opposed by the average viewer or listener—or even those who are above average. A national survey reported in *The People Look at Television*, by Gary A. Steiner, showed that the higher-educated, higher-income viewer turns to television primarily for relaxation and entertainment. The survey also showed that although this above-average American *said* that television should offer more education and information, he did not take advantage of such programs that were offered.

This desire by most segments of the audience for entertainment, almost to the exclusion of all but the daily news programs, is reflected in the total content of television. It is also at the heart of many of the problems faced by television newsmen in trying to obtain the proper time and format for news and documentary programs. In a speech delivered in 1958 to the Radio-Television News Directors Association, the late Edward R. Murrow declared:

> One of the basic troubles with radio and television news is that both instruments have grown up as an incompatible combination of show business, advertising, and news. Each of the three is a rather bizarre and demanding profession. And when you get all three under one roof, the dust never settles.

In the case of newspapers, entertainment is a guest in what is essentially a news medium. In the case of the electronic media, news is a guest in what is essentially entertainment media. This fact of life has implications not only for the style and content of news programs, but also for the *attitude* with which audiences approach such programs. For example, the news on television may be preceded by a situation comedy and followed by a western. The news items themselves, often of the most serious nature, are interspersed with commercials of the most trivial nature.

Broadcasters have indeed pointed out that there are also trivial advertisements in the most serious newspapers. But obviously the audience option to avoid such ads is quite different in each medium.

Keeping in mind these important influences, government control and the entertainment emphasis, we can now turn to a brief examination of the basic characteristics of the television medium and their effects on the *communicator, message, channel*, and *audience*.

Characteristics of Television

As a medium of mass communication in the United States, television has the following basic characteristics:

1. It is an audio-visual medium. It appeals to the eye and ear. It is therefore able to present not only words, but noises and music and inflections of voice. It is able to present not only pictures, but *motion* pictures, including nuances of body movement and facial expression (kinesics).

2. It is a time-locked medium. It exists in time, rather than in space. For example, a commercial exists for one minute, with the slow reader (viewer) being given no more time to absorb it than the fast reader (viewer). Because a television program exists in time, the viewer has no opportunity to select out specific portions or review the material he has seen. If two similar programs are telecast at the same time, he has no opportunity to compare then.

3. It has a limited number of channels. Part of this problem is due to the development of very high frequency before ultra high frequency. Licensing of more UHF stations and expansion of cable television (CATV) are increasing the number of channels available to the average American.

4. It is a highly complex and expensive medium to operate. Cameras, film, transmission equipment, and other paraphernalia require numerous specialists in addition to the communicator himself. The costs associated with operating the medium are accordingly high. A popular, hour-long program presented in prime time may cost in the neighborhood of a half-million dollars each week for production and network affiliate time.

5. It depends on advertising as the single major source of income. This may be only a temporary factor in the United States, but it is a factor that has existed since the establishment of television, and prevails now. Public broadcasting and pay television, though they exist, have not made major inroads into the American tradition of commercial broadcasting.

Because of the above characteristics, television as a news medium in the United States evolved to its present state—and as these characteristics change, television will evolve even further. The following pages, however, will attempt to show how the various communication processes of television have been affected by these characteristics as they currently exist.

Effect on the Communicator

As television became more of a "mass-mass" medium, attracting huge audiences for its news programs as well as for its entertainment programs, it began to attract quality newsmen. They came from other media and also directly from the universities. Because television is an audio-visual medium, those who appeared on the air had to have certain qualities of voice and looks. Because television is also supported by advertising, and advertisers are interested in ratings, television networks and stations encouraged the "star system"—featured personalities who attract a regular audience.

In network television, there are implications to the star system that bear more examination than they have so far received. First, in order to become a star, one must receive exposure. In order for a correspondent to get exposure, his story (and, along with it, his face) must be selected for use on a news program. Since competition for the limited amount of time on a news program is usually severe, the correspondent is sometimes tempted to help his cause by emphasizing the sensational aspects of the story.

Or consider a network anchorman. His voice and face are more familiar to the average American than are the voice and face of the President of the United States. And while Presidents come and go every four or eight years, the television anchorman stays on, speaking to his public night after night, year after year. Belief in a favorite anchorman might exceed the viewer's belief in any other personality or institution in the United States.

The necessity to utilize a handful of proven stars rather than a much broader corps of specialized reporters and commentators has also served to blur the distinction between news and comment. On one night, a television newsman may be delivering a straight reporting job; on the next he may be called upon to analyze a political situation. Sometimes, there is confusion in the viewer's mind about whether he is hearing news or analysis. Because the television reporter is a star, highly paid and certainly highly qualified, there is the danger that he will tend to think of himself as omniscient, that he will see himself as the audience's representative on the scene, there to make assessments rather than to report the news.

Effect on the Message

Messages on television are often quite different from messages in newspapers. In television news the emphasis usually is upon that which can be pictured. As one American broadcast executive described it, television is more likely to emphasize the "goings and comings" of diplomats than the issues that they are discussing. At the very least, good "footage" of a trivial nature will probably receive inordinately more air time than important news for which "footage" is unavailable. A veteran BBC public affairs reporter and program producer has pointed out that this emphasis on pictures has caused television news to adopt the "tabloid vices of sensationalism and superficiality." He added:

> . . . the fact is that television's dependence on pictures (and the most vivid pictures) makes it not only a *powerful* means of communication, but a *crude* one which tends to strike at the emotions rather than at the intellect. For TV journalism this means a dangerous and increasing concentration on action (usually violent and bloody) rather than thought, on happenings rather than issues, on shock rather than explanation, on personalities rather than ideas.*

The visual nature of the medium has also forced television away from the "inverted pyramid" style of news presentation used by newspapers for a hundred years and, with modifications, by radio for more than half a century. Motion pictures do not lend themselves to a style of identifying the most important facts first; rather, they accommodate a chronological order of narration traditionally associated with the feature story. Stylistically, then, the anchorman on a news program is the straight news reporter; the correspondent in the field is the feature writer. Sometimes a "news" story will have both elements, the anchorman introducing the story in a straight news fashion, then switching to the correspondent in the field for feature commentary.

Television has also added new devices to the store of news presentation. Two of these are the "speculative indefinite" (. . . What he would do if the union rejects the agreement, he did not say . . .) and the "editorial fade" (. . . Death lurks in

---

*Robin Day, "Troubled Reflections of a TV Journalist," *Encounter* (May 1970), p. 79.

the coal mines near this mountain community, but the state has a history of ignoring the danger until it is too late . . .).

The fact that television is a time-locked medium also means that many important stories of the day will never be presented on network news and other important stories will be reduced to a few lines. A half-hour newscast, since it exists in time, cannot be stretched. The total amount of news delivered over a network news program on an average night would, if set in type, hardly fill the front page of a daily newspaper. Such limits, of course, are man made. A nightly network news program could be one hour or two hours. But if it were, it would probably lose a large part of its mass audience, and be unable to attract advertising sponsorship.

The complexities and/or attendant expense of the medium further reduces the range of stories available to television. It is expensive (and sometimes physically impractical) for camera crews to accompany reporters on all assignments; television cameras are also dependent on light—artificial or natural. Further, authoritarian regimes can restrict the movement of equipment and censor film more easily than they can restrict the movement of an individual reporter or censor his notes when he is departing the country. This does not mean that information thus missed by the television crew does not get on the air. But its chances of receiving air time commensurate with its importance are reduced. It also means that television is likely to give far more attention to the problems of democracies than it is to the problems of authoritarian states, resulting in a comparative advantage to the authoritarian regimes.

Television's limited number of channels has had two striking effects on news messages: 1. It has virtually eliminated overt, meaningful editorial messages, and 2. it has forced television news to disguise editorial opinions as news or interpretation, blurring the difference between fact and opinion.

Because of the limited number of radio frequencies, Section 315 of the Communications Act of 1934 included the "equal time" doctrine—if free time is made available to one political candidate during a campaign, equal time must be made available to all other candidates for that office. (In 1959, Section 315 was amended to exclude certain types of news programs on which candidates might appear from the "equal time" provision.)

In 1941, the Federal Communications Commission ruled that broadcast editorializing was illegal. The FCC reversed itself in 1949 and again permitted editorializing, with the proviso that stations also "provide the listening public with a fair and balanced presentation of differing viewpoints. . . ." The "fairness" doctrine was thus established. It was later extended to force broadcasters to give a reasonable amount of rebuttal time to opponents of any controversial ideas aired on radio or television.

A combination of the "equal time" and "fairness" doctrines has served to subdue most overt editorial functions in the broadcasting industry. Few stations editorialize; many are reluctant to grapple with controversial subjects unless they can give clinically even balance to all sides. Those that do editorialize or openly criticize run the risk of giving up valuable sponsored time to those who would make a rebuttal. If they refuse to offer such time, they face costly litigation and, in the last analysis, possible loss of their license at renewal time. For many stations, the safest course is to avoid editorializing and controversy. Government regulation, rationalized on the grounds of limited channels, has thus largely removed from the electronic media one of the basic functions of the press—criticism of government and nongovernment institutions.

Barred in fact if not in theory from overt editorializing, television newsmen editorialize in more subtle ways, often unwittingly. Because of the audio-visual nature of television, the personality of the anchorman or correspondent is bound to color the message; the newsman appears physically between the message and the viewer. The anchorman bridges two news items with an editorial comment ("Meanwhile, in another action frought with danger, the prime minister . . .") and correspondents end their reports from the field with an editorial conclusion ("State police escorted the candidate to his car and away from the violence that has been the signature of his campaign . . .").

The television news reports themselves are frequently highly interpretative, often without being identified as analysis. The result has been to confuse fact and opinion, in contrast to the newspaper tradition of clearly separating the two.

Effect on the Channel

The electronic media encounter special government regulations because of the limited number of frequencies and channels. Broadcasters have argued that these regulations should be relaxed and electronic media given the same First Amendment rights as the print media. They point out that they can hardly be called a monopoly when there are more television and radio stations in most cities than there are newspapers; in fact, there are four times as many AM and FM stations as there are dailies in the nation, and more than eight hundred television stations. The courts have held that numbers in the electronic media, especially in the case of television, are deceptive. Because of the expense of programming, most stations must affiliate with one of the three major networks and carry network programs for almost all of the television day. In practice, then, a three-way monopoly exists and entry is restricted, since those stations that were able to obtain a network affiliation in the early years of television now occupy a preferred position.

As a result of the nature of broadcast transmission, local stations occupy a position quite different from that of independent newspapers. Dailies are able to exercise a gatekeeping function vis-a-vis wire service and syndicate copy. Local television stations, however, are unable to edit any part of the regular network news programs. They are simply "paperboys" in the transmission of such programs. And since the news programs frequently carry interpretative material closely akin to editorial opinion, the local stations are in the ambiguous position of transmitting opinions for which they are legally, but not editorially, responsible.

It is ironic that newspapers in the United States have a dual tradition of political advocacy and objectivity, while television stations are apolitical, but less objective. Part of this contrasting situation is due to the nature of the medium and government regulation. But one is left with the impression that network news has a lower degree of objectivity than newspapers for two other reasons: television correspondents are given more leeway to interpret the news than are newspaper reporters, and television does a poorer job of separating and identifying news and opinion.

Effect on the Audience

The audio-visual nature of television news, and possibly even the fact that it is tightly compressed and therefore more easily absorbed, make the daily network programs a favorite with the mass audience. A majority of Americans now consider television their primary source of news. The majority also finds it the most credible source of news. This is probably due to their belief in the integrity of familiar and favorite anchormen, to their feeling that television is editorially neutral, and to their conviction that "seeing is believing."

At the same time, there are sizable numbers of viewers who are disgruntled about the presentation of network television news. Broadcasters credit this to the desire to "kill the messenger that bears bad news." Undoubtedly this is part of the explanation, but not all of it. The point is that television has a vast heterogeneous audience and only a tiny selection of networks. Consider this contrast: the early evening news programs of the three major television networks reach about 40 million Americans daily; 1,750 daily newspapers reach a little more than 62 million subscribers each day. It is true that the average subscriber possibly has even less choice of papers in his hometown that he does of networks. But the newspaper probably comes closer to appealing to his political and sectional prejudices than does network news. And whereas the reader can avoid the "bad news" in the newspaper and ignore the editorial opinions, he can do none of these with television. He must take all the news, the good and the bad, the straight and the interpretative. Given such conditions and such a varied audience, large numbers are bound to react adversely to news which, in their own minds, is presented "unfairly."

A Case Study

Many examples could be presented to show how news in the electronic media differs in content and form from news in newspapers. It would be difficult to take an example from a television broadcast and transfer it to print since much of the content (pictures and sound) would be lost. The following example from an actual radio network news program, however, might illustrate the point.

After the resignation of Supreme Court Justice Abe Fortas in 1969, President Nixon nominated Clement F. Haynsworth of South Carolina for the seat. The Senate refused to confirm him. Nixon then nominated G. Harrold Carswell of Florida, whom the Senate also rejected. The day after Carswell's defeat, Nixon made the following statement to the press:

> After the Senate's action yesterday in rejecting Judge Carswell, I have reluctantly concluded that it is not possible to get confirmation for a judge on the Supreme Court of any man who believes in the strict construction of the Constitution, as I do, if he happens to come from the South.
>
> Judge Carswell and, before him, Judge Haynsworth have been submitted to vicious assaults on their intelligence, on their honesty, and on their character. They have been falsely charged with being racists.
>
> But when you strip away all the hypocrisy, the real reason for their rejection was their legal philosophy, a philosophy that I share, of strict construction of the Constitution—and also the accident of their birth—the fact that they were born in the South.
>
> Four of the present judges of the Supreme Court are from the

East. One is from the Midwest, and two are from the West. One is from the South. Over 25 percent of the people live in the South. The South is entitled to proper representation on the Court.

But as I have often said to members of this White House press corps, more important than geographical or other kinds of balance in the Court is philosophical balance.

I have concluded therefore that the next nominee must come from outside the South, since this Senate as it is presently constituted will not approve a man from the South who shares my views of strict construction of the Constitution.

I therefore asked the Attorney General to submit names to me from outside the South of judges from the State courts, appeals courts—as well as the federal courts—who are qualified to be on the Supreme Court and who do share my view and the views of Judge Haynsworth and Judge Carswell with regard to strict construction of the Constitution.

I believe that a judge from the North who has such views will be confirmed by the Senate.

On April 10, the morning after Nixon's press conference, the CBS radio network featured a report by Washington correspondent Robert Pierpoint on its daily "World News Roundup," anchored by Dallas Townsend. The reader must keep in mind that voice inflections are missing from the following transcript of that report and that CBS undoubtedly transmitted numerous stories giving some of the facts of the Nixon statement on its hourly news programs during the afternoon and evening before this broadcast:

Townsend: Repercussions persist in the capital today from the Carswell affair. President Nixon's obvious anger over defeat of the appointment, and the explanations he gave for the Senate's rejection of Judge Carswell and of Judge Haynsworth before him, have drawn heated reactions of both disagreement and support. Now, as we hear from CBS News White House correspondent Robert Pierpoint, the struggle is obviously moving into the political arena with emphasis on the upcoming congressional campaign.

Pierpoint: The majority in the U.S. Senate has won the first two battles; but President Nixon could still win the war. The President's clear political strategy now is to turn those two defeats in the Senate on Haynsworth and Carswell into Republican victories in the fall election campaign. The first move in that campaign took place yesterday when the President made his strong statements claiming the Senate rejected his two Supreme Court nominees merely because of prejudice against their southern backgrounds. That was clearly calculated to solidify Mr. Nixon's support among southern voters. Now he moves into other areas, where he hopes to help the Republicans pick up some Senate seats. Democratic Senator Gore from the border state of Tennessee is sure to feel the heat, since he voted against Carswell, and the same goes for Senator Yarborough of Texas. The real question is whether President Nixon's strategy will work in Northern and Western states. But this President has established something of a record by appearing to lose and then coming out on top. Robert Pierpoint, CBS News, White House.

Townsend: A high official in the American Bar Association today calls for change in . . .

After examining both the statement and the newscast, one should attempt to answer the following questions:

1. Did anchorman Townsend make any interpretative or editorial comments in introducing correspondent Pierpoint?
2. Did Townsend identify Pierpoint's report as news or news analysis?
3. Was it "clear" that Nixon planned to make political capital out of the Haynsworth and Carswell defeats?
4. Did Nixon say that the Senate rejected the two candidates "merely" because of their southern backgrounds?
5. How did Pierpoint know that the statement was "clearly calculated" to solidify southern support for Nixon?
6. How did Pierpoint know that Nixon planned to inject this issue into the Texas and Tennessee campaigns?
7. Is the Pierpoint report, taken as a whole, news, interpretation, or editorializing?

6.

Advertising: The Ubiquitous Salesman

THE INFLUENCE OF ADVERTISING IS SO PERVASIVE THAT ONE has difficulty in clearly identifying its role in mass communication. The fog surrounding this identity is thick, and perhaps it can best be lifted by first considering the statements of two men who see advertising from completely different angles. Richard A. Posner, a Stanford University law professor who served on a presidential task force on productivity and competition, sees advertising as playing an indispensable social role. He wrote:

> A modern economy requires the generation of a vast amount of information on the identity and location of sellers, on types and changes in product, and on prices and other terms of sale.
>
> It is not surprising, therefore—and certainly not to be deplored—that there is a vast amount of advertising: A practical alternative, not involving economic stagnation, is not immediately evident.*

The second statement takes a less charitable view of advertising. George F. Kennan, former U.S. ambassador to Russia and

---

Advertising Age (June 23, 1969), p. 1.

a presidential adviser, wrote:

> [The] phenomenon of American advertising . . . has been per-
> mitted to dominate and exploit the entire process of public com-
> munication in our country. It is to me positively inconceivable that
> the whole great, infinitely responsible function of mass communica-
> tion, including very important phases of the educational process,
> should be farmed out—as something to be mined for whatever profit
> there may be in it—to people whose function and responsibility have
> nothing to do with the truth—whose function and responsibility, in
> fact, are concerned with the peddling of what is, by definition,
> untruth, and the peddling of it in trivial, inane forms that are posi-
> tively debauching in their effect on the human understanding. After
> the heedless destruction of natural environment, I regard this—not
> advertising as such, but the consignment to the advertiser of the
> entire mass communication process, as a concession to be exploited
> by it for commercial gain—as probably the greatest evil of our na-
> tional life. We will not, I think, have a healthy intellectual climate in
> this country, a successful system of education, a sound press, or a
> proper vitality of artistic and recreational life, until advertising is
> rigorously separated from every form of legitimate cultural and in-
> tellectual communication. . . .*

The Posner and Kennan statements appear to be contradictory. Actually they are not, although the Kennan passage certainly exaggerates and oversimplifies advertising's effects.
Posner is saying, "Advertising is necessary to the proper functioning of the American economic and social system." Kennan
is answering, "Possibly so, but it corrupts the media and therefore should be eliminated from them." Posner would undoubtedly be content to have the media exist without advertising, if this were possible. Kennan would be satisfied to let
advertising live if it were separated from the media.

Advertising is a salesman substitute, and salesmen are necessary in our competitive, free enterprise society. In an econ-

---

*George F. Kennan, *Democracy and the Student Left* (New York: Bantam
Books, 1968), pp. 201-202.

omy of mass production, mass distribution, and mass consumption, we need salesman substitutes (advertising) to tell us the benefits of the product, its price, and where it can be purchased. The problem with advertising vis-a-vis the mass media is this: Should the salesman's role extend beyond selling his product?

Critics of advertising make an analogy between advertising and an encyclopedia salesman. The encyclopedia salesman may offer us a free gift to get into our homes. But once in our homes, does he have a right to stay as long as he likes, interrupt our activities at will, and determine the subject of our conversations? Like the encyclopedia salesman, advertising is allowed into our homes because it brings us a free gift—subsidy of print media and free television. However, we are then bothered to find that advertising dominates the space in the print media, takes an inordinate amount of time on the television screen, interrupts the message in most of the media, and above all, apparently determines the content of popular publications and television.

One may gain a deeper insight into these allegations by attempting to answer the following questions: 1. Does advertising give the media audience a free gift? 2. Does the media audience want advertising? and 3. Does advertising determine the content of the media?

A Free Gift for the Audience?

Although some media manage to survive without advertising, notably books, recordings, and movies, advertising subsidies provide television programming free and reduce the cost of magazines and newspapers. Just how much cheaper magazines and newspapers are as a result of advertising is not to be found in the balance sheets released by publishing enterprises. For example, income from circulation is slightly less than one-third of daily newspaper revenue, while income from advertising is slightly more than two-thirds. But from sixty-five percent to seventy-five percent of the average daily is devoted to advertising. The reader thus pays only one-third the cost of a newspaper, but he is also getting only one-third or less of the space.

Many of the expenses incurred by newspapers and magazines are directly attributable to their advertising function: paper, printing costs, business staff, etc. This is not to say that a newspaper or magazine could do just as well, and sell as inexpensive a product, without advertisements. Some have tried— and failed. But it does indicate that advertising does not carry the burden sometimes claimed for it.

And one must ask, does the media audience get a free gift when it receives magazines and free television?

Postal subsidies, in the form of cheaper rates for newspapers and magazines, were instituted shortly after the founding of the Republic. Postal rates for periodicals intentionally covered only a fraction of the actual cost of delivering the publications, because Congress believed that "diffusion of information" was a cornerstone of democracy. Although the majority of space in newspapers and consumer magazines is now devoted to advertising, second-class mailing rates—subsidized by the taxpayers—enable such publications to maintain their cheaper prices *and* advertising rates.*

It not only costs each American additional federal taxes for the delivery of the advertising portions of his newspapers and magazines, but also additional local fees and taxes for disposal of the newspapers and magazines once they become waste paper.

The proliferation of advertisements also costs the reader something in wasted time and annoyance. Because of the ads and additional pages to accommodate them, the reader frequently has difficulty finding a story, and related stories may

---

*Operating under a new "non-subsidy" philosophy, the United States Postal Service sharply increased second-class rates in 1971, and announced further increases for a four-year period thereafter. It should be noted that publishers and postal authorities disagree about the validity of the Postal Service's cost accounting procedures.

well be in scattered pages or even different sections because of the scarcity of news space on a given page.

As for television, the viewer must "pay" for his free programs by devoting fifteen to twenty percent of his viewing time to commercials. If the average American watches television almost thirty hours a week, this means that he spends about five or six hours of his time each week watching commercials. If the viewer could apply this figure to the value of his time, per hour, he would come to some conclusion about whether free television is completely free.

Does the Audience Want Advertising?

Advertising is a message, albeit a paid message. As a message, it is either news, information, or entertainment, and sometimes all three. The reader or viewer's desire for an advertising message is therefore related to his need for the product, the information and/or entertainment value of the advertisement itself, and the unobtrusiveness of the presentation.*

Readers undoubtedly do have a strong desire for the retail ads in newspapers and for many advertisements in specialized publications. For example, the grocery ad in the daily paper may be more interesting to a housewife than anything else in the publication. It gives her news of special sale items. A reader of a camera magazine may find the ads as interesting as the articles, because they are directly related to his specialized interest. Few print media ads are obtrusive, since the reader can largely control selection.

The media audience probably desires least the commercials that appear on network television. Their entertainment value is usually high, and in that sense they certainly appeal to the viewer, but the viewer has little need for the specific brand. About eighty percent of the networks' commercial income is

---

*These factors relate to the *reader's* desire, not particularly to the *effectiveness* of the advertisement. From the point of view of the *advertiser*, an obtrusive ad may be more effective than an unobtrusive one.

derived from what one advertising executive called "economic pipsqueaks": deodorants, cosmetics, beverages (alcoholic and nonalcoholic), soap, toothpaste, hair preparations, patent medicines, breakfast foods, etc. Above all, television commercials are obtrusive. The viewer can hardly avoid them, though most of the ads may not remotely relate to his individual interests. In that sense, and in the sense that they interrupt the message, he finds them unappealing. The extent to which broadcasters permit—and advertisers demand—insertion of commercials in the middle of entertainment and news programs reflects their estimation of the viewer desire for such messages.

From the point of view of the audience, the optimum ad is the one to be found in the classified section of the newspaper. It is categorized so he can easily find it, yet he may also easily avoid it if he so desires. The entertainment value is low, but the information and news values are high, and the ad he seeks out relates specifically to his own special interests. From this optimum point, all other print advertisements and electronic commercials fall off on a continuum, perhaps hitting rock bottom with the underarm deodorant commercial that interrupts a news program and ends with the husband in the commercial skit coming very close to smelling his wife's armpit.

Does Advertising Determine Media Content?

The late Howard L. Gossage, who was a San Francisco advertising executive, contended that advertising "will tend to shape all the contents of any communications medium that it dominates economically, and in our society that is very nearly the lot." He added that this control is "not by intent, but through the simple ability of advertising to bestow or withhold favors."

The popular notion of advertising influence sees the advertiser as telling a publisher to print or not to print a specific story in his paper; it sees the advertiser as a censor over the material to be included in a program that he sponsors. This overt interference does occasionally occur, but to a much rarer degree than the average reader or viewer suspects.

The more closely an advertiser's product name is associated with editorial or program material, the more concerned he is about presenting material that will win friends, not alienate potential customers. This is natural. But when Gossage spoke about advertiser control of "contents," he was referring to the overall character of the publication, or programming day, not the specific message.

In the print media, where advertisements are rarely associated with (or blamed for) the editorial content, advertisers are concerned with *audiences*, not *messages*. The advertiser wants to know how many people read the publication and how they rank according to criteria such as age, education, income, number of children, etc. Indirectly, advertisers control the content of the print media they subsidize, since the publications attempt to attract an audience that will be most satisfactory to current and potential advertisers. For a general magazine, the articles may consciously be aimed at young, high-income urbanites, because that is the audience the advertisers want. For a newspaper, the content may be geared to attract the largest possible numbers of middle-class citizens, because this is what advertisers want. In the words of former British press lord Cecil King, "The sobering truth remains that the survival of the daily newspaper depends not on their social indispensability, but on their ability to attract advertising." Paradoxically, it is this advertising concern with *audiences* that has played the largest role in the trends toward monopoly of the daily newspaper and proliferation of the specialized magazine.*

In the electronic media, especially television, the advertiser is concerned with the *audience and* the *message*. Unlike the print media, television depends on the individual program to attract an audience. Since each program has its own "circulation," advertisers insist on sponsoring a program rather than a

---

*Advertising influence on these two trends is discussed in Chapter 4.

random part of a programming day, and their names become closely associated with the content of the program. Also, unlike print media, television has a three-way monopoly that controls the greatest part of the television audience, so the potential audience for each network's offerings is in the "mass-mass" category. Advertisers who want a mass audience, as opposed to a specialized audience, naturally turn to television.

All of these factors encourage network television to produce programming that is attractive to the "mass-mass" audience, and so noncontroversial that the sponsor's product will incur no backlash. Entertainment programming is obviously more likely to fit these two criteria than news and documentaries.

Thus, sponsors do not often act in a *positive* manner to deliberately censor programming material, as is commonly thought. Rather, their influence on the total programming picture is *negative*. Their reluctance to sponsor a program that is either controversial or likely to attract a small audience assures that such programs will not be shown frequently. The television medium is unsurpassed in its ability to present live coverage and analysis during times of national and international debate and confrontation. Yet television networks, except in dramatic emergencies, hesitate to preempt entertainment programs and forfeit their advertising revenues. In the words of CBS newsman Alexander Kendrick, "It is not required for television to be a marketplace of ideas, only a marketplace."*

Responsibility of the Salesman

In many ways, the difficulties in extracting advertising's advantages while barring its disadvantages derive from the advertising industry's similarity to the press. It is relatively unregulated by government and it has only minimal self-regulation

---

*A full and sober analysis of the condition of television programming is included in the first chapter of Kendrick's *Prime Time, the Life of Edward R. Murrow* (Boston: Little, Brown and Co., 1969).

since it is not a profession and consists of thousands of independent units. But there is an important difference between advertising and the press: A newspaper or television station is a medium, and bears responsibility for the content of its total product (e.g., the whole newspaper, the whole magazine). Advertising is not a medium; it is a message. As such, it is responsible only for the content of the advertising message and not for the magazine or programming day in which the advertising message appears. It is therefore far more concerned with advertisement's effect on the audience than its effect on the medium. To repeat in a slightly different way, advertisers are neither responsible nor irresponsible where overall content of the publication is concerned. They are "a-responsible"; that is, they take no responsibility at all. They are responsible for *their* message, not the message of the publication. In television, advertisers involve themselves, to some extent, with the message of the program they sponsor because they are closely associated with this program in the viewer's mind. However, it is significant that even here advertisers are primarily concerned with the effect of the program's message on their product, not with the effect of their commercial message on the program.

In the final analysis, it is the medium that must regulate advertising. For example, daily newspapers do not sell space on their front pages for display ads. That is a method of controlling advertising. Television networks have time after time increased the number of commercial minutes per hour instead of adequately raising the advertising rates on existing commercial minutes. This is a failure to control advertising.

Perhaps we can bring the problem of "advertising and the mass media" into better focus by asking and answering these simple questions:

Should advertising be included in the mass media? Yes. The audience has a need for the news and information content of advertisements; the advertiser has a legitimate right to distribute his messages in the most economical and effective manner;

and the publisher or broadcaster has an obligation to provide his periodical or program at the lowest possible cost to the consumer. In addition, advertisements are an important means of bypassing clogged-up communication channels; they provide an avenue for the expression of minority attitudes, opinions, and grievances, for the transmission of political messages, and for the conveyance of public service messages by industry and government. In this respect, individuals or groups can become their own publishers for a limited period at a relatively low cost.

   Should advertising be regulated in the mass media? Yes. Government agencies must regulate misleading and unfair practices. The media must regulate taste and position—offensive advertisements and commercials, and placement of advertisements and commercials.

   Ideally, commercial messages of all kinds should be placed in sections by themselves, with the reader, listener, or viewer having an option to seek them out or avoid them. This would mean that even display advertisements would be "classified," and commercials would either precede or follow the complete program being sponsored. Considering the tradition of the media, one realizes that such a suggestion may be considered unrealistic.

   Separation of advertisements from the regular media messages would make the media more attractive. It would not, however, reduce the power of advertising to shape the content of the media it subsidizes. But this has always been a more serious problem for the electronic media than for the print media. With more channels available through cable television and UHF stations, advertisers will be less able to find the "mass-mass" audience. They will thus be less likely in the future to demand common-denominator programming that appeals to that disappearing audience. And they will also find it safer to sponsor programming with controversial content.

Part II

The Communicator
and His Audiences

7.

The Press as an Institution

THE "PRESS" IS COMPOSED OF THE MASS MEDIA OF COMMU-
nication that are predominantly, or largely, journalistic. Media
such as newspapers, news, magazines, radio, and television
are largely journalistic in that they deal with news and views.
They may be considered social institutions. Of course, mass
media of all types—even books—may be institutionalized, but
they are of a different nature than the journalistic media mentioned above. Mass media are organized, structured social entities which presumably perform definite functional roles for
the general, or a specialized, public. In a sense, as has been said
earlier in this book, a mass medium is an "institutionalized
person." It acts and reacts in a social setting of other institutions in much the same way an individual person acts and reacts
in a less complex interpersonal group situation.

The press, that is the predominantly *journalistic* media, of
a country can be thought of in a collective sense as being a
social institution; or, each unit or medium thereof can be
thought of as being a social institution. So, we can speak of *the
press* as an institution in American society, or we can speak of a
particular newspaper or magazine as a social institution.

Institutions: A General View

Institutions, like persons, are difficult to generalize about, since they come in so many kinds and sizes. But there are certain commonalities among them, and it might be well to look at some of these in a general way before discussing the press specifically as a social institution. Sociologists, of course, are most interested in institutions for they see the whole process of socialization, the weaving of orderly and functional social relationships on community and national levels, as essentially a process of institutionalization.

Organized groups of individual persons can accomplish certain things that the individual persons cannot accomplish. Individual tasks are therefore, in the face of overwhelming social complexities, assumed by social organizations or institutions. Therefore, it is quite obvious that as societies become more complex, as populations grow and specialization is more in demand, institutions proliferate and, themselves, become more complex. In a very advanced nation, for example, it is not uncommon for many subinstitutions to spring up within a parent institution.

Always there is a tendency toward institutionalization, and as this takes place the individual person tends to become a mere cog in the social machine. He has, in a sense, been forced by social complexity to sell more and more of his individuality and his independence of action in order to continue to exist and function in a mass, institutionalized world. As he becomes ever more institutionalized, he progressively becomes an adaptable personality who thinks more and more about the "collective," the society, the institutions that subsume him.*

Social institutions are by nature conservative. They are set up in the first place, by and large, to conserve the social heritage and to achieve, through a kind of social conformity, some goal.

---

*Very good discussions of the forces in man which contribute to his collectivizing and institutionalizing are found in C. G. Jung, *The Undiscovered Self* (Boston: Little Brown & Co., 1957) and Erich Fromm, *Escape from Freedom* (New York: Holt, Rinehart & Winston, 1941).

They have a very large measure of social control vested in them, and they struggle to retain and to exercise whatever control they have acquired and to extend it if possible. There is the natural tendency for social institutions to become inflexible, reactionary, and decadent. And there is a tendency for them to become dominated by conservative—even reactionary—administrators. This is not really strange, for the very nature of the institution actually dictates that this be so. What has just been said does not mean that institutions do not change; certainly they do grow, progress and adapt, but their adaptibility usually follows the society in which they function.

Simple societies, underdeveloped or "new" nations, have a minimum of institutionalization and a maximum of individual freedom. In the realm of communication, then, we naturally find few if any institutionalized media attempting to reach the masses of the simple society. People speak to people more or less directly, person to person, in an unstructured way. Really it is not a very efficient system, albeit quite pluralistic. Very few citizens of an underdeveloped or transitional nation understand what their government is doing; there is no institutionalized press system to tell them. They get their news and views in bits and pieces, and in an *unsimultaneous* fashion. The splintered nature of the society is reflected in the splintered—almost chaotic—manner in which a very small portion of the population receives its social information.

Complex, highly institutionalized press systems are found in highly developed, highly complex nations. Even when the press institutions (media, units) are pluralistic or diversified, they form a well-organized part of a total national press institution that in some meaningful way synchronizes the pluralism into a unified or functional whole. In other words, a highly developed press system—at least in a Western democracy such as the United States—might be considered the epitome of institutionalized pluralism.

Institutions are organizations formed to serve a social function.

Institutions are structures set up to fill concepts.

Institutions are extensions of personal needs, designed to satisfy those individuals who become a part of them.

Institutions are individuals functioning collectively in society as the persons who make them up would want to function individually.

Institutions are the primary building blocks of a socialistic, collective society.

Institutions are social organisms that drain the individuality and personality from individuals and stir it all together in a common pot.

And institutions are much, much more. Many readers will quite likely not like some of the implications of the above statements about institutions, and will feel that at least several of them are subjective or even biased. There is no doubt that some, such as institutions are building blocks of a socialistic society, contain considerable subjectivity. But such a statement, we believe, is basically valid and follows logically from the very first principles of institutionalization. If institutions come into being to systematize and organize activities so as to be socially functional, then it would follow that institutions are based on *social* goals, not on individual goals. Social goal achievement, i.e. institutionalization, must assume a kind of collective or cooperative activity; therefore, it is difficult to come to any other conclusion than that institutionalization is a step in the direction of socialization. Even so-called "capitalistic" institutions lead to more social conformity, more "mass-oriented" activity, and ultimately to a more monolithic society. As institutionalization increases, *in whatever kind of political or economic context*, one will find individual decision making decreasing and "group-related" decision making increasing. Therefore, without passing judgment on the ultimate implications of institutionalization at this point, we feel we can safely say that the process is a form of depersonalizing and social standardizing.

Institutional Concept and Structure

Sociologists tell us that a social institution must have: 1. a concept, and 2. a structure. The *concept* would be the purpose to be served, the social aim or objective. It would entail the idea, notion, doctrine, interest or philosophy *behind* or *in* the institutionalizing process. The concept would answer the *why* of the institution? The *structure*, on the other hand, would be the *means* used to bring about the concept. It would consist of the framework or apparatus of realizing the purpose of the institution. It would include not only the *physical* apparatus (such as buildings or printing presses) but also the *human* apparatus (reporters, editors, printers)—in short, the persons or functionaries who cooperate in prescribed ways to achieve the goals.

In order for the institution to change, the concept must first change. The structure, then, is dependent on the concept, and it usually changes slowly as the concept is modified. The concept changes and then the structure must be brought in line with it. When the structure is so well adapted to the concept that the goal is reached (the expectation produced), then what is called *institutional equilibrium* is achieved. It may well be that this equilibrium is not very often reached in many of our institutions, and particularly not in our press. Why this implication that the press' structure is not very well adapted to its concept? Very simply because the press' *structure* is generally very advanced but has developed largely *divorced from the concept*. Said another way, the structure is well developed and the concept is undeveloped or underdeveloped.

Now, this is not to say that there is not some kind of extremely general (and vague) *concept of the press* in any society. In the United States, for instance, one could say that the press has as its main social functions (its concept) basically to inform, to interpret and lead, and to entertain. When we have said this, however, we have said very little. Obviously the press' concept is more profound than that. What is the overriding concept of the press (philosophically speaking) in the United States? Although we shall discuss this more fully in Part III of this book, the point should be made here that journalists do not appear to be sure; they are not really agreed on a basic press concept. Some might say that the basic function would be free expression; others might say profit or incentive to the total economy; others might say political guidance; others might say support of the social and political status quo; others might say social change.

In other words, there is probably no one *concept* of the press (in a collective sense) in this country. Or if there is, we know of no student of the press who has isolated it. It is quite possible that in a country like the United States the main characteristic of the press is that there is *no* concept—no goal or aim of journalism. Philosophically, one can understand why in our type of pluralistic society there is no press concept understood by all press people and media. However, it is a little more difficult to understand why individual media or units of the national press system do not have institutional concepts. No doubt many press people would say that their respective media do have concepts, generally understood and worked toward by the functionaries in these individual media. If this were true, however, it would be very strange indeed, for where is the mass medium in which all personnel ever get together and even discuss the medium's function or concept, much less *agree* on it?

What does this newspaper stand for? Where is it going? What overriding objective does it have? How does it go about determining its concept, if it does at all? Does every functionary even think about a concept, or does he in fact simply work, producing his little isolated bit which is fed into the total product *without any meaning* being attached to it? Many persons would equate the newspaper's concept with the philosophy or ideology of the *publisher* of the newspaper. But how could this be when most of the newspaper personnel do not have the slightest idea *what* the publisher considers the aim or objective of the paper? If the publisher represents the newspaper's workers, it is only in the same way that the President of the United States represents the people of the country; and certainly we cannot say that the President represents the people *conceptually*, philosophically, or ideologically. In fact, it may well be that this very atypicallity of the leaders in the country is at the root of much of the growing social discord and rebelliousness. And, it may well be that functionaries in our mass media will increasingly (it has already begun) demand a voice in the day-to-day policies and activities of their institutions.

In spite of what has just been said about the absence of, or vagueness of, a basic overriding press concept in the United States, it is safe to say that there are some functions of the institutionalized press system accepted by various sectors. Let us briefly look at these, which are derived from our American tradition.

Traditional American Press Concepts

One of the basic functions of the press in this country is that of presenting news and presenting it *objectively*. For most of our journalistic history we have heard that news stories must be objective. The term "objectivity" is, of course, a very difficult one to understand. But generally journalists have considered objective reporting to be that which is free (or virtually so) of bias, reporting that is factual—and could be verified. The problems of objectivity in journalism will be discussed more in detail in Chapters 14 and 15.

A second concept or objective of the press in the United States is that of *fairness*. Most journalists (at least those over thirty) in the country would not hesitate to say that their aim is to be fair. This, like most traditional concepts, is a glittering generality—vague but virtuous—and leaves us with many questions. One of the most important is: Fair to whom? For often we know that when we try to be "fair" to one party, the result is unfairness to another. Usually American journalists relate the concept of fairness to that of balance—to "equal time" and other ambiguous and fuzzy ideals.

A third traditionally held function of the American press is that of community and national *leadership*. The word somehow got out that a mass medium should exert influence, should affect people's opinions and actions. Although most media probably would extol the leadership function unreservedly, it might well strike most observers that media generally reflect and follow, rather than strike out in new directions, going beyond the typical thinking of their communities.

A fourth concept quite common in this country is that of the press as a *freedom-seeker-and-defender*. The press normally presents itself as being for an "open society," with the restraining doors of secrecy everywhere being pounded down by the freedom-loving functionaries of the mass media. Most journalists would probably look upon themselves as "liberals"—in the sense of being libertarians concerned with the free marketplace of ideas and information. They would insist that they were against would-be and actual restricters and censors of information that they feel the public has a right to know.

Few journalists seem to realize that there is something amiss here, that their concept of *freedom-seeker-and-defender* tends to lose meaning when it comes up against the very nature of the press as a social institution. Institutionalization, as we have seen, implies systematic ways of doing things—of having a kind of sanctioned mode of behavior, a socialized prescription for concerned action. In reality, then, an institution is diametrically opposed to freedom. As we institutionalize, as we define social roles, we are really losing freedom and acquiescing in its loss.

Related to this freedom-seeker concept is the idea that the press is a check on the power structure, a kind of anti-Establishment "watchdog." Most traditional textbooks in American journalism speak of the press as a public servant, as a critic of government, as a defender of the people's right to know, as a "fourth branch of government." It is only recently that astute observers and critics have recognized that this "watchdog" itself needs some watching, that this Establishment critic has in effect become an Establishment, that this crusader for the people's right to know has itself become a withholder and manager of information. Other persons have begun asking: If the press is in fact the fourth branch of government, how then can a "branch of government" criticize government dispassionately? Others are asking why it must be that the government is further removed from the people in our democracy than is the press? Why is it that the people should support the press in its *anti*government stance, when, at least in theory, the government is more closely related to the people than is the press? Who among the people elected the journalists to their important positions to be "watchdogs" on anything?

A fifth traditional press concept in this country is that of a "forum for the people." We are told that the press exists so that a democratic people can express themselves, argue issues, make themselves heard. This, of course, is compatible with the pluralistic, free-expression, open-society, free-clash-of-ideas concept. Everyone must have access to the press, we are now being told by those who would even legally force media to publish certain information. Pluralism, then, is carried to the limit of being *forced* pluralism. Forcing anything into the media, of course, is contrary to freedom of the press, is reactionary in nature, but this is seemingly overlooked by some of the self-styled "progressives" who would try to reconcile their type of *guided* journalism with an unrestricted freely working press. Here is one case where concepts tend to cancel one another out: the right of a mass medium to make its own free decisions versus the right of people to use the press as a forum.

What is probably happening, albeit slowly, in the United States and in most countries, is that the press concepts are increasingly minimizing the desirability of *freedom* and emphasizing importance of *guidance* in the name of a social responsibility. Even those press spokesmen who continue extolling the virtues of freedom would place controls and guiding hands upon the press in order that it would be "free" in *their* sense of the term. Today there are many people who seem to believe that freedom to control the press is as important as, or more important than, freedom of the press.

Many readers will wonder why so much emphasis is being placed here on the concept of freedom in a discussion about the press as an institution. In our opinion the concept of freedom is basic to a discussion of institutionalization; it begs to be dealt with. And although we plan to examine it in far more depth in Chapters 12 and 13, some attention must be given to it here. Actually the concept of freedom is so important that it is possible to say that in all the world there are but *two fundamental* press concepts: 1. a concept of a press integrated into government itself so as to insure ideological agreement, social progress, and stability, and 2. a concept of the press that considers itself, and is considered, to be outside government completely, free from all external restraints, and with no obligation to support the government.

The first of these two fundamental concepts is related to a press system which is a *supporter* of government, either because it is actually a part of the governing apparatus, or because it sees itself in a role of support and not of antagonism. The second of these basic concepts relates to a press system that sees itself generally in a role of antagonist and critic of the governing apparatus. A good example of a country embracing the first type is the Soviet Union, while the United States exemplifies a country with a press system of the second type.

Institutionalized Media

Now, let us look more closely at the mass media as institutions. Taking the United States as the context for discussion, we might say that the *concept* of the newspaper press is that of observer and critic of government, and protector of pluralism. This is about as much as we can say (and some will disagree even with this) about the institutionalized press concept in this country. The *pluralism* built into this concept is what really keeps the newspaper system of the country from having a more discernible concept.

Different newspapers seem to have different concepts; or, at least we can say they appear to disagree on many fundamental aspects of journalism. For instance, there is no generally agreed upon understanding of what *news* is. Here is the very foundation stone of journalism—at least of a *news*paper, and there is no real agreement as to the nature of news. Also there is no generally accepted understanding among American newspapers as to the desirability of *fairness or balance* in the treatment of minority groups, issues, kinds of content (e.g., politics, economics, sports, society, comic strips). Most newspapermen in the United States, if they have actually tried to ascertain an overriding goal for journalism at all, would probably agree that newspapers in this country really have no *concept* beyond pluralism—and, of course, money making. For even the opinion relative to government support or criticism seems to be ambiguous and fuzzy when scrutinized closely.

And when we have said that pluralism is the newspaper press concept of the country, we have not really said very much about the system's objectives, aims, purposes, goals. We have only said, in effect, that these objectives and goals are somehow intrinsic in the concept of pluralism and will in due course work themselves out in some kind of mystical manner. Newspaper people in this country, usually falling back on John Milton, have traditionally maintained that pluralism leads to a free encounter of information and ideas and somehow out of this battle of contradictions will emerge Truth. Therefore, *pluralism* has been enthroned conceptually in our press—in fact, in our entire media system.

There have always been persons, of course, who have challenged this concept. But, by and large, it has stood firm in this country. Why should Truth automatically emerge out of a clash of opposing opinions, ideas, or sets of facts? It would appear, many critics contend, that what might actually emerge would be confusion and frustration. In theory, perhaps, Truth might emerge in the sense of being evident to some persons receiving some messages at some times in some situations. But, even then, those persons would probably not recognize what they had as Truth. What is more likely is that in a conflict of ideas, some persons come away with some of the ideas and other persons come away with other of the ideas—more than likely those compatible with their predispositions. People are basically looking for supportive messages—facts and opinions—rather than for Truth.

We certainly have a pluralistic press system in this country. A wide variety of information and a fantastically broad range of ideas and opinions flood in upon us today from a multitude of sources. But how close to the Truth about anything are we? Or, said another way, if we are close to it, do we ever realize that we are? Pluralism may well make for a more interesting, a more exciting media system, but just how much truth we get from it is difficult to tell.

Now that we have examined briefly the *concept* of the American press, let us turn to the *structure*. While the concept of the press appears to be rather unclear and perhaps even weak, the structure is clear and strong. Technical facilities, buildings, organized functionaries dominate the mass communications scene. What is rather strange is that this press *structure* has risen like an imposing monument from the foundation of so weak a concept. But it has, and the daily pounding of its mechanistic heart appears to keep the press' institutionalized body functioning. In fact, one might say that the structure of the press is large and vital enough to obscure the fuzziness of the institutional concept.

It is certainly easy to see, on visiting any of the great newspapers, magazines or television stations across the country, where the emphasis is. A visitor would do well to simply gaze on the costly equipment, impressive buildings, complex inner workings of the staff, asking questions about circulation, production problems, hiring practices, and not inquiring into the philosophy of the mass medium—its purposes, its values, its *concept*. It appears to us that in the case of mass media as institutions, the structure has developed independently of a concept, or *in spite of* a vague concept. A gigantic mechanism, a complex structure, has come into being that manages to do rather haphazardly a large number of things without particular relevance to any *concept*. So in this respect we do not have what the sociologists would call institutional equilibrium in that the structure is not designed to bring about the concept. But we do have something institutionalized that works. It may well be that the fact that there is no unified or single goal (concept) in the American press is the reason so-called "professional" schools of journalism often appear to be thrashing about wildly in the academic woods trying to do everything in the absence of any kind of unified goal, ethic or body of professional lore.

Journalistic Orientations

Although it is next to impossible to discuss concepts in journalism as they relate to a whole media system as an institution, it is possible to talk about orientations as they relate to individual media or to individual journalists who are part of the institutionalized press. Media or journalists can be classified in many ways as to their basic orientations, inclinations, or concepts. It seems to us that a simple ternary typology is helpful in describing these basic orientations. Each mass medium and each journalist is predominantly inclined to accept one of these three concepts: 1. Neutral or Reflective, 2. Ambiguous or Multi-role, 3. Leadership or Directive.

It may be difficult to assign any one of these roles or concepts to an entire mass medium, e.g. to *The New York Times*, but we do believe that in a kind of generalized, overall way every mass medium does basically adhere to one of them. However, it is somewhat easier to describe individual journalists as accepting one of the three orientations. Each journalist, we believe, has his own individualized concept or role of journalism; he may work with others who have differing concepts and his own concept may undergo change, but at any time he is inclined to accept one of these three conceptual orientations:

1. Neutral. The journalist accepting this basic concept is the believer in "objective" journalism, a kind of journalism of non-involvement, of non-advocacy. He thinks journalism should essentially be concerned with reflecting the world, not changing or directing it. He is basically a reportive, nonpartisan journalist who tries to keep himself and his biases out of his work. He is dispassionate and non-judgmental, concerned with fairness and balance. He is a journalist who stands aside, apart from the turmoil of an event, and tries to soak up the reality of the event and transmit it, untarnished by distortion, to his readers, listeners, and viewers. He sees himself as neither critic nor supporter of government or the "Establishment."

2. Ambiguous. The journalist accepting this middle-area concept might be called a multi-role person. He sees his responsibility in journalism to do almost everything; he assumes many roles, none of which really dominates. He is, at times, an advocate; at times, he must provide facts. He, too, believes in objective reporting, but is willing to experiment with interpretive reporting replete with all of its judgmental overtones. He is sometimes passionate, sometimes dispassionate. He generally considers himself an open-minded journalist, capable of flexibility and change. He is the rider of many journalistic horses, feeling a special attachment for none of them. He tries to lead, as well as follow, public opinion. He sees himself as both critic and supporter of government or the "Establishment."

3. Leadership. The journalist who is inclined toward this concept sees the role of journalism as mainly directive. He is as convinced of journalism's leadership or directive role as the Neutralist is of journalism's reflective role. Any journalism worth its name, he believes, must be advocative, judgmental, catalytic. Journalism must lead, not follow. It must be subjective. He thinks that there is no such thing as objective journalism, although many cowardly, spineless journalists try to act as if there were. It is probably safe to say that Leadership journalism is propagandistic journalism. The journalist is a propagandist, with a belief, a program, an objective, and he systematically tries to implant it all in others. In a real sense he is an elitist; he believes he has answers for the masses. He uses his journalism to try to spread his values, to foist his ideology on others. He is passionate, personal, and forceful; he is involved and, to varying degrees, radicalized. He usually is inclined to be critical of government or the "Establishment"; however, a Leadership or directive journalist may just as passionately support the government or the "Establishment."

Many readers may object to this ternary typology just presented, saying with considerable truth that a journalist is too complex to be classified in any one of these ways. Surely, no journalist does fall snugly into any one of these classes, but there is good reason to believe that every journalist is oriented toward one of these three concepts. It certainly has been our observation that journalists, as well as journalism students, are basically neutralist, ambivalent, or advocative. Of course, each journalist may be a little of all three—and undoubtedly he is—but his basic orientation or predisposition would cause him to gravitate toward one of the three.

In the next chapter communicators will be considered in different terms, from a different perspective. But it is well that we have begun an analysis of mass communicators by looking at the broad concepts or roles that they bring to the mass-media system. So, as we leave this discussion of the press as an institution, we should realize that the institutional complexity comes about when the "concept" is considered. And since the concept, to the degree that it exists at all, is generated and crystallized by persons (functionaries) concerned with, or working in, the press, it is natural that we turn next to an analytical discussion of these persons—these *communicators.*

8.

Communicators

HISTORIES OF AMERICAN JOURNALISM ARE USUALLY BUILT around the outstanding personalities of the press. However, an argument could be made that inventions and social forces played a more prominent role than did men in shaping the content and nature of mass communication throughout U. S. history. This proposition does not deny the influence of forceful, and even flamboyant, publishers, editors, and reporters. But when one looks at the sweep of journalistic history in this country he is struck by the incidence of similar men appearing on the scene at the same periods of time and then, with notable exceptions, disappearing from prominence in the American press.

Thus, we could describe the history of news in America in terms of the kinds of men created by conditions of the press and society at four specific periods of time: *publisher-printer* (eighteenth to mid-nineteenth centuries), *publisher-editor* (mid-nineteenth century to 1900), *institutional editor* (1900 to mid-twentieth century), and *reporter-personality* (mid-twentieth century to present).

During the era of the *publisher-printer*, the proprietor of the press was essentially a servant of a hand-operated press. He was a skilled craftsman, but his inability to achieve high circulation as a result of the primitive state of press mechanics meant that his staff was small, and that he could not free himself from duties such as writing some, if not all, of the news copy, in addition to setting type and operating the presses. The "job-shop" nature of his operation and the extremely limited circulation meant that the *publisher-printer* was likely to accept material from outside "contributing editors" and cater to the political tastes of his select group of readers. In such circumstances, the newspapers of that period often became vehicles for political and literary essays (many of them reprinted from other sources), as well as for news and editorial items. The publisher had to stand responsible for the controversial content, although he was not always totally involved in its creation. Toward the latter part of the period, coincidental with the rise of political parties, newspapers became more partisan, and the "contributing editors" moved into the more formal position of functioning editors.

This situation provided a bridge from the period of the *publisher-printer* to the period of the *publisher-editor*. Inventions such as the steam-driven rotary press, coupled with the social phenomenon of public education, allowed the publisher for the first time to reach a mass audience. Newspapers could now maintain larger production and reporting staffs, emancipating the *publisher-editor* from everyday involvement in the details of both the printing and news operations. For the first time, he could afford his own division of labor: as publisher, he laid down general business and news guidelines; as editor, he gave more attention to the editorial page. The *publisher-editor* was personally responsible for the editorial tone and position of his paper, and, in the reader's mind, the paper itself was closely associated with the personality of the *publisher-editor*. The period began with such memorable personalities as Benjamin Day, the James Gordon Bennetts, and Horace Greeley; it ended with men of similar force, Joseph Pulitzer and William Randolph Hearst.

Adolph Ochs's purchase of *The New York Times* in 1896 inaugurated the third period, the age of the *institutional editor*. In assimilating the technological innovations of the late nineteenth century, the newspaper had become a costly and complex machine dispensing news and advertisements. This industry called for publishers who were first and foremost businessmen, albeit businessmen well-grounded in the total functions of the press. These publishers set overall policy, but generally were dissociated from the news operation and all but the basic tone of the editorial page. Having turned their attention to the business side of the newspaper operation, they delegated editorial supervision to *institutional editors*, retailers of the production of reporters, the wire services, and syndicated features. The newspaper achieved a rather bland balance of straight news and not-too-controversial editorial opinion. It was a period in which the newspaper as an institution achieved greater recognition than publishers or editors. The inception and full flowering of the news magazine during this period epitomized the virtual anonymity of the communicators themselves. Highly skilled publishers amalgamated and forged newspaper groups. Equally skilled editors arrayed the glut of news. The volume of news and its credibility reached new heights. But the editorial page lost its punch, for it had begun to represent institutions rather than the human beings with whom the reader could identify. Names of publishing families and groups stand out during this period: Scripps-Howard, Annenberg, Newhouse, Gannett, Knight, Chandler. The names of great editors come less slowly to the surface of recognition.

Reporters of the caliber of Henry M. Stanley, Arthur Brisbane, and Richard Harding Davis achieved fame throughout the nineteenth and twentieth centuries, and outstanding columnists and commentators—Walter Lippmann, Arthur Krock, and Edward R. Murrow, to name only a few—cast their giant shadows prior to the mid-twentieth century. But these were the exceptions to the typical subordination of the reporter to the *publisher-editor* and later to the *institutional editor*. Television was the catalyst that, for the first time, permitted the *reporter-personality* to dominate the news scene in the United States. Radio had given the reporter a voice. Television gave him a face, and it put this face in the living room each weekday night. The immediacy and brevity of television news, however, gave newspapers an opportunity to compete through offering perspective and detail. The resulting interpretative stories and opinion columns emphasized the personalities and names of their authors. Television was only one factor associated with the arrival of the *reporter-personality*. By the mid-twentieth century, daily newspaper monopolies existed in all but a few American cities. The newspaper had a dilemma: how to fulfill its function of offering a variety of controversial opinion without antagonizing large segments of its heterogeneous audience. The answer was the syndicated columnist, who wrote under his own by-line and spoke for himself rather than for the newspaper in which he appeared. The number of syndicated columnists has mushroomed, as has the syndicate services; and newspapers today are likely to run regularly four or more political columnists, covering the broad spectrum of political opinion.*

It may well be that we are still barely into the era of the *reporter-personality*. But most observers would agree that this type of newsman has captured the imagination and interest of the American audience. It is the *reporter-personality* who draws the premium salary, especially if he is syndicated or in network television. Novelists abandon fiction for subjective news assignments by magazines. Reporters, rather than editors or publishers, run for elective office. And television anchormen on

---

*For an interesting analysis of the world of syndicated columnists and how they are featured by "liberal" and "conservative" newspapers, see two articles in the *Columbia Journalism Review* written by Ben H. Bagdikian: "How Newspapers Use Columnists" (Fall 1964) and "Journalism's Wholesalers" (Fall 1965).

"location" at political rallies are apt to draw larger crowds than major political candidates.

Some media units, of course, still operate under the *institutional editor* philosophy, and one could find a few magazines and newspapers, generally of small circulation, that even today are *publisher-printer* or *publisher-editor* operations. The development of offset printing has made it comparatively simple for a person with something to say, or something to sell, to become a newspaper publisher. As a result, underground and suburban weeklies have proliferated in recent years. Generally, in the early years of publication they are *publisher-editor* operations. The few that survive find it necessary to fill more space and offer a wider variety of content to their readers. As this occurs, they are likely to undergo a change to a *reporter-personality* orientation.

Who Becomes a Communicator?

Gay Talese, in his book about *The New York Times*, observes:

> Not only on *The Times*, but on other newspapers, the news staffs were largely populated by products of the lower middle class—by liberal Jews and less liberal Irish-Catholics from the North, by progressive Protestants from the South and Midwest; and, not unexpectedly, by relatively few Italo-Americans. The immigrants from Italy took longer to become familiar with the English language and its literature, as did other ethnic groups to whom the English language was difficult; they did not produce many newspaper reporters. . . .*

Talese contends that only those from the lower middle class had the "drive, patience, and persistence to succeed as reporters." Journalism, he explains, provided men from this group with a vehicle for upward mobility. Talese's generaliza-

---

*The Kingdom and the Power (New York and Cleveland: World Publishing Co., 1969), p. 326.

tions about the source of reportorial manpower is certainly superficial. But he touches upon two important points that deserve amplification: the exclusion of certain groups from journalistic professions, and the tendency of the profession to be dominated by liberal, as opposed to conservative, personalities.

Generally, reporters do not come from the racial and ethnic minorities in the United States. This has often been attributed solely to discrimination by the mass media. Although media in all sections of the United States have been guilty of racist hiring practices, there are factors in addition to outright bias that have perpetuated this situation. As Talese implies, language is an important qualification for journalistic personnel, and a facility with English has always been a prerequisite for entrance into the print media. Blacks in America have historically had schools of inferior quality to those in white sections. In addition, English has been one of the least successful courses in their schools because the grammar of the textbooks has been almost a different language from that spoken in the ghetto. Language also has been a problem, obviously, for those students from bilingual communities, where, say, Spanish is the language of the home and neighborhood, and English is the language of instruction. Their lower degree of facility with mainstream idiom and accent have made blacks and Mexican-Americans poor candidates for either the electronic or print media. Fortunately, improved educational opportunities and active recruiting by the media are helping to correct the existing imbalance.

An explanation such as that given above would explain why first-generation Italian-Americans were less qualified than more established Americans for jobs as reporters, but indicates that second generation Italian-Americans did not face a similar handicap, since the process of language assimilation had been completed by that time. In cases where language barriers are perpetuated by social and cultural immobility—as with blacks and large numbers of Mexican-Americans—succeeding generations have only a slightly better chance than their parents of entering journalistic professions.

Talese also declares that those who enter the ranks of reporting tend to be "liberals," rather than "conservatives." This is a widely held view, and is probably correct. Writers, in a sense, are word performers. Communicators engaged in radio and television news work are actually on the fringe of show business itself. All are creative people, and, like other creative personalities in the arts, they tend to be more sensitive to the social ills that they observe and describe in the course of their professional work. They are also people who initially, at least, enter their profession as salaried employees; many become at the same time members of an AFL-CIO union, the American Newspaper Guild. For all of these reasons, it would be surprising if the average reporter were not more liberal than conservative, just as it would be surprising if the average trainee in banking were not more conservative than liberal.

Responsibility of the Communicator

In the days when the publisher or editor fully controlled the content of his newspaper, it was the publication's responsibility to see that some order of fairness in reporting the news was maintained. Now this responsibility has shifted more than ever to the reporter. The newspaper has little control over the copy of the syndicated columnists, who are increasingly taking more of the newspaper's space for interpretative stories on events of domestic and foreign interest. Television is able to exercise only limited gatekeeping on sound-on-film reports from its far-flung correspondents. Copy usually cannot be examined in advance; the filmed report often cannot be edited at all.

In such circumstances, where a reporter does not come under the tight reins of an editor, there is a tendency toward subjectivity. The loaded adjective, the inflection of sarcasm or incredulity, remain in the final report. However, this natural tendency of television to force a shift away from objective reporting in the electronic and print media has been accelerated by a new attitude apparent in many young reporters. They consider objective reporting to be an impossible, if not a cowardly, act. They feel they must be personally involved in the stories they are assigned to cover. They must do this for the sake of humanity and for the sake of their own self-respect.

The feasibility of achieving "objectivity" is discussed in detail in Chapter 15. The consequences of personal involvement, however, must be considered at this point, because they are closely related to the role of the newsmen in the *reporter-personality* era.

Earlier in this book, in discussing the problem of press monopoly, we compared it to the problem of monopoly in the soap industry. We pointed out that a soap monopoly would still offer the product that consumers want, but monopoly of the press threatens to remove the product itself, variety of criticism. In a similar fashion, we can say that there are many professions whose practitioners can involve themselves completely in the problems of individuals or society as a whole without damaging the service they perform. In the case of a reporter working for a truly *mass* medium, involvement threatens to destroy the reporter's product, a factual report arrived at by professional newsgathering methods.

This example is sometimes given: A press photographer observes one man preparing to fire a pistol at the head of another man. Does he stand his ground and take the photograph, or does he rush to the aid of the intended victim? If he takes the picture, it will undoubtedly be a dramatic photograph that may have significant effect on the minds of the audience. If he doesn't take the photograph, perhaps he will be able to save the man's life. Under a circumstance like this, we would hope that the photographer would instinctively act to save a man's life, a human life being worth more than a photograph under any conditions. But, unfortunately, the lines are not always so clearly drawn or dramatically presented. In most cases a reporter has to consciously determine whether to serve his readers or serve a cause, and when he tries to do both simultaneously it is usually the readers that are shortchanged.

A communicator who, by dress or action, identifies himself with a controversial cause damages his own credibility for impartiality. Some sources who properly identify him will withhold all or part of the information he needs to produce a factual story. Some members of the audience who properly identify him will doubt the credibility of his report, and some of this doubt will be transferred to the publication or broadcasting station that employs him. If the doubt becomes strong enough, many readers or viewers will turn to what they consider a more credible source, or they will (in the case of electronic media) demand government intervention to assure fairness.

It is the responsibility of every individual, of course, to make his own decision about personal involvement, but he must remember that his decision affects the credibility of his publication or station, also. A reporter who believes that he must become personally involved in political or controversial causes has other alternatives that he should consider, too. These include asking that he not be assigned to a story in which he has a personal involvement, participating in the cause after working hours,* taking a leave of absence from his publication or station in order to work for the cause, and going to work for a publication that is clearly identified as an organ of opinion.

For those who persist in identifying themselves, their reports, and their medium with a partisan cause on the grounds that this is the proper function of mass media in a free society, we can only suggest that the inevitable result will be media that are no longer "mass," operating in a society that—from the point of the view of the press—will no longer be free.

Control of the Communicator

With the individual reporter, columnist, and commentator playing a more important role in the communication process than ever before, some critics have suggested that communicators be held personally accountable for the quality of their product. A physician recently wrote in his county medical bul-

---

*This would not be an acceptable solution for a communicator so well known that his private personality could not be dissociated from his professional personality. Some television anchormen, for example, decline to express a private opinion on highly controversial topics, even when off the air, for fear that the credibility of their entire newscast will suffer.

letin that, considering the newsmen's "tremendous, almost unlimited power in shaping public opinion," they should be licensed. A newsman, the doctor wrote, should be required to
show proof of ability, training, and qualifications before being
allowed to practice his profession, and he added:

> Almost all professions and even most skilled and some unskilled
> trades are so regulated. There seems to be no justification for the
> exclusion of news reporting, a profession, from identical regulation.
> This would not limit free speech and would give at least minimal
> assurance as to ability, reliability, and veracity.

What the doctor failed to note is that, aside from the
clergy, journalism is the only profession open to all under a
guarantee of an Amendment to the United States Constitution.
Most trades and professions that license practitioners do so for
one of two reasons, to artificially limit the number of persons
who can engage in that work, or to protect the lives and property of those who purchase their skills. Journalistic reports offer
no direct threat to the lives and property of readers and viewers,
and any effort to limit entrance to the profession would undoubtedly be declared unconstitutional. If the license were
automatically issued to any literate person who wanted to write
for a publication or work in broadcasting, it would be meaningless. If the licensing procedure called for any qualifications at all
on the part of the applicant, it would pose a basic threat to
freedom of the press. As in so many other cases where the press
is concerned, a gain in "responsibility" means a loss in freedom.

Few in the journalistic profession have ever seriously called
for licensing of newsmen. The closest the profession has ever
come to enforcing a standard among its practitioners was a
famous episode involving the American Society of Newspaper
Editors and its "Canons of Journalism." The ASNE adopted the
Canons, a code of ethics, shortly after the founding of the
organization in 1922, but the first effort to enforce the Canons
shattered when it ran against the figure of Frederick G. Bonfils,
editor and co-publisher of the *Denver Post*. The case concerned
Bonfils' involvement in the famous Teapot Dome scandal,

which rocked the Harding administration. The principle was one of basic journalistic ethics—Bonfils had apparently accepted money in return for surpressing advance information about the scandal. The ASNE moved to toss him out of the society. Bonfils threatened to sue each member of the Board of Directors if that occurred. The ASNE did not expel Bonfils (he later resigned from the organization) and never again attempted to expel a member for violation of professional ethics. Some members of the society contended at the time that, reprehensible though Bonfils' action was, any effort to make a pariah out of him by expelling him would in itself be a violation of the spirit of the First Amendment. In the words of Benjamin Franklin, "Abuses of freedom of speech ought to be repressed, but to whom dare we commit the power of doing it?"

Codes of ethics can be found in many newsrooms, on the walls of most journalism schools, and in the annals of state press associations throughout the land. But those who have created and adopted them would agree with Benjamin M. McKelway, former editorial chairman of the *Washington Star*, who said: "Codes and canons may be helpful outlines of desirable conduct, like the Sermon on the Mount. But a vital characteristic of a free press is the guarantee of freedom for what may be regarded as the worst, as well as the best, among its practitioners."

Education of the Communicator

Journalism education, pioneered in the United States, is now available in some form in every developed country of the world. In America, courses in all aspects of mass communication have been incorporated into the curriculum of most colleges and universities. The purpose of the undergraduate curriculum remains much the same as that foreseen by University of Missouri President A. Ross Hill during the School of Journalism's first year of operation in 1908: "I believe it is possible for this school to give dignity to the profession of journalism, to anticipate to some extent the difficulties that journalism must meet and to prepare its graduates to overcome them, to give prospective journalists a professional spirit and high ideals of service, to discover those with real talent for the work and discourage those who are likely to prove failures in the profession, and to give the state better newspapers and newspapermen and a better citizenship."*

The lack of a journalism degree, however, does not bar any college graduate from employment in the mass media. Indeed, there are numerous editors who prefer that beginning reporters have a degree in some other field, and still others who do not require educational standards beyond the high-school level.

Often, those editors who disdain journalism degrees are those who do not have them themselves. Self-made men usually feel that the best avenue to success is the one that they themselves followed. If medicine and the law were unlicensed professions—if "reading for the law" or learning the medical trade by practicing with a licensed physician were still as popular now as they were a hundred years ago—similar attitudes would exist in those professions, too. In the sense that no uniform educational standards prevail for entrance to the professions, journalism is anachronistic. But the severe demands of the First Amendment, permitting access to all, perpetuates this anachronism, and in the long run this is a benefit to society.

Even so, there are serious long-range handicaps to a journalistic tradition of "learning on the job." Tom Hopkinson, who established courses in journalism in several African countries for the International Press Institute, came back to England with a different perspective toward the British bias against journalism education:

> My own conviction about the "rubbing-off" or "sitting next to Nellie" system is that it is wasteful and ineffectual. There is no

---

*Quoted in Walter Williams, *Twenty Years of Education for Journalism* (Columbia, Mo.: E. W. Stephens Publishing Co., 1929), p. 25.

reason why a young man should spend years crawling up the ladder of journalistic competence, if he can learn the technical side of his calling in a year. But the system in-builds a far worse defect. It tends to perpetuate existing faults, because new people coming into journalism are indoctrinated not simply with the knowledge, but with all the prejudices, of their so-called teachers.

. . . Since I have been back in England I have talked to dozens of young men and women going into journalism. Most, it seems to me, reject the false sense of news values so enthusiastically accepted by their seniors. But they lack journalistic expertise and know-how. In five years' time, when they are in a position to affect decisions about what goes into the paper and how it is to be treated, they will have been thoroughly indoctrinated with the views they now reject.*

Journalism offers each person complete freedom of choice in shaping his own education. If the student chooses to go the route of an accredited school or department of journalism, only about a quarter of his courses will be in the communication curriculum, and a number of these will be more akin to classes in the social sciences than to "nuts and bolts" technique courses. In effect, he will have "majored" in journalism in the same way that another student majors in history or sociology. At the end of his college course work, he should have an education as broad as those who majored in another field in liberal arts colleges, and at the same time he should be equipped to produce higher quality work than beginning communicators with nonjournalism degrees.

Where journalism schools and departments do not exist, talented students who could best serve their fellow man in the profession of journalism are attracted to other fields of learning that do present courses and dedicated professors. It must be noted that some private universities that do not offer journalism education on either the undergraduate or graduate level traditionally produce outstanding communicators, who have learned journalistic techniques through work on university publications

---

*Tom Hopkinson, "Sitting Next to Nellie," *The Listener* (October 16, 1969), p. 502.

and broadcasting stations. But these schools also furnish fewer men to the mass communication fields than they should, and fewer men than the country needs, simply because they do not offer a full range of scholastic incentives.

It has been the authors' observation that few students embark upon journalistic careers because they believe this is the way they can best serve the cause of democracy. They enroll in journalism courses because they believe they have special talents in communication fields, and because they think they would enjoy exploiting these talents to earn their daily bread. However, the student who leaves with a journalism degree should have an awareness that goes above and beyond a facility in journalistic skills and a broad knowledge of the liberal arts.

He should have an understanding of the ethics of journalism, a knowledge of the relationship of press freedom to political democracy, and a commitment to the role of journalism in a free society. Hopefully, he will assimilate this information in all his courses—technical and theoretical. If he does not, he may enter publishing or broadcasting as a craftsman, but it is unlikely that he will enter it as a professional.

9.

Audiences

THE CONSUMERS OF MASS COMMUNICATION—THOSE WHO EX-
pose themselves to the mass media—comprise what might be
called audiences. The term "audience," however, is very difficult to deal with analytically, especially when we are thinking
about a *mass* audience. If we want to study and describe the
persons sitting in an auditorium listening to a lecturer, we can
do this with some degree of competence and success. We can at
least count them and observe their reactions to the message and
to the communicator. And, if we are so inclined, we can get
their names and do various in-depth studies in which a very substantial body of data will be gathered. We could, then, say that
it is possible to know this type of audience very well.

It is not so simple with the mass audience, or more correctly, with mass *audiences* that continuously expose themselves to various types of mass messages. Since the members of
these audiences are scattered, fluid, anonymous, unseen, and
heterogeneous (see Chapter 1), it is impossible for us to know
very much about their consistencies. The very nature, then, of a
mass audience defies careful analysis, although many sociologists have attempted to do this in a kind of statistical way. Most

generalizations that can be made about mass audiences must stem mainly from intuition; in other words, our ideas about mass audiences must be formed by a rather unscientific method of limited observation and inadequate induction.

Two Main Audience Types

In spite of the impreciseness with which we can discuss mass audiences, it is possible to suggest several possibilities of classification that might prove beneficial in analyzing them. For instance, it appears reasonable to say that there are two main types or kinds of mass audiences. One of these would be the very broad, *completely* heterogeneous and anonymous, audience that is often referred to as the *general public*. The other type of mass audience would be a more specialized audience that appears to be formed by some kind of common interest among its members. In other words it is rather *homogeneous* in at least one important aspect. Let us look a little more closely at these two basic types.

The General Public Audience. Although some writers think this general mass audience is really mythical,* it does seem to have some meaning and is probably the type of audience to which most persons refer when they talk about "mass" audiences. When we say that television (at least in its network programming aspect) is a mass medium, we are implying that it reaches, or has the potential of reaching, a very broad, heterogeneous *general* audience. Certain programs on television may be aimed primarily at specific portions or specialized segments of this broad general audience, but television itself—or its message output *in toto*— is not specialized, but is general.

The member of this amorphous, general, heterogeneous audience has no sense of relationship with other members. He has nothing (that he is aware of) really in common with them;

---

*Robert C. O'Hare in his *Media for the Millions*, for example, contends that the mass audience is "one of the great fallacies of mass communication"; in spite of the fact that it has been discredited, he says, it still persists (pp. 35-36).

he is, in fact, exposing himself to the mass media in an atom-
ized, individual, personal way. He has no sense of camaraderie
with others of like mind or interest. He does not think of himself as one of a *group* of any type. This member of the "general
public" audience, then, reacts independently to mass media
messages. In one sense, therefore, he is really more *independent*
or *individualistic* in his exposure and response to the mass media than is the member of the second main type of mass media
audience, which we shall look at now.

The Specialized Audience.   This type of mass audience,
although scattered, basically anonymous, and in most ways
heterogeneous, is made up of individuals who have a common
interest or orientation that causes them to be members of the
same audience.* For example, people with a certain interest or
concern subscribe to the *Wall Street Journal*; usually they are
homogeneous at least so far as economic interest is concerned.
Not that they are all wealthy, but they are interested in finance,
in economic matters, and more than likely they are members of
the upper-middle and upper classes. So, this audience is specialized in the sense of interest in economics; it is also homogeneous in that this manifest interest in financial matters is a
common bond and probably evidences a homogeneity in many
other areas—e.g. in social and political ideologies, values, and
general life-styles.

The readers of the *New Republic,* without personally
knowing each other, can assume that a kind of intellectual cohesion exists among them. They can, in effect, *know* a considerable amount about one another, and the publisher, editors, and
writers for the magazine can assume much about their audience
members. One thing that can be assumed about a reader of the
New Republic is that he is vitally interested in serious social

---

*This type of audience is, in many ways, quite similar to what Gustave Le Bon
refers to as a "psychological crowd"—not necessarily in one place, perhaps comprising thousands of isolated persons. See Le Bon's classic work, *The Crowd* (1895); *The
Crowd: A Study of the Popular Mind*, paperback ed. (New York: Ballantine Books,
1969).

problems, in politics, in war and peace, in international issues. It can also be assumed that he considers himself a "liberal," whatever such a term may really mean. He is probably to the left politically, a person concerned with civil and minority rights, with what he sees as exploitation of other nations, with injustices in the legal system, with excesses by the police, with the drift toward militarism, and the allocation of an inordinate proportion of the wealth to war and war-related enterprises. These are a few of the basic "concerns" that bring audience members to the *New Republic* and similarly oriented publications. The audience of the conservative *National Review* would be politically homogeneous also, but would draw a quite different type of audience member than would the *New Republic.*

It should be pointed out, however, that although the two publications named above may attract different types of audiences, they draw readers who have something in common. For example, readers of both magazines are concerned with *issues,* and are basically *political* persons. Each audience is not concerned with issues in the same way or for the same reasons, of course, but they share a certain common passion, intellectual curiosity, and considerable political egotism and arrogance. In this sense the dedicated audiences of "liberals" and "conservatives" are very much alike.

Audiences, then, can be mass and at the same time can be united or specialized in one way or on one main interest. We can think of audiences that seek out media that will feed one or more of their common interests: politics, economics, country-and-western music, hunting and fishing, boating, stamp collecting, gardening, sex exploits, and on and on. And in a mass society such as that of the United States there are enough persons who have common special interests that communications media can afford to exist to satisfy these extremely sizable specialized audiences.

Before turning to some more specific types of audiences or subgroups of the all-inclusive mass audience, it might be well to say a few things that would apply to audiences generally.

Audiences vary in at least four essential ways: 1. in size, 2. in composition, 3. in degree of homogeneity, and 4. in longevity.

Every mass media audience is large, but when we have said this we have not said very much. "Large," "medium-sized" and "small" mass audiences evidently do exist but in a kind of fuzzy, undefined way. At any rate, it is safe to say that mass audiences vary in size. Different numbers of persons at different times are exposed to (become audiences of) various of the mass media.

Not only varying *numbers* comprise distinct audiences, but different *persons* are involved. Although undoubtedly there is some overlap among audience members comprising mass audiences, we can say that each audience differs in composition. The makeup of every audience, while possibly partly the same, is fundamentally unique, with one audience having within it not only different *individuals* but often quite different *types* of persons.

The degree of homogeneity varies considerably between or among audiences. Usually, but not always, the larger the audience the less the degree of homogeneity; the smaller the audience the more homogeneity. The general mass audience (the *potential* public) lacks much homogeneity; the smaller sub-audiences tend to become more specialized and thereby more homogeneous. But every audience differs from every other in its degree of homogeneity.

Lastly, audiences vary according to the length of time they stay "in tune with" the particular mass medium and message. *Exposure cohesion* this might be called. In one sense, however, no audience remains completely cohesive or intact during the entire communication of the message. Audience members, to be sure, are *mentally* tuning in and out; in addition, they are *physically* coming to and going from the message. All audiences, then, are in a constant state of flux, but if we can accept that and pass over it, we can then say that audiences differ from one another in *longevity*. In other words, some audiences essentially stay "together" or adhere without major change much longer than do other audiences. So we can refer to audiences of short exposure and audiences of long exposure, although we may not be able to say precisely what "short" and "long" exposures are. On television, for example, the audience watching a football game differs considerably in *exposure cohesion* from the audience watching a half-hour network newscast. In the print media, the audience reading articles in the *New Yorker* is quite different in respect to exposure cohesion from the audience reading articles in *Reader's Digest* or in a local newspaper.

Three Basic Subgroups

The kind of audience member a person is largely depends on his attitude, his values, desires, his philosophy of life—as the Germans say, his *Weltanschauung*. Since publications and other mass media must aim, where possible, at persons with similar interests or orientations, it is important for journalists to recognize the basic types of persons making up the mass general audience. Media, then, can aim at a specific type of person who, in a way, symbolizes a sizable segment of the public. Of course, there are many ways these basic audience segments may be classified, but a fairly simple and useful one is this ternary typology:

The "Illiterates." The reason that quotation marks are around this type of audience member is that many of these persons can actually read and write. So this segment of the mass audience includes those who can read, but who are not inclined to do so. Then, there are those true "illiterates" who do no reading, but do expose themselves to picture publications, movies, television, and radio. Therefore, we can say that the "illiterate" audience member is either truly illiterate or that he is attitudinally illiterate. At least, he is not a *word-oriented* person. His adherence to the mass media is a very surface kind; he exposes himself to the most superficial and action-filled of media messages. He is entertainment seeking; he is searching for excitement in his media exposure.

The illiterate audience member savors vicarious thrills from his media messages. He is a superficial consumer; he may read light fiction that gratifies his emotional appetites; he may read captions with pictures; he may read headlines and certain action-type stories in the newspaper. *But basically he does not like to read.* He exposes himself to *picture media* where he can expend a minimum of effort as he receives the messages.

He is not idea-oriented. In fact, it is safe to say that he is self-gratification oriented. To some extent he is "thing" oriented, but oftentimes he evidences a callousness or disdain for material possessions except those of a very simple type that will give him momentary satisfaction.

Basically, this type of audience member is mentally lazy. This is why he is a "looker" and not a "reader"; this is why he is an "actor" and not a "thinker"; this is why he is satisfied with a superficial picture of the world around him and not with a full interpretation of or understanding of events and issues.

The "illiterate" reader-viewer-listener is unimpressed with participation in political and social activities. In a sense he is a "loner"—at least in the sense of involvement in the workings of the larger social world outside his own family or neighborhood. He feels that he can have little or no impact on major decisions of any type, and so he largely retires from the main current of human activity.

His "communication world" is thus turned inward. Self-gratification is the primary motive for his interest in any of the mass media. Since he is not concerned with social involvement and activity, he is naturally not interested in any kind of mass communication that attempts to activize him, to get him to participate, to consider problems and issues, to think, to discuss, to become concerned. What the "illiterate" audience member takes in from the mass media, he keeps within himself. He is not a "message sharer" except in a very narrow way—with his wife, perhaps. He absorbs his messages for his own emotional benefit, for his own escape from the routine world of existing.

As to his socio-economic status, he is generally found at

the poverty or near-poverty level. However, it is important to note that he exists in rather large numbers in the lower-middle classes. For it should be remembered that his communication activities stem largely from his *interests*. Many people are even quite well off financially and are still "illiterates" when it comes to being concerned mainly with reading, viewing, and listening to messages that will give them personal and immediate enjoyment. However, since one's socio-economic status does have considerable impact on his education, and thereby on his interests, it is not hard to see that most of these attitudinal "illiterates" would fall in the lower income levels of society.

A person's native intelligence (IQ) is also a related, but peripheral, factor in determining whether or not he will be a mass media "illiterate." Many persons have great mental capacities, great intellectual potential, but do not have the motivation, the interests, or the energy to make the effort. One can only speculate as to the number of persons with extremely high IQ's who go through life being satisfied with only superficial messages of a self-gratification type, designed to erase their boredom for the fleeting moment.

There is no way to know what percentage of the total audience comprises this "illiterate" group, but it is probably safe to estimate that it consists of at least sixty percent of all readers-listeners-viewers. It would certainly be the largest of the three segments of the general mass audience of the United States. Let us turn now to the next largest—and probably the most important to the mass communicator: *the practical audience.*

The Pragmatists. Probably thirty percent of the total mass audience can be found in this important middle group, which has been referred to as the pragmatic or practical audience. These pragmatists are social beings in that they like to involve themselves in the machinery of their society. They participate. They work. They campaign. They vote. They belong to organizations. They have hobbies. They travel. They build homes.

They buy automobiles. They watch television. They read newspapers and magazines. They buy recordings, and listen to radio.

The practical audience members, therefore, are *not lazy—* mentally or physically. They desire to be accepted by others. They are ambitious; they want to rise in their system. They want promotions and salary increases. They want to keep up with, or get ahead of, the Joneses. By and large, they are the ones who exercise social power today.* They are interested in *status*, and since material possessions are symbols of status in our society, they are interested in accumulating possessions.

These pragmatists, since they basically may be characterized in the terms used above, form the primary audience for a commercially oriented mass media system. Their concern with status and their ambitions cause them to be great consumers of mass messages. Advertisers, and by projection all of our commercial mass media, love them and try to satisfy their desires. Since these practical audience members want to advance, and since they are pragmatic in that they want to know how to do things that will help them get ahead, they feed regularly at the troughs of expository journalism. How to live more meaningful lives. How to get the most out of that trip to Europe. How to win friends and influence the boss. How to build your own patio and save money. How to be stimulating and knowledgeable at the company party. How to live a spiritually satisfying life. These are the kinds of concerns the practical audience member has. And he exposes himself to media of mass communication which will give him what he wants.

He, unlike the "illiterate" audience member, is seeking information that will help him advance, progress, get on better with others, involve himself more usefully in his community and nation. He has a practical reason for his communication

---

*See José Ortega y Gasset, *The Revolt of the Masses* (New York: W. W. Norton & Co., 1932), for a look at these middle-class pragmatists, these typical "mass men" who dominate in society. Cf., for a more recent analysis of these persons—from a U. S. perspective, William H. Whyte, Jr., *The Organization Man* (New York: Simon and Schuster, 1956).

habits—a socially practical one. For he is essentially a *social* person, one who is actually lonely and restless when he is not with others. He is in a way a snob, but not one who sits in seclusion from society; he is an involved snob—a snob in the sense of having a kind of arrogant demeanor because of his *doing*, his social accomplishments, his physical possessions, his neighborhood, his title, his circle of friends and associates. He is snobbish, then, toward the *inactive*, the uninvolved persons who do not appear to be ambitious and who seemingly make no real contributions toward the ongoing of the country.

The pragmatist is much like the "illiterate" in that he does not really like *ideas*. He, too, is essentially a thing-oriented person. He does not like to think, to contemplate and philosophize, to analyze and scrutinize, to play with concepts. He is an *action* man. However, he often accepts serious, thoughtful messages in the course of his media exposure, because he knows that he *might be expected* to know something about these things. He must at least appear interested in ideas and issues, not because he really is, but because he feels it will "pay off" in the long run. In effect, he is interested in issues and ideas for a very *practical* reason.

The "Intellectuals." Intellectuals, and the term should be in quotation marks to indicate a basic orientation or attitude, comprise the smallest segment of the mass general audience—probably no more than ten percent. The intellectuals (not necessarily the "intelligent ones") of the mass audience are those who are concerned with issues, aesthetic matters, philosophical problems, and concepts. They take serious things seriously.* They are not thing-oriented persons; in fact, they are prone to disdain material values and to enthrone *ideas* among those things man is concerned about. Again, it is a matter of

---

*Ayn Rand in *For the New Intellectual* (New York: Random House, 1961) describes intellectuals as "all those whose professions deal with the 'humanities' and require a firm philosophical base." This entire book is a forceful description of intellectuals as persons guided by *intellect*—not as "zombies" guided by "feelings, instincts, urges, wishes, whims, or revelations."

concern, a matter of priorities, a matter of what is most important to a human and *humane* being, a matter of being rational
and thoughtful. The intellectual is concerned with the broad
strokes of human existence, with the more nonpractical aspects
of life (from the point of view of material success). He is the
practicing humanist; he is the thinking man, the conceptualizing
individual, the creative person. Or so he sees himself.

The intellectual is not so much antisocial as he is non-
social. He is usually self-centered or clannish, generally intro-
vertish, and prone to gravitate to those nonconformists who fit
into his image of the intellectual; he, like all other persons,
seeks the company of his own brand of people. He conforms,
then, to his own kind of nonconformity, and this is a rather
detached elite group of *idea people* perpetually fascinated with
some avant garde concept, food, ideology, wine, music, or man-
nerism.

The intellectual, the "thinker," is a person who basically
is against the whole *mass* concept. Fundamentally suspicious of
the intellectually "unwashed," hoi polloi, he is antidemocratic
in his basic orientation, although he would probably deny it. He
and his colleagues are elitists; they are would-be directors of
society, assured of their own "insights" and suspicious of institutionalized or group decision making. They are cultural aristocrats, ideological autocrats, the saving remnant of humanity;
they are those who are not simply living in this world but who
are concerned about it philosophically, who are seeking through
their high-level dialectic a better world for tomorrow.

Since the intellectuals care little for mass society, they
naturally care little for the mass media of communication. *Mass*
communication, they say, is necessarily low level, aiming its
superficial and bland pabulum at a fundamentally naïve, un-
caring, mechanistic, self-seeking audience. Intellectuals feel that
the mass media, giving the masses what the masses appear to
want, are leveling society and are not recognizing the important
responsibility of raising the thoughts and aspirations of the gen-

eral public. The intellectual, since he takes serious things seriously, would like the mass media to do the same. One would be led to doubt, however, the sincerity of the intellectuals in this respect, for if the mass media were to really make intellectuals of the members of the mass audience, those elitists who now enjoy the status of their minority position would find themselves lost in the mass again—and this, to the intellectual, is the worst of all possible fates.

Whereas the "illiterates" read adventure-and-sex fiction and comic strips, and the practical audience members glean their pragmatic informational diet from *Reader's Digest, Time,* the local newspaper, and the *Wall Street Journal,* the "intellectual" audience member reads journals such as *Harper's, Saturday Review,* and their particular brand of political journal. Of course, to many intellectuals even magazines like *Saturday Review* and *Harper's* have become rather "middle brow" as the number of intellectuals continues to grow, and the circulations of those journals increase. So the avant-garde intellectuals are pushing always further and further out, seeking magazines, newspapers, recordings, and books that are "different" so as to isolate themselves more securely from the encroaching mediocrity.

And whereas the pragmatic audience member embraces serious material because he thinks it will help him progress in the practical world, the intellectual audience member embraces serious material for its own sake, because he likes it. He receives thought-provoking information because he wants to think, enjoys thinking. He likes being stimulated mentally; he needs aesthetic and catalytic communication in the same way the pragmatist needs directive and normative communication. Of course there are "fakes"—pseudo-intellectuals who have no real, genuine desire to think and create, and who have joined the intellectual world for some *pragmatic* reason, but we will not deal with these persons. It is enough to simply say that they are intellectual "leeches," sucking the elitist blood from the intellectual community so as *to pass* for something that they are really not.

One type of intellectual, really different from the pseudo-intellectual, is the *ideologue.* He is an intellectual gone wild on one subject, a dedicated crusader for a particular cause. Usually he begins as a balanced intellectual, truth seeking and open-minded, but slowly one particular idea takes precedence over ideas in general. He increasingly focuses on one area of interest, on one political orientation, on one concept, on one research methodology, on one intellectual concern. He becomes obsessed with one idea, which becomes a consuming interest, leading him to a kind of monolithic world-view that in his eyes is the panacea of all problems. He is an intellectual crusader, who becomes ever more dedicated to his "program" until he becomes biased, extreme, and intolerant of dissenting positions. The ideologue, often extremely intelligent and articulate, makes a good propagandist. Usually he is persuasive, well informed (at least in his one area) and is, essentially, a missionary out to convert others to his way of thinking.

It is often difficult to tell an intellectual from his doctrinaire brother, the ideologue. In fact, many writers seem to feel that most intellectuals are *at times* ideologues. It does seem that the passionate concern most intellectuals have for ideas and ideological positions often tends to turn them into polemic zealots of almost fanatic fervor. The true intellectual, it has been said, has no great mission other than speculation, contemplation, and meditation. He is not trying to impose his ideas on others. But the ideologue thinks *in order* to persuade, to crusade, to campaign. The true intellectual likes to think and create, if for no other reason, for his own satisfaction. Not so the ideologue; he must be talking, writing—pushing his concepts, his ideology, on others.*

---

*See Eric Hoffer, *The True Believer* (New York: Harper, 1951), for a fascinating discussion of intellectuals and of mass movements, Cf. Gustave Le Bon, *The Crowd.*

Audience Behavior and Motivation

Now that we have looked at three segments or types of audiences to which mass media must appeal, let us turn briefly to a more general view of the mass audience. Why do members of the audience make media and message selections of the media in the way they do? Why do they accept the offerings of some media and not others, and why do they accept certain offerings of one medium and not other of its offerings? A large number of factors affect the selections an audience member makes from among and within the mass media. Certainly two of the most important of these factors are: 1. the availability of the message, and 2. the potential for personal gain.

The first of these general principles of selection states that the audience member takes the path of least effort, that he naturally tends to read, view, and listen to media and messages that are most accessible. The second of the principles of selection assumes that audience members expose themselves to messages that will give them the greatest reward. Of course, it should be said that, in a sense, all messages offer some degree of reward, even if it is a kind of "escapism" or momentary enjoyment. It should also be noted that audience members are seeking—often unconsciously—messages that reinforce their opinions, their preconceptions, and biases. They, in effect, take in those messages compatible with their mental and psychological predispositions. They perceive those messages that cause them no "pain"—that tend to substantiate their beliefs. A person's past experiences and his philosophy of life play important parts in determining which media and messages he will select. This factor in message receiving is usually called *selective perception*.

In addition to those factors above, there are others related to a person's reading a certain newspaper, watching a particular television network program, subscribing to a certain magazine, or selecting certain messages from any of these. Leisure time, state of health, political orientation, media availability at the time, special interests, finances, and habit—all these contribute in varying degrees to media and message selection.

Now that we have looked briefly at these factors in the audience's selection of media and messages, let us consider some reasons why audiences turn to the mass media in the first place. What motivates them? Although motivation differs with the person, there does seem to be a rather basic core of relevant motivational factors.

Three main motivational factors suggest themselves:

1. Loneliness. People are basically lonely. They do not like to find themselves unoccupied or detached from others. This gives them a sense of social estrangement, of frustration, of anxiety, and of fear. The next best thing to being with other persons is being with a mass medium of communication. In fact, for many persons it is *more satisfying* to be with a mass medium than with other persons; there are no social or conversational pressures on them. Television, especially, satisfies the longing for companionship; the TV set becomes a friend helping to fill the time with pictures and sounds—and really asking very little in return. The print media are "friendly" time consumers and companions, too, but perhaps to a lesser degree. At any rate, loneliness is a very powerful motivating factor that pushes people into the presence of the mass media.

2. Curiosity. People are basically curious. They are interested in what is happening about them—what others are doing, saying, thinking. Outside their very immediate surroundings, there is no way really to satisfy this curiosity other than turning to the mass media. Persons are curious about, interested in, a myriad of things—and not only in those things that will affect them in some direct way. Curiosity, in fact, is probably the prime factor in a person's exposure to the mass media. What is happening? Who is involved in it? Why is it happening? And, of course in many cases: How might it affect me? Man's curiosity appears practically insatiable; the mass media can depend on the audience to continue consuming vast quantities of material about isolated happenings, quirks of nature, eccentric persons and groups, and all kinds of gossip and rumor. Curiosity may have "killed the cat," as the old saying goes, but it has proved the very life blood of mass communication.

3. Self-aggrandizement. Human beings—audience members—are basically selfish. They desire information that will help them achieve their individual ideas of success and happiness. They want help in their idealistic and/or realistic pursuits. They seek substantiation of their prejudices and biases. They want philosophical and religious reassurance and guidance. They want practical and aesthetic messages that will be of personal service to them. They want information that will be of immediate, and also of long-range, value. They want messages that will help them make decisions, purchase products, and derive rewards from their activities. They also want to be humored, cajoled, and entertained. In short, they want their practical, philosophical, and religious natures served by the mass media.

In conclusion, it might be well to reiterate what was said at the beginning of this chapter: It is very difficult to discuss and analyze mass-media audiences thoroughly and meaningfully. However, in spite of the extreme complexity of this subject, it should be dealt with more often. Most books on mass communication give audiences little or no attention, concentrating instead on communicators and mass media. This is understandable, of course, since most persons tend to place major emphasis on the *sending* rather than the *receiving* of messages. Also, in mass communication the *sender* (the mass communicator or the mass medium) is relatively simple—a person or an institution—that can rather easily be observed and described. The mass audience, on the other hand, is basically nebulous, fluid and unobservable—a "distributed" entity without real structure. It is hoped that we have, in this chapter, helped to give some much-needed attention to the audience—the body of essential consumers, the mass media's *raison d'être*.

10.

A Search for Communication Effects

THE EFFECTIVENESS OR CONSEQUENCES OF A MESSAGE CAN only be determined by coding and analyzing the reactions of the receivers. Even if the communication researcher were dealing with only one receiver, his task would be most difficult, since that one receiver is a complex and unique person. The need to record the reactions of large segments of the *mass* audience makes the job even harder.

The difficulties in this type of research, of course, do not stop here. Frequently, it is important to know the precise content of the message in order to evaluate its effect on the audience. With print media, this was relatively simple; the message could be carefully examined and the various parts of it catalogued in a process called *content analysis*.

Radio and television, however, have defied this kind of analysis. By their very nature, they are difficult—sometimes virtually impossible—to review. But even if one were able to review them, he would still have to devise an acceptable system of cataloguing not only words, in regard to radio, but voice inflections, background sounds, and pauses, as well. In regard to television, the researcher would have to code body movements, including facial expressions. Kinesics, the study of this "body language," is now in its infancy—even though kinesicists estimate that most human communication is nonverbal rather than verbal. In that sense, television has returned human communication to its natural, preprint state by imparting qualities of sound and motion to the mass media.

Communication researchers, recognizing the near impossibility of coding the sound and motion messages of the mass media, have largely avoided any meaningful diagnosis of this kind of communication. In an age when a majority of Americans consider television a primary source of information, researchers are still churning out content analyses of magazines and newspapers, producing what one critic called a "plethora of 'definitive' statements about the irrelevant and inconsequential." By the 1970s they still have not developed the most elementary devices for cataloguing sound and motion bias. For example, researchers employed by one network gave the company's television news program a clean bill of health after carefully analyzing all of the *scripts* for a specified period. This at a time when one observer has pointed out that the sentence "Did she buy two tickets to that play?" can be given at least seven different meanings by word emphasis alone.

Other researchers have bypassed the difficulties of coding radio and television message meaning by turning their analytical guns exclusively on the audience itself. Obviously, the audience does not have to be aware of the precise content of the message in order to react in various ways. In fact, they may react as a result of receiving only part of the message. This is especially true of electronic media audiences, as evidenced by the panic of those who missed the first part of the famous "War of the Worlds" radio broadcast in the 1930s.

And it must be added that a large part of the audience can be aware of the precise meaning of the message, yet still disregard it.* A majority of the nation's newspapers opposed the

---

*One research study has shown that the average American is exposed to 1,600 advertising messages each day, but is moved pro or con by no more than 15 of them. Another study by the Batten, Barton, Durstine and Osborne advertising agency in-

presidential candidacies of Thomas Jefferson, Andrew Jackson, Abraham Lincoln, Woodrow Wilson, Franklin D. Roosevelt, Harry S Truman, and John F. Kennedy.

None of these observations is intended to denigrate the value of relevant communication research. Humans *are* affected by the messages they obtain from the mass media, and we must depend upon communication research to describe effective and ineffective messages and their positive and negative results. The student of mass communication should have an intellectual respect for research in his field, but he must also treat such research with healthy skepticism. He must be able to recognize the limitations of communication research; he must know that findings are usually fragmentary, since the researcher can delve only a tiny distance into the uncharted complexities of messages and men.

Practitioners in the media are sometimes critical of communication research, although they have become dependent over the years on practical aspects of the discipline such as readership and readability studies. Without communication researchers, the media would find it impossible to challenge the persistent charges that the mass media narcotize their audiences, produce conformity, weaken the nation's capacity for criticism, retard participatory democracy, and inculcate habits of violence and delinquency. Researchers, of course, are not able to prove or refute every charge made against the media, since the vast number of variables involved assures that there will always be unanswered questions. But this poses a handicap for the critic, also. It is equally impossible to support many of the charges that are gratuitously flung in the direction of the mass media.

The criticisms directed at mass media are frequently unsupportable and the findings of mass communication research often contradictory for the following reasons:

---

cluded only those messages disseminated by mass media and outdoor advertising. The findings, released in 1970, show that the average American male is exposed to 285 advertising messages a day—35 television commercials, 38 radio commercials, 15 magazine ads, 185 newspaper ads, and 12 outdoor messages.

The messages of mass media cannot be isolated from the personality of the receiver. Innumerable personal variables will cause the same message to have a different effect on two receivers. A person's health, religion, sex, economic status, education, race, prior experiences, etc., will affect his reaction to a message. What is "good" news for one person will be "bad" news for another. Yet, as mentioned earlier, the mass communication researcher is usually interested in the reactions of the total audience rather than the reaction of one individual in the audience.

Other personal variables involve the attitude of the receiver to the source of the message, to the communicator, and to the medium itself. An accurate message coming from what the receiver believes to be an untrustworthy source, an unfair reporter, or an error-prone medium may be considered completely inaccurate. Inaccurate messages may be completely credible if the receiver has a positive attitude toward the source, the communicator, or the medium.

That these multiple variables pose a severe handicap to the communcation researcher has been demonstrated in studies on the effects of violence in the mass media, especially the effect on children. Some psychologists have declared that even if an effect could be proved—that is, that violence in the media caused some children in the audience to become violent—it would be a minor factor when compared to the more dominant factors of the child's own individual personality, his socio-economic position, and the influence of his parents.

The best that researchers have been able to come up with in this area is that mass media violence may tend to trigger antisocial behavior in an *abnormal* child, or cause a potential delinquent to imitate aggressive actions depicted on television. Like adults, most normal children have an ability to separate aggression in the real world from aggression in the unreal world of drama or cartoons. One British study showed that children were less frightened by violent acts in television dramas than by scary background music. Mayhem on the screen upset them less than a mother and father arguing or a parent scolding a child in the same drama.

This suggests only a few of the complexities in this type of study. There are hundreds of other variables. For example, although violence in the media may have a more negative effect on abnormal than on normal children, it has also been determined that delinquent children read fewer books and magazines than normal children, and that aggressive children do not have the patience to watch as much television as do more passive normal children. Further, one study has shown that delinquent children *perceive* more aggression in the media than do nondelinquent children, and there are also indications that violence in the media may serve as a vicarious release (the "safety-valve" or "catharsis" effect) for certain violence-prone children. Even though virtually all researchers agree that violence in the media can be harmful for "some" children under "some" conditions, they disagree about the actual threat to the average child, and whether violence in the real world of news—which cannot be easily excised—may not have a greater effect on the child than does violence in the unreal world of fiction and drama.

One medium cannot easily be isolated from other media. The average person in a modern society is bombarded with messages from a variety of media. He may see or hear different versions of a message in newspapers, radio, television, and magazines. It is extremely difficult for him to remember precisely where he heard or saw a specific message. In fact, he may have received the information from a friend rather than from a medium of mass communication.

There have been some outstanding examples of the reader's inability to sort out the source of his information. One mass magazine, in a readership survey, gave interviewees a list of news events and asked which ones the magazine had covered with the greatest competence. The readers gave one of the highest scores to a story that the magazine had never covered at all.

Individuals in the audience not only confuse their sources of information, they also are unable to recall accurately how much time they spend with a specific medium. For example, the average American *admits* to watching less than three hours of television a day, but he actually watches more than four hours of television each day.

Surveys conducted by Roper Research Associates have shown that Americans consider television to be the most "believable" medium.* But the unanswered questions in the surveys are these: How many respondents received virtually all of their news from television alone, and therefore had no real basis for comparison? How many gave this answer as a justification for the time spent watching television? How many believe in the accuracy of a televised event that they see with their own eyes, but consider a newspaper "report" more accurate than a "report" by television correspondents or anchormen? How many are simply unable to recall clearly the source of the information they consider the most accurate?

The message cannot be isolated from the physical conditions surrounding the receiver. The message transmitted by a medium is affected by certain characteristics of the medium itself. A book, magazine, or newspaper can easily be put aside while the reader is in the middle of a message. A television message is interrupted by commercials; a movie message is not. A television message is seen in lighted conditions when the viewer is often accompanied by members of his family; a movie message is seen in darkened conditions when the viewer is either alone or has the feeling of being alone. An individual may withdraw from a television message by changing the channels or leaving the room temporarily; a movie goer is held more closely to the total message.

All these and many other factors surrounding reading and viewing play important roles in message impact. What happens, then, when the communication researcher sets up artifical con-

---

*Burns W. Roper, *A Ten-Year View of Public Attituues toward Television and Other Mass Media, 1959-1968* (New York: Television Information Office, 1969), pp. 4-5.

ditions in order to conduct his tests more conveniently and more precisely? He may be getting reactions quite different from those that would be obtained under normal reading or viewing conditions. The dilemma for the researcher is this: laboratory conditions are unreal and may seriously affect the results, yet the results would be impossible to obtain under normal receiver conditions.

There is great difficulty in getting representative "control" groups. When attorneys involved in a sensational murder case seek jurors who have read or seen nothing about the case, an observer is bound to wonder if the life-or-death decision will be made by a panel of idiots. A communication researcher seeking data about the acceptability of a specific advertisement might easily find one group that he can expose to the ad, and another group that can be isolated from it. But it is almost impossible to find representative "control" groups for research into problems that are of vital concern to society—problems involving obscenity, violence, racial coverage, and political bias, for example. The mass media penetrate and saturate the total American environment. A person not exposed to information on these subjects is likely to be completely unrepresentative of the important sectors of American society.

If one is attempting to test the effects of television violence, how does he obtain a control group of normal children who are not exposed to regular television fare? And, if the researcher works the other way, attempting to pick out a control group of normal children and expose them to concentrated television violence, then he is placing them under "abnormal" laboratory conditions, if not running the additional risk of harming their psyches for the sake of science.

Obviously, good researchers are frequently able to obtain control groups under near normal conditions. But because of the pervasiveness of mass communication, some problems defy accurate research.

There is difficulty in determining long-range effects. Under laboratory or normal conditions, a television viewer may register a startling reaction to a particular message. A half-hour later he may have forgotten it. Other viewers may not have reacted so strongly, but this and similar messages may have a cumulative force that, in the long run, will affect him more severely.

It is virtually impossible for communication researchers to determine in any scientific way the cumulative effects of certain kinds of communication messages. The researcher cannot remain with the receiver for anything but a limited period of time, nor can he isolate the receiver from hundreds of other influences that are affecting the messages and the personality.

Some psychologists, for example, have said that the constant exposure to violence in the mass media "conditions" children over a period of time until finally the child feels less sympathy for victims of violence. Another observer complained about the impact of the "lone man" theme of many movie and television dramas, particularly westerns. In these dramas, he said, the recurrent theme is of a brave little "good guy"—surrounded by an indifferent or cowardly populace—who achieves his one great moment with one act of violence against the big "bad guy." These dramas had a cumulative effect, he said, on men like Lee Harvey Oswald, James Earl Ray, and Sirhan Sirhan, and resulted in the assassinations of the two Kennedys and Martin Luther King.

Hypotheses such as these are contributed by men who can offer little supportive data. The inability of researchers to make controlled, long-term tests of communication effects, of course, opens the way to this kind of speculation, which may or may not be valid.

There is difficulty in determining whether the message is the cause or the effect. Is the audience being affected in a harmful way by certain messages of the mass media, or do the messages simply reflect the present state of the audience? Do the mass media force certain harmful messages upon the audience, or does the audience hunger for such messages and demand them? These are questions seemingly without answer, but they strongly affect the validity of accusations against the media and the validity of communication research.

To a certain extent, segments of the audience can avoid messages that are distasteful to them. By the same token, they can seek out those messages that particularly appeal to them. One study has shown that delinquents read more comic books and seek out more aggressive and exciting television programs than normal youths. A psychiatrist recently declared:

> I believe that the vast amount of violence on television is basically a reflection of the violent interests of the viewers; it is a symptom, not a cause; it graphically portrays the violence in our souls. I doubt that it is a serious cause of much of it.*

And, the psychiatrist added, neither the message nor the receiver's interest in the message may be "causes" or "effects." Both may be symptoms of something else that exists in American society.

Whether the message is generated by the audience or the communicator, there remains the tangential problem of control. How does one alter or censor messages in a free society, especially when the effects of phenomena such as violence, real and unreal, cannot be properly measured?

The "Fear" of Effects

Some effects of mass communication can be proven; others cannot. But in certain cases, society would not be convinced even if the overwhelming results of communication research showed a particular genre of message had no ill effects. For example, the majority of Americans are opposed to messages that they deem to be pornographic, especially if those messages are available to children. The fear of this ill effect could be called an effect itself, and even the Supreme Court has recognized this by upholding laws barring the sale of porno-

---

*Ner Littner, "A Psychiatrist Looks at Television and Violence," *Television Quarterly* (Fall 1969), p. 11.

graphic material to youths, despite contradictory evidence on the subject.

All the handicaps of communication research are multiplied when one attempts to pursue the effect of obscenity on children. One cannot imagine a researcher assembling a "control" group of children to bombard with concentrated doses of obscenity in order to measure the effects. And those children who are available for interviewing in this area are usually delinquent or deviant.

In the absence of empirical evidence, then, there is an abundance of speculation. Here, however, many psychologists who contend that obscenity has no ill effects on adults believe that it could have ill effects on children. Children, they say, do not yet have the perspective to compare pornography with the traditional view of sexual experience and are not yet mature enough to control sexual feelings once they have been aroused.

The overall problem of assessing mass communication effects can be exemplified by examining just two areas of recent communication research—effects of political polls and effects of pornography.

The Effect of Political Polls

A problem exists regarding the possible influence of political polls and election predictions. It is a problem that communication researchers have been able to study with beneficial results.

Political polls with a high degree of reliability have been on the American scene since the mid-1930s. Few people seriously question the relative accuracy of the major polls, although there are doubts about using polls for predictive purposes. With narrow margins allowed for error, surveys conducted by major polling organizations are accurate for the day or week in which the field work took place. But people have a habit of changing their minds, and the finding of the poll may be quickly outdated.

Recent controversy has surrounded the possible effects of polls and—in the case of presidential elections in the United States—early election-night predictions. In both cases, charges have been made that this information can have one of three effects: 1. the "stay-away" effect, causing the voter to remain away from the polls in the belief that his candidate is an easy winner or doesn't have a chance; 2. the "bandwagon" effect, causing voters to choose or switch to the favored candidate in order to have the personal satisfaction of voting for a winner; and 3. the "underdog" effect, causing voters to choose or switch to the losing candidate out of sympathy or to make him a closer contender and possible winner.

The potential effects of poll results have not been lost on the candidates themselves, who quickly release the favorable findings of polls which they have personally financed, while withholding the unfavorable results. Harry S Truman contended during his 1948 campaign that the polls predicting a Dewey victory were "Republican polls" designed to keep Democrats away from the voting booths on election day. But the most convincing evidence of a "stay-away" effect came during the British Parliamentary elections of 1970, when four out of five major polling organizations erroneously predicted a substantial Labor victory. Unlike the Gallup Poll during the 1948 American presidential election, the polling organizations surveyed the electorate virtually to the eve of election day, so could not blame the mistake on a last-minute change of mind by voters. A few months before, favorable polls had convinced the Labor Party to call an election in mid-1970. These earlier polls, widely publicized in the British mass media, apparently had some effect on many persons who had said they would be voting for the Labor Party, but did not go to the polls to cast their ballots.

Scientific research is available on a similar problem in the U. S.—the fear that early election returns and predictions from the East Coast could strongly affect the voting on the West Coast on the evening of presidential elections. Polls on the West Coast, of course, had always closed three hours later—and, in some sections, four hours later—than polls on the East Coast, but by the time significant returns could be broadcast from the East Coast, polls were already closing on the other side of the country. Two developments changed this situation: 1. the establishment of the News Election Service, a cooperative of the three major networks and two major wire services designed to coordinate coverage of the 165,000 precincts in the country for instant gathering of results, and 2. the programming of computers for analysis of early returns from key precincts and "projection" of final results in each state. In some cases, the broadcast networks could predict the final vote in major states on the East Coast when only a fraction of the vote was in, and this information could be broadcast to the West Coast up to three hours before many of the West Coast polls closed.

Some congressmen proposed bills making it illegal to broadcast such predictions before all the polls had closed; others suggested a uniform voting day that would have polls open and close earlier on the West Coast to compensate for the time difference.

There were at least two major independent studies and three network-sponsored studies of this phenomenon during the 1964 presidential election. They consisted of random sampling of voters across the nation and depth interviews of those voters who cast their ballots after the polls had closed on the East Coast.* The surveys showed:

1. The great majority of voters on the West Coast had voted before the polls closed on the East Coast.
2. Only about one-fourth of the voters could have been influenced by election returns or projections from the East Coast, and less than half of these were exposed to such electronic media reports.
3. Very few of the persons who had heard returns or projections changed their votes; in fact, a larger percentage among those who had *not* heard the returns and projections changed their minds on election day.

---

*See Kurt Lang and Gladys Engel Lang, *Politics and Television* (Chicago: Quadrangle Books, 1970), pp. 250-88; and Robert P. Knight, "Voters, Computers and TV Forecasts," *Freedom of Information Center Publication No. 169,* University of Missouri (October 1966).

All the surveys generally agreed that the early reports by electronic media did not cause a significant "stay-away," "bandwagon," or "underdog" effect on the West Coast. The surveys further showed that even those who had heard the broadcasts were uncertain whether they had heard actual returns or network predictions, and there was evidence that they further confused the reports of opinion polls *prior* to election day with the whole lot.

The research showed that the overwhelming majority of the voters have too strong a commitment to a decision by election day to be influenced by early returns, even if they are in the small minority exposed to these broadcasts. Only in the very closest election could such forecasts, spread by the broadcast media, affect a national election. And in a very close election, it is unlikely that the networks could or would make clearcut predictions so early.

The careful research conducted on this problem exploded the myth that the network broadcasts could influence a sizable segment of the voters. The proposed bills barring such broadcasts died in Congress and new ones have not been proposed. Because it presents more complex research problems, the influence of preelection polls has not been defined in the same manner. The British election of 1970 suggests that research in this area is needed, especially regarding the possible "stay-away" effect. It is unlikely that anyone would suggest that mass media bar dissemination of such reports, even if a strong influence could be found, but the findings may suggest that the voter needs more education in placing these opinion polls in proper perspective.

Sex in Denmark

Communication researchers are faced with a great number of variables when dealing with the relationship between pornography and sex crimes. Their findings, therefore, can never be as definitive as those of researchers investigating problems with more limited variables, such as the effect of election-day predictions on voter behavior.

Even so, there have been observers who are willing to draw hasty conclusions about the consequences of liberalizing obscenity laws. In 1965, the psychiatric department of Denmark's Council for Forensic Medicine reported that "no scientific experiments" could lead one to the assumption that pornography or obscene pictures and films contributed to the committing of sexual offenses by normal adults and youths.* In response to this report and substantial supporting sentiment in the country, the Danish parliament repealed the legal prohibitions against written pornography in 1967. Two years later, it ended film censorship for adults and legalized the sale of pornographic pictures and photographs to anyone over the age of sixteen. Sex crimes dropped sharply in the year following the 1967 government action, and dropped again after the repeal of virtually all pornography laws affecting adults in 1969. Sales of pornographic material in Denmark have also shown a steep drop since the initial boom in sales in 1967.

Outside Denmark, persons who are opposed to obscenity laws have pointed to the Danish experience as proof that pornography does not contribute to antisocial behavior, and further that elimination of pornography laws actually leads to a decline in sexual crimes. They also contend that the sales drop in Denmark proves that most people are completely revolted by pornographic literature and films once such material becomes freely available.

The Danish situation is another case where uninformed speculation moves in, in the absence of thorough research. Such research is now underway in Denmark, and undoubtedly numer-

---

*In the United States, the Commission on Obscenity and Pornography transmitted a formal report in 1970 to the President and Congress with a similar finding: "Extensive empirical investigation, both by the Commission and by others, provides no evidence that exposure to or use of explicit sexual materials play a significant role in the causation of social or individual harms such as crime, delinquency, sexual or nonsexual deviancy, or severe emotional disturbances." See *The Report of the Commission on Obscenity and Pornography* (New York: Bantam Books, 1970), p. 58.

ous reports will be produced in the coming years regarding the incidence of pornography and antisocial behavior. But any person reading these reports must see if the researchers make note of the following points:

1. The years 1966 or 1967 are poor base years on which to make comparisons regarding the sale of pornography. There is evidence that there was a flood of pornographic material published in 1966 in anticipation of repeal, and that there was lax enforcement of pornography during this period by authorities for the same reason. "Curiosity" sales were therefore at their peak in 1966 and 1967. Figures on sales since 1967 should be compared with more normal years, say the years preceding 1965 or following 1969. If sales are indicated by expenditures rather than number of items produced, the researcher should indicate how much of the lower total expenditure is a result of reduction in prices (because of market glut) rather than a result of fewer items sold.

2. Any data concerning "sex crimes" should make some compensation for the revised definition of this term in Denmark. Prior to repeal, pornography itself was a crime; it no longer is. Acts which were considered offensive and subject to punishment prior to 1966 are now permissible.

3. Data should make adjustment for the increasingly permissive nature of Danish society, reflected also in police attitudes. Offenses that are perhaps still punishable by law are not prosecuted in many cases.

4. Data should also make a comparison of precise categories of sex crimes. There has been some evidence that while the number of trivial sex offenses (e.g., voyeurism) has diminished, the number of serious sex offenses (e.g., rape) has remained about the same.

Obviously, reliable data that showed no appreciable increase in sexual offenses would be a first step toward proving that the availability of pornography does not, in and of itself, cause unacceptable antisocial behavior. However, even this is still circumstantial evidence in the absence of a clear cause-and-effect relationship. Further, the communication researcher who is able to come up with significant findings regarding Denmark would probably be unhappy if his conclusions were lifted wholesale and applied to another country, because the question of pornography involves the attitudes of the individual as imposed by parents, religion, and society.

Danish society has long had a reputation as a sexually permissive society, and the State Lutheran Church, to which ninety percent of Danes belong, brought no effective pressures to bear against repeal of pornography laws. In other countries, society and organized religion impose a different set of attitudes upon the individual, and this would go into the mix of variables that could cause different effects.

Even in Denmark, initial research will show the short-range effects, but will leave unanswered for many years the long-range effects on morality, marriage, etc. Rhetoric, rather than communication research, has so far advertised the results of Denmark's experiment. Many countries, especially the United States, are now awaiting the results of serious research on this relevant subject. It is the kind of research that will severely tax the methodology and objectivity of the researcher.

11.

Media Evaluation

EVALUATION AND CRITICISM OF THE MASS MEDIA OF COM-
munication are becoming commonplace. It seems that the layman—the person who is the consumer of media messages—has
taken it upon himself to criticize, appraise, and evaluate the
media and their performance. The world is full of media
critics—speaking in pulpits, classrooms, streets, Rotary Clubs,
political campaigns, conventions of all kinds, in small select
conferences and at mass rallies. Everybody seems convinced
that he has the answers for the questions that plague, and have
plagued, media managers and functionaries.

Nonmedia people, especially intellectuals and politicians
(sometimes they are the same), are articulating their opinions
about the mass media more often, more loudly, and more assuredly. It has been a short step, indeed, from the critical appraisal of the press by the controversial Hutchins Commission*
in the 1940s to the many sorties into the area of media criticism

---

*Formal name of the self-appointed and self-styled "Commission" which
studied the American press in the 1940s was the Commission on Freedom of the
Press; its chairman was Robert M. Hutchins, then Chancellor of the University of
Chicago.

triggered by the equally controversial blasts by Vice President Agnew in the late 1960s and early 1970s. Criticism of the media has increased greatly, but its nature has not changed very much.

Criticisms of Media Systems

Certain patterns emerge from the general criticism that has been, and is being, hurled at the mass media in the United States. One of the most common is that media owners are too concerned with their own interests, are too interested in making money, and are not interested enough in public service. Another criticism, ranking right along with that one, is that there is not enough diversity in the mass media, not enough competition, and that a monopolistic trend toward group or "chain" ownership, coupled with the high cost of getting into the media business, is contributing to the shrinking pluralism.

Other critics believe that advertisers are wielding too much influence on the media, that a single socio-economic class (the upper) controls the mass media, and that the media are basically conservative and therefore tend to perpetuate the status quo. Another common criticism of the overall media system is that atypical, eccentric, and destructive persons and groups are given too much emphasis, and that trivia, sensation, sex, and violence are getting undue, disproportionate, and unrealistic attention.

The Hutchins Commission set up five main requirements for the mass media in their 1947 report,* and, after submitting the American media to these standards, concluded that they were not really socially responsible. The Commission maintained that the media of the United States should:

1. present a "truthful, comprehensive and intelligent account of the day's events in a context which gives them meaning";
2. provide a "forum for the exchange of comment and criticism";
3. project a "representative picture of the constituent groups in the society";

---

*See Chapter 2 ("The Requirements") in The Commission on Freedom of the Press, *A Free and Responsible Press* (Chicago: University of Chicago Press, 1947), pp. 20-29.

4. present and clarify "the goals and values of the society"; and
5. give "full access to the day's intelligence."

Judged by these impossible standards (at least all but the second one are), it is little wonder that the Commission's verdict was that the American press was not responsible. This whole concept of "social responsibility" and journalistic ethics will be taken up more thoroughly in Part III of this book; presently it is enough to say that anyone vaguely familiar with the intrinsic problems of the mass media and of language itself will know that these "responsibilities" set forth by the Hutchins Commission are rather obvious *ideal* (unrealizable) cliché fantasies of impractical intellectuals.

Criticisms of Individual Media

When we come down from the mountain and begin looking at individual media in a direct, specific way, many less monumental and imposing criticisms suggest themselves. For instance, most media are careless with basics—spelling, punctuation, pronunciation and enunciation, names, quotations, statistics, etc. Almost anyone who has ever read a newspaper story about a speech he made or a program in which he participated knows full well the validity of this criticism.

Look carefully at any individual newspaper. Is it not superficial, not only in its selection of stories and pictures, but in the way it handles each separate story? Glance down and across the columns; notice the haphazard fashion in which unrelated stories and pictures are presented; notice also the unsynthesized mish-mash of bits and pieces of news and views. Look again and you will see that probably close to two-thirds of the total space is taken up by advertising scattered meaninglessly throughout the pages.*

---

*Why not put all advertising in a separate section of the newspaper? And why not classify it (even the display ads) for easy reference? We know the old reply: Advertisers want their ads adjacent to editorial matter so the reader will see the ad whether he wants to or not. But is not this somewhat contradictory to another advertising statement—that advertising is as sought after and popular with the reader as is news?

Notice a particular headline: it does not reflect what the story below it says—and it may say just the opposite. Take a closer look at all that white space around the type and headlines, at those large space-consuming headlines themselves,* at those typographical ornaments, borders, etc. Ask yourself why the headlines have to be so large, many of the pictures so large, so much white space here and there. Is it because the reader demands it? Do *you* demand it? How many additional stories and pictures could be in that newspaper if headline and picture size was scaled down? At least a fourth more!

One might be led to think that the newspaper editor is not as concerned about your knowing what is going on as he pretends; it appears he may be more interested in typographical experimentation and what he believes to be aesthetic appeal than he is in publishing news and views in as large amounts as possible. Take a close, careful look at any of the individual media and you will find similar aspects to criticize. There is no shortage of faults in any of the mass media.

Who Should Evaluate the Media?

Since there is plenty to criticize in the media, the next question that presents itself is this: *Who* is really qualified to criticize and evaluate the media? The professionals in the media generally think that nonmedia people know too little about the problems of the media, about intrinsic weaknesses and specialized procedures, to offer very meaningful and valid evaluations. Why, ask the media people, should a lawyer or doctor claim to know any more about the mass media than the journalist knows about medicine or law? Is it not presumptuous for a physics teacher or a state senator to tell the media workers what they should or should not do? These are pertinent questions and they are being heard more every year as the mass media, by

---

*A great majority of newspaper copies are delivered to the door or sent through the mails. There is no need for large, eye-catching headlines on most papers, and there is no evidence that readers demand them.

touching the lives of increasing numbers of the citizens, are inviting a growing torrent of criticism.

One of the main faults that press people found with the Hutchins Commission's evaluation of the press in 1947 was that none of the commissioners was a journalist or a media person. Therefore, many editors and journalists said that they could not take the criticism very seriously—it was uninformed, unrealistic, impractical, and that it tilted with journalistic windmills, which professional press people would have known really did not exist. The press has long considered itself the social critic, the "fourth estate," the "watchdog on government," or some such thing, and has been particularly sensitive when any outside person or group has dared criticize it or evaluate its performance. Newspapers traditionally evaluate and criticize. But very seldom do they criticize or evaluate themselves or one another. Throughout the history of world journalism, newspapers have found it easy enough to point out all sorts of weaknesses in every other social institution; they bludgeon this man, that party, this group, that law. But when someone points out the derelictions of these same newspapers, newsprint is filled with indignant screams. Television commentators can regularly evaluate politicians—even Presidents—but pity the poor person who scores a telling criticism against one of these television sages!

The same media that insist that it is impossible to evaluate in a valid way the performance of the press or to rank newspapers as to quality proceed daily to evaluate and rank politicians, colleges, universities, libraries, books, and any number of persons, places, and things. It is rather strange that they often appear to think that only communications media have the expertise to make intelligent, valid, and worthwhile value judgments.

All of this is not to denigrate the value of social criticism emanating from the mass media; we in the United States are extremely fortunate to have a critical journalism. And it is undeniably true, as newspaper apologists are quick to mention, that the Western democratic press serves as a check on government. But *who*, one should ask and keep on asking, is serving as a check on the press? Those who would say there are no press excesses are blind indeed; and those who would say that these press excesses do exist but do not need to be brought to public attention, have a peculiar ethical myopia. A nation's journalists are prone to cry in anguished tones about government secrecy, uncooperative sources, and unethical practices in various segments of their societies, and all the while go their way in their own "closed societies"—unexamined, uncriticized, and in all too many cases, unchallenged. Informed and perceptive criticism of the media would seem to be the best check on the press in a libertarian system. But, alas, criticism of this type is rare indeed!

Pockets of criticism of the press, of course, do exist in all countries; and individual voices do cry out periodically against press irresponsibility. Various press councils and journalistic groups mouth their platitudes, publish their codes, deal in generalities, and hope. But this criticism is sporadic and too often isolated; too seldom is it specific; too seldom is it positive. And too seldom does it result from vigorous study and thought.

Back to the earlier question: Who is really qualified to criticize and appraise the press? Perhaps every person would have his own answer to this question, but one thing is certain: There is no reason to believe that informed, intelligent, helpful criticism and evaluation cannot come from persons who themselves are not a part of any of the mass media. Mass communication is everybody's business. It is too public, too pervasive, too powerful, to be left completely to the rather small group of media people who prepare and disseminate the messages.

But we do not dare try to tell surgeons how to operate, the mass media apologists will declare. These media people, attempting to draw the protective cloak of professionalism about them, would have a difficult time drawing an analogy between their "profession" and that of the medical doctor. Actually, journalism (one aspect of the media industry or trade), which comes closest to being a profession, has no clearly defined body

of knowledge or professional "lore"; it has no licensing procedures that protect it and the public from corrupt, unscrupu-
lous, or incompetent practitioners; it has no generally agreed-
upon code of ethics or guidelines for what is the "correct"
conduct for journalists. So, it might be well if media people
would divest themselves of the illusion that they belong to a
profession and that their "professional expertise" makes them
singularly qualified to criticize the mass media.

Although journalism is not a profession in the same sense
that medicine or law are professions, the most prominent and
serious of its practitioners agree pretty well on many of the
fundamental aspects of what might be considered "good" journalism. For example, graphics people and page designers can
agree pretty well as to what is good typography and page lay-
out. Leading photographers can at least agree on what is *not*
good photography. Journalists who take writing seriously and
have concentrated on style and effectiveness generally agree as
to what is "good" writing and what is not.

In other words, serious practitioners in the mass media do
have a pretty good idea of what is quality and what is not. They
do recognize a hierarchy of value: they do have standards. In
spite of the high degree of subjectivity in journalism—as compared to medicine, for example—there does remain a rather
large area where there are standards of quality. All is *not* relative in journalism. One person's opinion is *not* just as good as
any other person's. Some media people *are* more effective than
others. Some stories *are* better written than others. Some TV
commercials *are* more artistic and effective than others. Some
radio voices *are* superior to others. Some foreign correspondents
are more accurate and perceptive than others. Some headline
writers *are* more skilful than others. And some photographers
are more imaginative and technically proficient than others.

So, it can be concluded that there are ways to evaluate
media and discriminate among them and that both media
people and nonmedia people can offer valuable criticism and
evaluation of these media. What it takes is intelligence, interest,

concern, systematic analysis, open-mindedness, and a desire to be fair and unbiased. A lawyer or a biology teacher who will criticize the media in this framework, might actually, because of his more neutral stance, provide criticism and evaluation that is more valid than that of the media person who stands too close to his object of criticism.

Evaluation: A Problem of Context?

In this age of relativity where special considerations have taken precedence over standards, it is easy to understand why many persons say that it is unrealistic to rate this newspaper as good and that one as bad, to say that this page makeup is better than that one, that this television newscast is more reliable and better produced than another one. It is really impossible to evaluate a mass medium or a portion of a mass medium's message, the relativists say, unless you know all the circumstances surrounding the medium and the specific context in which it exists. They would, in effect, make all media evaluation nothing more than a description of how well a particular medium is doing with what it has at the place and time and under the circumstances.

The context is all important, they say. How can you possibly say that *The New York Times* is a better newspaper than, say, the *Wichita Eagle*? The *Eagle* in its context (Wichita and Kansas) may be just as good as the *Times* in its context. It is doubtful that very many serious students of newspapers would accept this thesis, but the "context advocates" do have a certain amount of logic to their argument, and such a position appeals to large numbers of persons who see themselves as tolerant, progressive, and open-minded. The contextualist, if he took his concept very far, would find himself in the position of not being able to compare any mass medium with another as to quality; he would logically have to assert that every single medium is ultimately *in its own context* and cannot, therefore, be compared to any other medium.

Context is, of course, extremely important when one is evaluating media and comparing one with another. No intelligent critic, for instance, would fault the *Podunk Weekly Gazette* for having only eight pages an issue when compared to the *Washington Post*'s bulky edition. No critic would compare a television network's thirty-minute newscast with the news presentation of an edition of big American daily newspaper. No sensible critic would expect of the *New Republic* or the *National Review* what he would of *Time* or *Newsweek*. The person who would say that the *National Geographic* was a "better" magazine than the *Esquire* could not be taken very seriously as a critic. So, context is important for the media evaluator; the problem comes when the concept of context in criticism is taken too far—when the critic becomes like the man who grew weeds around his house instead of roses because "in their own context" they were just as good.

It would seem that a serious, educated person—in the media or out—would be discriminating and would reject, or at least question, the idea of qualitative relativity. He undoubtedly realizes that a large part of becoming educated is learning to see differences in quality, to pass judgments based on intelligent criteria, to discriminate and to tell the good product from the shoddy. As a person becomes better educated and more perceptive, he should become increasingly aware that all newspapers are not equal, that all communicators are not equally skilled, and that significant differences in quality exist everywhere. And, if he wishes to be a critic or evaluator of the media, he will seriously seek to ascertain what are the most useful criteria that he may use for evaluation and criticism.

Certainly he will not forget the importance of context as he searches for valid criteria of evaluation. For example, he must consider the theory or concept of the press under which a particular mass medium falls. One cannot evaluate a Communist newspaper *in the same way* that he evaluates a libertarian newspaper. The overall theoretical or ideological purpose, in other words, must be taken into consideration. And, it is extremely difficult to compare a small-town weekly newspaper with a cosmopolitan daily newspaper. Usually this is not done. Weeklies are compared to weeklies; medium-sized dailies to those of their own kind; big-city dailies to other big-city dailies; specialized dailies to specialized dailies.

This, then, is a basic assumption of media criticism: criticize, evaluate, and compare only within contexts—or rough or broad contexts. Usually this is done by serious critics. But an interesting question arises: Is it not possible to say that one magazine (in context A) is better than another magazine (in context B)? Suppose the magazine in one context does almost everything in a more careful, professional, discriminating, and qualitative manner than the other magazine does in its context? Is it not, then, a better magazine in a general, *non*contextual sense? Can not *The New York Times* rationally be considered a better newspaper than some little poorly printed, superficial weekly or daily in a small town—even though they are in different contexts? Obviously so. Therefore, we can assume that, although usually contexts are used in media criticism, it is possible to talk about *inter*contextual quality also.

In spite of the difficulty of evaluating and making distinctions among media, we believe that it can be done and done intelligently and meaningfully. Certain standards do exist among communications specialists. Criteria are available for evaluation. Basic standards can be used against which media are judged. Just as we speak of great music, great books, great paintings, we can speak meaningfully of great newspapers and great magazines. There is some way to recognize quality, to differentiate among media. There are better and worse ways to do things journalistically; if not, then journalism education is a fraud and the student is wasting his time and money.

There is a hierarchy of value or worth, or a quality, in the mass media. Too long have media people—and others—evaded this issue; too long have they been reluctant to pass judgment on the media; too long have they timidly gone along acting as if all newspapers were equally good (because *somebody* liked them and they fulfilled *some* purpose); too long have media people—and outsiders—been silent when they could have been saying loudly and clearly which media were good and which were bad and giving the reasons why. Let us now consider some of the criteria that can be used to evaluate the mass media of communication.

"Common" Criteria of Evaluation

Certain "common denominators" among evaluative criteria may be used in a kind of universalistic or noncontextual appraisal. In other words, there are certain common factors that must be considered if we are judging newspapers—*any* newspapers. And also, for example, if we are considering the quality of television newscasts—whether in the United States or in Russia—considerations such as pronunciation, voice resonance, and enunciation will enter into the appraisal. These are examples of "common" criteria that are useful regardless of the size of the medium or the *location* of the medium. They might be called *noncontextual* criteria. Let us take, for example, some common or noncontextual evaluative criteria *for newspapers*; these may be used for any newspaper—whether it is weekly or daily, communist or capitalist, large or small, urban or rural, general or specialized. The critic, of course, would not use only one of these criteria for passing judgment on a newspaper; rather he would attempt to make use of as many of them as possible.

First, there are at least eight *internal* (using the newspaper itself) criteria that the evaluator would find useful in appraising or criticizing a newspaper. Let us look at these eight:

1. *Good typography and makeup techniques.* In every country and language-system there are typographic and design specialists. They are the "experts" who, in a sense, define what is *good* typography and newspaper design. They know when type faces clash; they know when blocks of type or pictures and type are juxtapositioned in such ways as to offend good taste or aesthetic sensitivities of their culture. This criterion is, in a way,

relativistic in that what offends aesthetic sensitivities in one culture might not offend in another, but at least in a single "language system" this can be considered a common criterion. For example, Chinese language typographers or calligraphers know there are certain things they do not do with type, just as typographers using the Latinized alphabet know the same. And, regardless of the language, one does not "crowd" the alphabetical units or space them so as to disrupt the quick recognition, one does not "transpose" units or "mass" type, nor does one use differing varieties of type in the same sentence—and probably not in the same story. So there are some common denominators of good typography, and typographic experts or "professionals" in all countries know them.

2. Editing and proofreading care. Regardless of where the newspaper is published, a common criterion of evaluation is the care with which it is edited and proofread. Sloppy editing shows up in any language, in any size newspaper, in any nation, and is considered undesirable. Poor proofreading, resulting in numerous errors, is also deemed a factor that will contribute to low quality. Therefore, a critic or newspaper appraiser can use this criterion when he begins his criticism or evaluation of a newspaper.

3. Correct spelling, punctuation, grammar. Although permissiveness appears to be growing in this area, there are still basic and generally standardized rules for spelling, punctuation, and grammar that educated persons in any country understand and respect. What constitutes "good" writing may be considerably relativistic, but good (correct) grammar can be checked, as can spelling and punctuation. A newspaper that evidences care in such matters gives the reader the feeling that he can have confidence in what the newspaper has to say. Care in spelling and punctuation, with a few exceptions of course, implies general care in the total newspaper product.

4. Picture reproduction and printing excellence. Some newspapers have clearer picture reproduction than others. It is not difficult, even for the layman, to spot this common qualitative criterion when studying a newspaper. Likewise, the general printing quality is obviously better on some newspapers than on others. Care in printing is a good criterion to use, regardless of what newspaper you are studying.

5. Balance in editorial/news material. When you are considering general newspapers, this is a useful criterion for evaluation. The assumption is that a good general newspaper will be *balanced.* It will not be overloaded with any one type of subject matter; for instance, it will not have two-thirds of its news pages filled with foreign news. Just what the *proper* balance is, of course, nobody is certain. But a reasonably bright person can tell when the balance is *not* proper.

6. Concern with staff quality. An evaluator of a newspaper, observing and interviewing, can learn a great deal about the newspaper's concern with having a good staff—well-educated, skilled, intelligent functionaries with high morale. The evaluator can check into such things as salary levels, number of specialists, foreign correspondents, training and other educational programs for staff members, job assignments and their correlation with special training and interests, intrastaff communication, etc.

7. Concern with editorial policy. The evaluator could check to see how much emphasis is given to editorial policy. Does the newspaper seem to have one? Do the staff members know what it is? How well does the newspaper achieve this policy—or reach its goals?

8. Concern with self-evaluation and outside criticism. The assumption is that a good newspaper will evaluate its philosophy and practices regularly and that it will welcome criticism. The evaluator could very easily appraise the newspaper's activities in this respect.

Now that we have looked briefly at these eight *internal**
(or newspaper related) common criteria for evaluation, let us
turn to five others that might be called *external* (or audience
related)—for checking the reputation or "image" of the newspaper among readers:

1. Frequency of quotation and allusion. This factor
should be considered in evaluating a newspaper, although taken
alone it is not very meaningful. When a newspaper is often used
as a source in speeches, in conversations, in class lectures, in
other publications and various of the other media, this is an
indication that the newspaper has a good reputation and that it
is having some impact on opinion leaders and the people whose
opinions they lead. One does not quote a newspaper when he
believes it does not have credibility and qualitative status.

2. Frequency of library subscriptions. Although it is quite
true that many libraries subscribe to newspapers in a rather
haphazard and thoughtless fashion, it may be assumed that libraries try to get newspapers that are the best representatives of
their cities and nations. Certain newspapers, believed to be the
most reliable for researchers, are commonly found in libraries
around the world. A person can expect to find newspapers such
as *Le Monde* of France, *Neue Zürcher Zeitung* of Switzerland,
Die Zeit of West Germany, *Asahi* of Japan, *Corriere della Sera*
of Italy, the *Guardian* of England, *Pravda* of the Soviet Union,
and *The New York Times* in almost every large library in any
nation of the world. This indicates something of their quality
and value.

3. Reputation among journalists/historians. A good way
to get at the quality of a newspaper is to find out what journalists think of it. Also, it is well to ascertain the reliance histo-

---

*Another "internal" criterion may be considered: factualness or reliability or
accuracy of reportage. Although quotations, facts, and, in a sense, whole stories *can*
be verified by the careful and persistent critic, it is very difficult to test factualness.
However, it is a possible criterion which may be used to ascertain the quality of *any*
newspaper, regardless of its context.

rians place in it. Historians do use newspapers as sources—in spite of their constant criticism of the press generally—and it is useful to find out which newspapers they most frequently use, and why.

4. Reputation in politics, government, diplomacy. Which newspapers do politicians, government officials, and diplomats take most seriously? Which ones do they read regularly to get what they feel is reliable and insightful information about their localities, states, nations, and foreign countries? This is a key question when considering the quality of a newspaper.

5. Reputation in academic circles. College and university professors and administrators are among the most critical of the mass media appraisers. When a significant segment of the academic world—including students—thinks a particular newspaper is good, there is reason to believe that it is.

The thirteen evaluative criteria above (eight internal and five external) are certainly not all the "common" ones that might be considered, but we feel they form a usable and useful core of determinants of quality and provide a systematic method by which a newspaper may be analyzed. An analyst using these thirteen guidelines can go a long way toward forming an intelligent and valid impression about the quality of a particular newspaper or can come to a rational conclusion about how one newspaper compares to another in quality.

Many persons will discount the value of such criteria and will persist in their belief that "quality" is such a subjective and relative concept that newspapers (or other media) cannot be evaluated and compared as to quality. In practice, they do not accept the premise that it cannot be done for they proceed to judge and compare regularly. So, it would appear valuable to have a systematic set of evaluative criteria, despite their weaknesses, that can be used to make this criticism and evaluation more intelligent, complete, and valid.

Criteria for "Free" Newspapers

The criteria for evaluation that have been briefly discussed above have related to *all* newspapers, regardless of what political or ideological context they may represent. They would apply to the Soviet Union's *Izvestia*, Spain's *ABC* or to the *St. Louis Post-Dispatch* of the United States. What we need to consider now are a few other criteria that might help the student of the press evaluate a newspaper published in a free or libertarian nation. He could use the "common" criteria just discussed and then supplement them with these others that are especially relevant to the libertarian press.

1. Concern for "people's right to know." How conscientious is the newspaper about informing the people, the readers, especially in the area of governmental affairs? The libertarian newspaper presumably is dedicated to letting the people know, to breaking down walls of secrecy, to exposing governmental corruption, to making the people better informed voters. Is this mainly "talk" or does the newspaper evidence in its regular activities that it is really dedicated to this concept?

2. Concern for public service. Here is another plank in the platform of the libertarian press. How well does the newspaper indicate such a concern? What does the newspaper do in the area of public service? Public service here must be defined by the newspaper as being something more than simply providing the public with something to read.

3. Pluralism in news and views. How well does the newspaper achieve a diversity of news and views on its pages? Is there an attempt to provide some kind of balance of argument in the opinion columns and a realistic range of viewpoints and subject matter in the news columns?

4. Resistance to outside pressures. A foundation principle of a libertarian newspaper is editorial freedom. How well does the newspaper ward off outside pressures that might infringe on its decision making? What outside pressures are most dangerous to the newspaper and how are they dealt with?

5. *Separation of "news" and "views."* Traditionally in the libertarian press there is the concept of keeping fact and the reporter's opinion separate, clearly demarcated so that the reader knows what he is reading. Although this is beginning to erode as "interpretive reporting" and "advocacy journalism" make deeper penetrations into traditional libertarian journalism, it is still generally considered a firm principle. How well does a particular newspaper achieve this separation of reporting and analyzing/opinionating?

6. *Headline accuracy.* How well do the headlines of the newspaper reflect the substance and tone of the stories beneath them? Do they give accurate information and impressions or do they distort the story and deviate from the implications of the story?

7. *Reliance on own staffers.* To what degree does the newspaper use its own staff members to report the news, write the columns, features, and editorials?

8. *Economic stability.* In a libertarian press, it is very important that the newspaper be in good financial condition. This gives it an opportunity to improve its product, get better staffers, and ward off many pressures. How economically stable is the newspaper?

Criteria for "Controlled" Newspapers

Now we have looked at a body of common evaluative criteria and eight others that may be used also in appraising a newspaper in a libertarian society. Are there not, also, beyond the common criteria discussed, some that are relevant especially to newspapers published in authoritarian or "controlled" societies such as the Soviet Union, Egypt, or Spain? Undoubtedly there are many, but a few will be suggested here as this chapter is concluded, and it is believed that they might be of aid to an analyst critic in dealing with the newspapers of authoritarian societies. There are at least eight of these, also, as there were for the libertarian newspapers:

1. Understanding of, and achieving of, purpose or goal. How well does the entire staff understand the purpose and goals of the newspaper and of the press generally? How well is the policy communicated internally, and how well are the goals achieved?

2. Homogeneity of staff. Is the staff dedicated to the purpose and goals of the newspaper? Is the staff homogeneous in philosophy and journalistic activities? Do they, in other words, work together to achieve an end or do they often work at variance?

3. Self-criticism and evaluation. Does the newspaper have regular conferences for the purpose of self-criticism and discussion of press-government cooperation? Are there regular sessions where the total operation is scrutinized carefully and changes are made to permit the newspaper to better achieve its purpose?

4. Dedication to staff improvement. How much emphasis does the newspaper give to continuing education of the staff, to indoctrination, to critique sessions, to moving staffers from one job to another, to getting better people in every position?

5. General media system cooperation. How well does the newspaper integrate its activities with the whole media system? How much coordination is there with other newspapers, with television, radio, news agencies, government, and various social institutions?

6. Elimination of unstabilizing elements. How well does the newspaper keep out information—stories, pictures, etc.— that will harm social stability and a sense of national unity or that will tend to undermine social (government) progress?

Ideally, the whole editorial product must eliminate discrepancies, contradictions, frustrations, puzzling questions, and "negative" criticisms that will destroy people's confidence in their government and nation.

7. *Staff dedication and dependability.* Does the newspaper have staff members who staunchly believe in the system and the press theory and who are not dedicated to "rocking the boat"? How dependable are they? In other words, how little direct supervision do they need to function? Every journalist must be dedicated to seeing that his newspaper (and journalism generally) is harmonious with—not an irritant to—government policy and progress.

8. *Use of "resource" persons.* How often and how well does the newspaper make use of specialists and prominent persons outside journalism? The better newspaper will use, on a regular basis, such "resource" persons to write guest articles of all kinds. In fact, the more enlightened the newspaper, the more it will welcome to its pages the contributions of nonstaffers. Resource persons, of the *right kind* of course, are extremely important in the journalism of a "controlled" press system.

Part III

Media Concepts
and Ethics

12.

Media and Political Systems

SINCE AROUND THE END OF WORLD WAR II THERE HAS BEEN, at least in journalistic circles, an increasing emphasis on an analysis of mass media *systems* throughout the world with a concomitant concern with typologies by which they may be differentiated and explained. Media systems are, of course, closely related to the kinds of governments in which they operate; they are, in essence, *reflective* and *supportive* of the governmental philosophy. At least we believe this is generally the case; when it is not the case, some kind of national revolution is undoubtedly taking place, which is being precipitated quite likely by the media system. Basically, then, it is our contention that media systems are supportive, not directive; they are more to be considered extensions of a nation's political philosophy than determiners of its philosophy.

Certainly, we would not discount the interplay of influence between government and the mass media; obviously the media do have some impact on governmental dynamism, but their impact must be *within* the limitations of existing political philosophy. Media impact must be "tolerated" by the system, thereby making the media no more than *a part of the system*, in theory responsible to, and reflective of, the government. When viewed in this way, it is possible to say that *all* press systems are *enslaved*—tied to their respective governmental philosophies and forced to operate within certain national ideological parameters.

It is possible, then, to speak of all press systems as controlled in this respect. A realistic view of media systems would be to admit this ideological limitation of freedom and place the emphasis on the degree of freedom *practiced*, not simply permitted, in the various media systems. No press system is truly free, regardless of how freedom is defined. Restrictions of every kind—but in differing degrees—are exerted on all national press systems. For example, the Inter American Press Association has, for years, prepared an annual report of press freedom in the Western Hemisphere, in which for certain countries the brief statement "There is no freedom of the press" labels the press situation in those nations. Such a statement could, of course, be made about *every one* of the countries in the report.

Press freedom is on a continuum and the only sensible way to talk about it in an international, comparative way is by using a systematic methodology that would focus on similarities and differences. At this point, there is no need to get deeply into press freedom as such (certainly not into ways to "measure" it); this will be discussed in the next chapter. When dealing with media systems and political systems, however, it is impossible to ignore the subject of freedom.

A Basic Dichotomy

Before surveying specific ways media systems have been, are, and may be, classified and discussed, it might be useful to deal briefly with a basic "two-valued" consideration underlying all typologies and philosophical discussions. At the risk of offending those readers who, through a "general semantics" orientation, feel an intellectual repulsion toward any kind of either-or conceptualization, we will submit a few generalizations about such an approach.

Men, as well as nations, tend to be authoritarian or libertarian. Of course, they are all somewhat schizophrenic, but basically they are disposed toward either a well-structured, disciplined world view with definite rules and an ordered society, or they are disposed toward an open, experimental, nonrestrictive society with a minimum of rules and controls. Governments are designed on the philosophical base of one of these two basic orientations. Of course, no person or government is quite so simple. Authoritarians are more flexible and open than most would suspect, and libertarians are more assured of the validity of their position and more dogmatic than most would suspect. The same is true of governments. But this does not mean that men and governments are not primarily or basically inclined in one or the other of the two directions. A nation such as Spain, we may quite validly say, has an *authoritarian* press system, while a country like Denmark has a *libertarian* press system.

In light of what has been said, it is probably safe to divide the world's press systems into two basic classes: authoritarian and libertarian. Or, perhaps, it would be more accurate to refer to them as "authoritarian tending" and "libertarian tending." In order to really determine whether a media system/government apparatus is primarily one or the other, one must look very carefully at that total system, observing not only the philosophical literature of the nation, but the total cultural heritage that has manifested itself either in an open, competitive, laissez faire national "attitude" or in a closed, noncompetitive, highly structured, directive and paternalistic "attitude."

Some persons maintain that it is impossible to make valid statements about freedom in one country as compared to freedom in another. Why? Because, for example, "freedom" does not *mean* in the Soviet Union what it *means* in the United States. This, we feel is simply an intellectual "cop-out"; no reason exists why freedom (of the press, for instance) cannot have a rather pure meaning that can be applied to the press system of *any* nation. How much criticism of the government, for instance, can Country A tolerate as compared to Country B? How many laws restricting the expression of opinion or of the printing of "pornographic" books are existent and used in one country as compared to another? Such matters will be taken up in the next chapter, but suffice it to say here that the concept of "freedom" is not *just relative*, meaningful only in the particular context of a nation. It *can* have a generalized, universal meaning.

Now, returning to our premise that a basic philosophical dichotomy exists among nations and press systems, it might be well to look briefly at the two orientations:

Authoritarian Orientation. The philosophical base for countries that subscribe to this concept may be traced back at least to Plato, the first great proponent of "law and order" and advocate of rule by *an aristocracy of the best.* This is basically an elitist orientation, reflecting a suspicion of the masses; therefore, it may be considered—in the Western sense—an "antidemocratic" stance. People in general are not intellectually capable, psychologically rigged or educationally competent to make many decisions for themselves, say the elitists. The masses, in fact, are frightened and frustrated when they have power in their hands and, having it, pose a great danger to the whole society. They basically want to escape from the problems of decision making—especially as it relates to governing. Special people must rule—people interested and competent, people dedicated to accumulating and wielding power.*

Many important writers and thinkers since Plato have con-

---

*For excellent discussions of the authoritarian personality and the function of power, see Karl R. Popper, *The Open Society and Its Enemies* (Princeton: Princeton University Press, 1950); T. W. Adorno and others, *The Authoritarian Personality* (New York: Harper & Brothers, 1950); Erich Fromm, *Escape from Freedom* (New York: Rinehart, 1941); George Orwell, *1984* (New York: Signet Books, 1950); Bertrand Russell, *Power: A New Social Analysis* (New York: W. W. Norton & Co., 1938); Niccolò Machiavelli, *The Prince* (many editions); and Richard Hofstadter, *Social Darwinism in American Thought* (Boston: Beacon Press, 1955); Carl Friedrich and Zbigniew Brzezinski, *Totalitarian Dictatorship and Autocracy*. 2nd ed. revised by C. Friedrich (New York: Frederick A. Praeger, 1968); Robert Tucker, *Philosophy and Myth in Karl Marx* (London: Cambridge University Press, 1969).

tributed to the development of the closed, totalitarian, elitist political philosophy; a few of them are Machiavelli, Hobbes, Hegel, Nietzsche, Treitschke, Fichte, and possibly even Rousseau. A desire for strong government, a fear of the masses, an inclination to personal arrogance based on a felt superiority, a respect for power, a hatred for anarchy, and a desire to control: these—among others—are the natural proclivities of the elitists and authoritarians.

In a basically authoritarian society there are many things that the populace—the people in general—must not know. The mass media must keep these things secret. There are things that the people need to know. The mass media must publicize these things. The power elite will either encompass the mass media or will control and dictate to them. The mass media will, in effect, be instruments of the governmental leadership. The goal: political and social equilibrium and harmony. This is true whether the country is an authoritarian nation of the right or of the left. Actually, as Friedrich Hayek demonstrates in *The Road to Serfdom* (1944), there is no real difference in the basic philosophy of rightists and leftists: both advocate statism and control. Plato may well be considered the grandfather of both Fascism *and* Communism, as is Hegel quite likely the father of both.

The basic characteristic of the authoritarian orientation is political and intellectual arrogance by a small elite group having a deep-rooted suspicion of the masses. This orientation filters down into the media system in many ways, depending on the particular type of government the nation has. In theory, then, right meets left so far as basic philosophy is concerned, the emphasis being on cybernation of the populace with the mass media being the instrument of direction and control.

Libertarian Orientation

This philosophical stance has many roots. "Freedom lovers" undoubtedly have always existed, but it was not until the seventeenth and eighteenth centuries that the libertarian emphasis began to infiltrate the press. John Milton with his "self-righting process" and John Locke with his insistence on "popular sovereignty" were seventeenth-century pioneers. Thomas Jefferson in eighteenth-century America supported the concept, and John Stuart Mill in nineteenth-century England added further theoretical foundation to the orientation of libertarianism.

All these men, and many others, propounded a philosophy that was quite different from that of the authoritarians. They basically trusted the "mass man"; they believed that all kinds of information and ideas should be made public; they despised secrecy; they believed that there should be no prior censorship, and that free criticism was essential to happiness and growth. They were fundamentally "democrats" and not autocrats or some other variety of aristocrats. Of course, there are certain paradoxes in this generalization, which are very well exemplified by Jefferson, the southern, slave-holding, aristocrat who was also early America's leading libertarian.

A national libertarian orientation is one in which the leadership relates closely with the followership. It is one in which there is a trust of the masses, a belief that the majority can come closest to the truth and can make good decisions. This trust of the people is related to the mass media in that it is the media that must inform the people so they can know and so they can intelligently elect their representatives, direct them, and change them when necessary. *In theory, the libertarian nation is one in which the people cybernate their leadership instead of the other way around, as in an authoritarian nation.*

Two Libertarian Ideas. Two important ideas related to a libertarian press system have come to stand out and, in a sense, define such a system. They relate to: 1. the press as "the fourth branch of government," and 2. the "right of the people to know." Theoretically, the people, at least in the United States, have the media system checking on their government Establishment, keeping it honest. And, also, as theoretical rules of their country, the people have a right to know what their governmental apparatus is doing. These two ideas have become generally accepted as foundation stones of media libertarianism.

Briefly let us consider the "fourth branch of government" concept. It is based on the assumption that the press is an integral part of government—that it, theoretically, supplements the executive, legislative and judicial branches. This, of course, is really not the case at all. Another related assumption, heard very often, is that the press serves as a "check on government." This, of course, would *exclude* the press from the government and would tend to contradict the "fourth branch" idea.

Since the people do not elect the press to represent them in any way, it is quite probable that the press itself, rather than the people, has developed this "fourth branch" concept. In effect, the press is a self-appointed part of government and a self-appointed check on government. Yet, neither the United States Constitution—or the constitution of any other country—gives the press the responsibility, the obligation, to watch government and to check on its actions.

"Fourth branch" apologists will immediately say that traditional practices in American journalism plus "common sense" tell us that our mass media have this responsibility and obligation. And, certainly, these persons will insist, the press recognizes this obligation. But, *does* the press really recognize this obligation? If so, why can so many newspapers and other media be found that do not serve as "watchdogs" on government, checks on government, critics of government? Obviously many segments of the "press" *do not* recognize this obligation.

If any conclusion can be drawn from the questions raised above, it might be simply that the press is not any "fourth branch of government" and has no reason to consider itself even a critic of, or check on, government. After all, does not freedom of the press include the freedom of the press *not* to be a "fourth branch of government," a critic of anything, or a check on anything? So, perhaps the mere setting up of a premise of *what the libertarian press is* automatically restricts its freedom and demolishes the whole concept of libertarianism.

Now, let us turn briefly to the other assumed aspect of

libertarianism in the mass media: the "people's right to know."
If the source of this "right" is ever thought of at all, it is
generally assumed to be implicit in the "free press" clause of
the First Amendment to the American Constitution. But is it
really? The question might be asked if a free press should not
have the *freedom to withhold* certain things from the people—
the freedom, if you will, to keep the people from knowing.*

Even if we can pass over this basic conceptual contradiction, many other puzzling questions arise. For instance, if there
is a "right to know," one might ask—the right to know *what*?
(Surely the people *cannot* know, do not *need* to know, and do
not *want* to know, everything.) If the answer to the above
question is that the people have the right to know "public
business," then we have the problem of defining "public business."

Let us look again at the basic question: "The right to
know *what*?" If we agree that it is basic and important, then the
next question arises: *Who*, then, must decide what is appropriate for the people to know? Somebody or some group must
make this decision since not all information can be disseminated.

This person (or institution) then, must serve as a gatekeeper or censor—or "definer" of what the people have a right
to know. If this is true, then the concept of the "right to know"
is abridged; it simply means now the "right to know" *certain*
things that *somebody* wants us to know. In effect, then, the
"right" is not a right at all. If we really had a "right" to know
government business, the media could *insist* (by law) that the
government provide them with any or all of its information.
And beyond that, we citizens could insist (by law) that the mass
media provide us with any or all of the government information
they obtain. But if we were to insist that the press do that, we

---

*This is a modern variation on the well-known "paradox of freedom," first
pointed out by Plato. Free men, said Plato, may exercise their freedom by curtailing
their state of freedom and deciding to live under a tyrant.

would be contradicting the concept of press freedom—which includes the freedom to make editorial decisions.

We have examined briefly the two basic orientations—authoritarianism and libertarianism—and have considered some of the questions that may be posed related to the latter, the one with which we in the United States are most concerned.

So, before looking further at ways of describing media systems, we propose that these two orientations are prime shapers of the world's media philosophies and structures. And considering the nature of governments and institutions, it is probably safe to say that the natural drift of *all* governments and media systems is in the direction of authoritarianism. The forces of libertarianism must constantly fight (and it is an uphill battle) to keep the elitists from dictating, the censors from managing and restricting, and the antidemocrats from cybernating the people.

Now, from this rather simple dichotomous view of basic orientations affecting the media systems, let us turn to a more discerning, discriminating, and complex method of describing and analyzing media concepts and systems.

The "Four Theories" Concept

Probably the best-known typology of press systems is the "four theories" concept. Although these "theories" had long been discussed singly from time to time by a large number of authors and speakers, it was not until 1956, when three professors of communication—Fred S. Siebert, Theodore Peterson, and Wilbur Schramm—brought out their *Four Theories of the Press*, that this kind of typology was considered seriously. Now the little volume (in paperback since 1963*) has become stan-

---

Four Theories of the Press (Urbana: University of Illinois Press, 1963). Cf., a good discussion of the four concepts by William L. Rivers in Chapter 2 of Rivers and Schramm, *Responsibility in Mass Communication*, revised edition (New York: Harper & Row, 1969).

dard reading in journalism departments and schools and has implanted the "four theories" concept rather firmly in minds of journalism students, faculty, and practitioners. Almost every article and book dealing with philosophical bases for journalism has alluded to this book, commented on it, or quoted from it. The book has definitely made an impact.

Siebert, Peterson, and Schramm discuss journalism philosophy by presenting these four theories ("concepts" might have been a less pretentious term): 1. the authoritarian theory, 2. the libertarian theory, 3. the communist theory, and 4. the social responsibility theory. Briefly, here are the main characteristics of each of these "theories":

Authoritarian. The highest expression of organizational structure, the state, supercedes the individual and only with state domination is the individual able to acquire and develop the attributes of a civilized being. Mass communication, then, must support the state and the government in power so that the society may advance and the state may reach its objectives. The state (the "elite" that runs the state) directs the populace, which is not considered competent or interested enough to make political decisions. One man or a few men are placed in a position to lead. Part of their duty is to control the mass media, which must be used to push the leadership and its goals.

The media, then, under authoritarian theory, are "educational," directive, and propagandistic. They are instruments of control, not truly educational in the sense of sponsoring free and open information flow and discussion. Generally the media are privately owned, although the leader or his clique or party may own units in the media system. This theory revolves around the idea that a person engaged in journalism is so engaged as a special privilege granted by the national leader; therefore he owes an obligation to the leader and his government. This press philosophy has formed, and now forms, the basis for many press systems of the world; in each case it owes its existence to the state and operates to support and perpetuate the authority that permits it to survive. The mass media have only as much freedom as the national leadership will permit them to have at any time.

Libertarian. The concept of press "libertarianism" can be traced back to the seventeenth century where it took roots in England and in the American colonies. The philosophy that looked upon man as a rational animal with inherent natural rights gave rise to the libertarian press theory. One of these natural rights was the right to pursue truth, and would-be interferers should be restrained. Exponents of this libertarian press movement during the seventeenth, eighteenth, and nineteenth centuries included Milton, Locke, Erskine, Jefferson, and J. S. Mill. Individual liberties were stressed by these philosophers, along with a trust in the people to make intelligent decisions *if* there was freedom of expression.

Theoretically, a free press functions to uncover and present the truth, splintered though it may be in a pluralism of voices. It cannot do this if it is controlled by some authority outside itself. The press must serve as the informational link between government and people, and if this link is cut by governmental censorship or secrecy, the concept of freedom of information is largely invalidated. Today the libertarian press accepts (or claims to accept) the obligations of keeping the public abreast of government activities, of watching and serving as a check on government improprieties. In theory at least, the libertarian press is a "fourth estate" or "fourth branch of government," supplementing the executive, legislative, and judicial branches. In addition, through its pluralism it represents the many aspects of society and serves as a "forum" of discussion for the people.

Communist. The first quarter of the twentieth century saw the birth of the communist theory of the press. Karl Marx was its father, drawing heavily on the philosophy of his fellow German, Georg W. F. Hegel. The functions of the mass media of communication in a communist society, said Marx, were basically the same as those of the entire ruling apparatus—the perpetuation and expansion of the socialist system. Means of communication should exist to transmit social policy and not to aid in searching for the truth.

Under this theory media of mass communication are instruments of government and are integral parts of the State. The mass media must be owned and operated by the state and directed by the Communist Party or its agencies. Self-criticism in the media is permitted (i.e., criticism of failure to live up to communist planning and goals); in fact, such criticism is actively encouraged. The communist theory is based on the premise (as is the authoritarian) that the masses are too fickle and too ignorant and unconcerned with government to be told very much about the workings of government. Mass media must do what is best for the state and party; and what is best is what the leadership elite say is best—in line, of course, with Marxist theory. Whatever the media do to support and contribute to the achievement of communism is moral; whatever is done to hinder the achievement of communism is immoral.

Social Responsibility. This theory is a mid-twentieth century concept of the press as it is recognized in the Western world. It has its roots in the libertarian theory, say its proponents and explainers. It goes beyond the libertarian theory, however, in that it places a great many moral and ethical restrictions on the press; it not only places restrictions on the press, but it proposes that the press do many things that it has not been doing.

The emphasis in the social responsibility theory is shifted from press freedom to press responsibility. The theory has been drawn largely from a report published in 1947 by the Hutchins Commission.* This new theory, which emerged from the Commission's publications and is named and systematized in *Four*

---

*See Commission on Freedom of the Press, *A Free and Responsible Press* (Chicago: University of Chicago Press, 1947).

Theories of the Press, maintains that the importance of the press in modern society makes it absolutely necessary that an obligation of social responsibility be imposed on the communications media. To many persons, including the authors of the present volume, there are many problems with this "theory" and these will be discussed in the following sections. A growing number of scholars, press critics, and even media practitioners, however, are becoming increasingly concerned with our "libertarian" press performance and are urging all manner of reforms. This would indicate that it may be, as the authors of *Four Theories of the Press* contend, that libertarianism in this country's media system is evolving into social responsibility.

It may well be that through using different terms and structuring the typology to permit more flexibility, the objections that many have to the "four theories" concept—and especially to the social responsibility theory—could largely be overcome. Let us now look briefly at one recent modification.

The "Two-Tiered" Concept

While teaching courses in "Controls of Information" and "Mass Media and Society" at the University of Missouri, Ralph Lowenstein found that the basic 1956 "four theories" concept raised a number of serious questions in his own mind and in the minds of many students. The publication of these four "theories" or concepts tended to freeze basic thought in this area, and, as Lowenstein contends, since that time no significantly new propositions have been added to the 1956 formulation. Many other journalsim professors around the country, using the "four theories" concept in their classes, have noted certain student dissatisfaction with the typology and rationale.

In a class lecture in 1970, based on a brief paper he had written, Lowenstein said that attempting to fit a nation into one of the four theories, or vice versa, has been comparable to fitting the proverbial square peg into a round hole. What philos-

ophy, for example, he asks, prevails in Kenya, Burma, the
United Arab Republic, or a few dozen other underdeveloped
nations?

Contending that the "four theories" concept lacks the
flexibility needed for proper description and analysis of all of
today's press systems and therefore should be modified, Lowenstein proceeds to do just that. The following is the gist of his
new "two-tiered" typology which, he says, can be applied to
both the *ownership* and *philosophy* of a given press system:

Press Ownership:

1. Private—Ownership by individuals or nongovernment corporations; supported primarily by advertising or subscriptions.
2. Multi-party—Ownership by competitive political parties; subsidized by party or party members.
3. Government—Owned by government or dominant government party; subsidized primarily by government funds or
   government-collected license fees.

Press Philosophies:

1. Authoritarian—Negative government controls over the press
   to stifle criticism and thereby maintain ruling elite.
2. Social-Centralist—Positive government controls to harness
   the press for national economic and philosophical goals.
3. Libertarian—Absence of government controls, assuring free
   market place of ideas and operation of self-righting process.
4. Social-Libertarian—Minimal government controls to unclog
   channels of communication and assure operational spirit of
   libertarian philosophy.

The three types of press "ownership" obviously consider
the press from the point of view of sources of financial support.
This is done for a purpose: In Lowenstein's opinion, the source
of support will, in almost every case, indicate important operational characteristics of the press. For example, to say that a
press system is *privately owned* is to indicate that its chief
source of revenue must come from advertising and/or subscriptions. It could be understood, then, that the system must be

immediately responsive to the needs of the advertising community and/or its subscribing public.

Slightly different titles are given to two of the four 1956 basic press philosophies. *Authoritarian* and *libertarian* remain the same; the philosophies they represent are clear, and the terms themselves have behind them centuries of usage. "Soviet-Communist," however, has been abandoned by Lowenstein to make way for *social-centralist*. The latter term admits a broad enough spectrum to include all the nations of the Eastern bloc, and yet removes the negative connotations of the word so it may also be used to describe those centrally guided press systems in many developing nations. The *social-centralist* philosophy is a modern modification of the authoritarian philosophy as set forth in the "four theories" concept. The clear difference is that this philosophy, in all its variations, controls the press not primarily to keep it from doing harm to the ruling elite, but to channel the power of the media into what the state sees as constructive educational, developmental, and political machinery.

The term "social responsibility" has been discarded by Lowenstein because the name itself is ambiguous. Instead, the term *social-libertarian* was chosen because of its clear descriptiveness. The social-libertarian philosophy bears the same relationship to the libertarian philosophy as the social-centralist does to the authoritarian. The difference is that the social-libertarian is only a short step away from the libertarian, a modification needed only insofar as it is necessary to make the libertarian philosophy work. Self-regulation to this end is preferable, but where monopolistic trends are pronounced, government regulation is unavoidable.

It must be pointed out that mixed "philosophies" are possible within a given nation, and it is also quite likely—especially in the West and in developing nations—for a country to have mixed "ownerships." One might find all three "ownerships" in the print media alone, or one type of "ownership" for the print media, and another type for the electronic media.

For example, England may be classified in the following manner under this two-tiered system:

Print media:
    Ownership: Private
    Philosophy: Social-libertarian
Television:
    Ownership: Government
    Philosophy: Social-centralist; social-libertarian
Radio:
    Ownership: Government
    Philosophy: Social-centralist

Classification of the media takes into account the overall pattern of the media, not the exceptions that exist in every medium. For example, there are a number of magazines in England produced by governmental or "publicly owned" agencies (*The Listener*, published by BBC is one example), but this is an exception to the general pattern in England. The classification of television, however, does take into account the dual programming system—BBC networks, on one hand, and Independent Television (ITV) networks, on the other. Government still owns the channels and broadcasting facilities of ITV, but programming is a private affair, partly dependent on advertising. ITV has therefore developed a different philosophy or rationale, and we can classify it, says Lowenstein, as *social-libertarian.* There are many who would argue that the philosophy of BBC is *social-libertarian* also, rather than *social-centralist.* But Lowenstein believes that government controls of BBC are not "minimal," and that there *is* the intent to harness broadcasting for educational and philosophical goals of the state.

Lowenstein also classifies a state—Israel—whose media are not so well known in the United States. This example demonstrates that much can be told about the media of a specific country in a few words, using this classification system:

Print media:
    Ownership: Private, multi-party, government
    Philosophy: Social-libertarian, social-centralist

Electronic media:
    Ownership: Government
    Philosophy: Social-centralist

The identification of these ownerships and philosophies in clearer terms also offers new insights into the relationships between the ownerships and philosophies themselves. For example, one might hypothesize that under the *privately owned* structure, there tends to be a "progression" of philosophies. Consider the following model:

Ownership: Private
Philosophic Progression: 1. *Authoritarian* (primitive)
                         2. *Libertarian* (revolutionary)
                         3. *Social-libertarian* (mature)

Other insights await, once this new yardstick can be applied to the press systems of the world. This new, two-tiered system, proposed by Lowenstein, will not be without its handicaps. There will still be nations whose press systems defy simple classification. Also, to modify and expand an existing concept is also to complicate it in some ways. The gates that will open in understanding and constructive analysis, however, should compensate for these relatively minor problems.

Some Concluding Observations

Although the "four theories" typology (1956) and Lowenstein's "two-tiered" concept (1970) permit more sophisticated analysis, the basic dichotomy with which this chapter began appears to dominate both. Either a media system is authoritarian in its dominant disposition or it is libertarian. Siebert, Peterson, Schramm in their *Four Theories of the Press* make the case for splitting this basic "authoritarian" disposition into what they call the *authoritarian* and the *communist* theories. And, they contend that the *social responsibility* theory is growing out of the *libertarian* theory. So, in effect, they have made four concepts out of the basic authoritarian/libertarian dichotomy.

Lowenstein, not satisfied with either the labels used in the "four theories" approach or the lack of emphasis on ownership, has attempted to come up with a more meaningful typology. But his typology, too, is tied rather tightly to the basic dichotomous press philosophy. He breaks the authoritarian philosophy into the "authoritarian" (emphasis on negative controls) and "social-centralist" (emphasis on positive controls). And, he likewise makes a similar type of distinction with his "libertarian" and the "social-libertarian" concepts.

The two typologies (1956; 1970) have certain obvious similarities. Both are rigged as dynamic concepts, in that they show how a press system may evolve,* contending that the direction of change (in noncommunist and nonauthoritarian countries) is toward "liberating" the libertarian system from its weaknesses and, as Lowenstein puts it, assuring the "operational spirit of libertarian philosophy."

It is the latter concept that is rather troublesome both in the 1956 typology that calls it "social responsibility" and in Lowenstein's 1970 typology that refers to it as "social-libertarianism." To achieve this presumably ideal press system, some controls would be necessary (Lowenstein says they would be "minimal") to keep the media system responsible to society as theoretically it should be under libertarianism. What is somewhat puzzling and disturbing about this is that when a government begins tampering with, or controlling, the libertarian functioning of the press system, the time is ripe for the control cycle of press development to begin all over again. When a government "forces" libertarianism to work, the country no longer has libertarianism, but control.

What is a "Responsible" Press? Unless duties and responsibilities for the media are spelled out by law (and they are not in the United States), the whole concept of a socially responsible press has little or no meaning. Is it not simply the kind of press that "supports my kind of truth"? Implicit in the recent Western preoccupation with "social responsibility" (or "social-liber-

---

*At least this is true of the "social responsibility" or "social-libertarian" concepts which presumably evolve from, or are refined out of, the libertarian concept.

tarianism") is the argument that some group (obviously a governmental one, ultimately) can and must define or decide *what* is socially responsible. Also, the implication is clear that publishers and journalists acting freely cannot determine what is socially responsible nearly as well as can some "outside" or "impartial" group. If this power elite decides that the press is not responsible, not even the First Amendment to the United States Constitution can keep the publishers from losing this freedom.

No one would deny that the press, in one respect, would be more "responsible" if some type of governmental supervision came about; indeed, reporters could be kept from nosing about in "critical" areas during "critical" times. News broadcasters and commentators would present "politically balanced" programs, and the amount of sensational material could be controlled in the media, or eliminated altogether. Government activities could always be supported and public policy could be pushed on all occasions. The press could be more "educational" in the sense that less hard news (crime, wrecks, disasters, riots, demonstrations, etc.) would appear, while more news of art exhibits, concerts, governmentally supportive rallies, and national progress in general could be emphasized. In short, the press would stress the positive and eliminate, or minimize, the negative. Then, with one voice the press of the nation would be responsible to its society; and the definition of "responsible" would be functional—defined and carried out by government edict and law.

Also this question must be considered: When we are talking about the responsibility of the mass media (or press) to society are we talking about the responsibilities of publishers, managers, editors, journalists, commentators, news sources, or what? Also: To whom are the media supposed to be responsible? To a given group or party? To a given country? To humanity? To a particular medium's particular readership or audience? Do not these various entities have conflicting demands that are fighting for dominance? It would seem that in a pluralistic society, with conflicting ways of life and divergent political ideologies, there can be no single concept of press responsibility. And, if there is no single concept of press responsibility, there is only a pluralism of concepts; therefore, talk about *press responsibility to society* (a kind of monolithic idea) in a libertarian, pluralistic country is a philosophical contradiction.

Rationale for Media Responsibility. The social responsibility proponents say that government should intervene "only when the need is great and the stakes are high." They assure us that the government should not be heavy-handed. The question arises, however, as to just when the need is great enough and the stakes high enough for government to intervene. And just how much intervention by government is enough to be "heavy-handed"?

We are told also that a "duty to one's conscience is the primary basis of the right of free expression under social responsibility theory."* This is all very well, but what relation does this have to the question of government intervention "if the need is great"? It would seem that "duty to one's conscience" is extremely relative and that a newspaper defending the U.S. military presence in Southeast Asia, for example, would do so in as good conscience as would the newspaper advocating immediate U.S. withdrawal from that part of the world. Which newspaper is responsible to society? To what or which society? To which segment of what society?

The American media system generally (FCC regulation of certain aspects of broadcasting being the exception) has proceeded on unregulated initiative. But the Hutchins Commission in 1947 and its ideological followers think this is of questionable value. Suggestions have been made by such persons as law professor Jerome Barron that media be forced legally to publish certain material submitted by certain groups. The trend is toward control. This is natural, of course, because when you start stressing "responsibility," you necessarily must begin defining it

---

Four Theories of the Press, pp. 95-97.

and this definition implies a restriction of options, a limiting of freedom.

The social responsibility advocates feel unregulated media operation is unwise because the citizen has "a moral right to information and an urgent need of it" and the implication is that the American press is not giving this information to the citizen. A moral right to *what* information? This is a significant question. Or, probably a better one: To *whose* information? Evidently Robert Hutchins and his twelve commissioners did not think that a pluralistic information system is good enough—or they implied that our system was not pluralistic enough to be good enough. But when is a media system *pluralistic enough?* The Commission did not really know, nor do we. But there is good reason to believe that our media system permits the citizen to get an extremely wide assortment of information in great quantities. Admittedly, there are gaps in it. But anyone vaguely familiar with information theory and semantics knows that there will always be gaps, and if different reporters observe and communicate it, there will always be variant versions.

Pluralism and Libertarianism. It would seem that press pluralism should be the objective of American society, and pluralism consists of the diversity of information and ideas, and not necessarily the *number* of media units operating. A single newspaper in one town may present a greater variety of viewpoints and ideas than a television station and four newspapers in another town. Pluralism is closely tied to libertarianism—or traditionally has been. The growing concern with, and emphasis on, responsibility to society tends to be directive and thereby restricts pluralism. It is possible, certainly, to *force* pluralism where there is little. But in so doing, press freedom is diminished. So, it might be well to recognize that if pluralism is the goal, the price that must be paid (if you have no faith that a laissez faire system will result in pluralism) for forcing pluralism is the erosion of press freedom.

The assumption of many today is that the libertarian press

(the "free market" operation of media) is not meeting its re-sponsibilities, not resulting in pluralism. Many persons, some of them in the media themselves, have lost faith in libertarianism, just as many others appear to have lost faith in democratic processes. They are embracing "social responsibility" with its directive and proscriptive overtones, rationalizing this position by saying that the results that *should* come from a libertarian media system must be *made* to come through some kind of control of the mass media.

Perhaps these critics of libertarianism are right. Perhaps their evolving theory of cybernated media responsibility will prove more beneficial to the nation's citizens and even more pluralistic than the old laissez faire libertarianism. Time will tell.

13.

Media Freedom and Controls

IT IS A POPULAR MISCONCEPTION THAT THE PRESS IN AMERica was more free in the years immediately following the Revolutionary War than it is today. Actually, the state legislatures inherited (and in many cases adopted into law) British restrictions on seditious writings, blasphemy, and press access to legislative assemblies. The fight against *prior*publication restraints did indeed end for the most part with the Revolutionary War. The fight against *post*publication restraints, however, still had a long way to go.*

Another misconception surrounds the First Amendment: "Congress shall make no law respecting an establishment of religion, or prohibiting the free exercise thereof; or abridging the freedom of speech, or of the press, or the right of the people peacefully to assemble, and to petition the government for redress of grievances." It was not, as many think, originally intended as a blanket guarantee of press freedom. Rather, there

---

*In *Legacy of Suppression* (Cambridge: Harvard University Press, 1960), Leonard W. Levy offers documentation to prove that America's founding fathers had no real understanding of freedom of speech and press as we know it today. It was not until about 1800, according to Levy, that true libertarian thought began to emerge in America.

195

is reason to believe that the entire Bill of Rights was an effort by anti-Federalists to prevent federal authority from superseding state authority. The First Amendment, if read with emphasis on the word "Congress," imposed limitations on national government only. The state legislatures were still free to enact laws regarding the press, and most of them did. Not until much later was the First Amendment applied to states as well as to the federal government.

The genius of the "founding fathers" lay in their locating the freedoms of speech and press in the same Amendment with three other basic protections. There have been times in our history when a majority desire to amend or abrogate the freedoms of speech and press was deterred only by their reluctance to tamper with the other three.

In any case, the press of the United States ranks today among the freest in the world. Its freedom is partly, but not entirely, due to the First Amendment. Every nation in the world with a written constitution "guarantees" press freedom. But having guaranteed it, most then pass restrictive legislation and engage in discriminatory practices against the press. The press in the United States is free because America is in fact a democracy with an unintimidated judiciary. Otherwise, our own guarantee would be as meaningless as those guarantees in the constitutions of authoritarian countries.

Most persons would agree that the press plays a vital role in a democracy by serving as a watchdog over government, providing channels for popular participation in government decisions, and reevaluating the standards of society. However, no democracy, including the United States, can offer the press complete freedom; otherwise the nation would run the risk of abridging the freedom of the individual and adversely affecting society as a whole. Few people could feel secure, for example, in a society that had no libel laws. Therefore, in many cases press controls are necessary, though in a democracy these are kept to a minimum by the press' vigorous appeal to the law and to public opinion.

Press controls are not always an obvious phenomenon. Governments in some countries manage to exert great pressure on the press by allocating newsprint, bribing or licensing newsmen, granting licenses for purchase of printing equipment abroad, distributing all foreign news through government-owned wire services, etc.

If we take a look at the press controls that exist in the United States, an acknowledged free press country, we may have a better idea of the rationale and potential dangers of press control. In approaching this subject, however, we must leave out all the contrivances of concealment exercised by individuals in government (ranging from the President down to the most insignificant municipal employee) and the activities of individual newsmen and press units to limit the flow of news.* Excluding these two vast (and unchartable) areas, controls of information in the U.S. can be divided into three major categories: 1. punitive laws for harmful publication, 2. regulations that prevent access to information, and 3. pressures on publishers and broadcasters to restrict the flow of legally harmless information.

Punishment for Harmful Publication

A number of laws involving the press protect the reputation or property rights of the individual. More than this, however, the laws are also there to prevent a breach of the peace. When a man's honor or property rights have been damaged, society can offer him an avenue for recompense or revenge other than a resort to violence. Those laws protecting the individual or organization include:

Libel. False or malicious reports affecting reputations open the way to civil libel suits, although it must be remem-

---

*An increasing threat to press freedom in this country is ownership of press units by "conglomerates." A parent corporation may exercise control over one subsidiary, a press unit, in order to promote or protect products sold by another subsidiary, a manufacturing plant.

bered that there are fifty different sets of libel law in the U.S.,
one for every state.* In order to protect—and even encourage—
freedom of speech and the press, the courts have sought to
place strict limitations on the law of libel. The *New York Times
v. Sullivan* ruling by the U.S. Supreme Court in 1964 greatly
extended freedom of the press. The ruling essentially held that a
public official could not recover libel damages, even for a false
report, unless he could prove that malice was involved. And
malice, according to the Court, exists only if the plaintiff can
prove that the defendant knew the material in question was
false or had a reckless disregard for its truth or falsity. The
Supreme Court declared that "debate on public issues should be
robust and wide-open, and that it may well include vehement,
caustic, and sometimes sharp attacks on government and public
officials."

Since 1964, the ruling has been consistently broadened,
primarily by liberally defining "public official," until it now
includes: 1. "public figures," 2. persons in whom there is a public interest, and 3. private citizens who engage voluntarily in
public discussion of matters of "grave public concern and controversy." The courts have indeed searched for the "outer limits" of this First Amendment right. Libel law in the United
States is considered by most observers to be among the most
liberal in the world.

Copyright and privacy. It may seem unusual to place
copyright and privacy under the same heading. But they are
both essentially protections of property rights. Copyright, of
course, prevents the poaching of literary and other creative
works. The concept of privacy as a legal right is less than a
hundred years old in the United States, one of the first countries ever to adopt it into law. In its broadest meaning, it entails

---

*"Criminal" libel suits, in which the state is the plaintiff, rarely occur in the
U. S. First, it is difficult to convince a public prosecutor to bring such charges;
second, any fines go to the state, not to the individual damaged. Such suits, when
they do appear, are usually brought on behalf of a public official who believes he has
been libeled.

the "right to be let alone." But in so far as publication or broadcasting is concerned, it involves unauthorized use of a person's name or likeness.

The law is applied strictly where advertising is involved. But as for news, news features, or biography, a "public figure" loses much of his right of privacy, under an extension of the *New York Times v. Sullivan* rule, and even a private citizen's name and picture can be used in television film, news stories, and feature articles without his consent, as long as the material was obtained in a public place. Supreme Court Justice William J. Brennan, Jr. has explained: "Exposure of the self to others in varying degrees is a concomitant of life in a civilized community. The risk of this exposure is an essential incident of life in a society which places a primary value on freedom of speech and of press." Even so, the public's "right to know," the courts have ruled, does not justify using identifiable photographs of people in humiliating acts or poses when the story can be told as well without so identifying individuals.

Other laws are designed to protect society as a whole from what is considered to be harmful communication. Such laws involve:

Fraud. The Post Office Department and the Federal Trade Commission are empowered to initiate action against advertisers and publications that seek to defraud the public, either through false advertisements or stories which publicize fraudulent schemes. There is a gray area between "legitimate advertising puffery" and outright falsehood, however, and this often defies satisfactory solution either by regulatory of self-regulatory agencies.

Sedition. Every country can be expected to protect itself from violent overthrow, whether from external or internal enemies. In order to "advocate" violent overthrow of the government, one must speak or write; the government's right to self-defense is thereby placed in opposition to the individual's speech and press freedom. There is still one sedition act on the federal books in the United States, the Alien Registration Act of 1940 (usually referred to as the Smith Act), which makes advocacy of violent overthrow of the United States government a crime. It was the first peacetime sedition law enacted by Congress since the infamous Alien and Sedition Acts of 1798. Although two Supreme Court justices have referred to it as an abridgement of speech, press, and assembly in violation of the First Amendment, the Court majority found it constitutional in the *Dennis* case of 1951. In the 1957 *Yates* case, however, the Supreme Court effectively emasculated the act by ruling that lower courts had to distinguish between advocacy of forceful overthrow of the government as an "abstract doctrine" and advocacy of action to that end. Preaching an "abstract doctrine" of forceful overthrow is no crime, the Supreme Court implied, since this does not demonstrate a "clear and present danger" to the United States government.

Obscenity. The legal aspects of obscenity are affected by two questions: 1. Is pornography harmful in that it incites sexual offenses?* and 2. To what degree is pornography protected by the free speech and free press rights of the First Amendment?

Some contend that obscenity is illegal not because it is harmful, per se, but because it is offensive. It is a punishable offense, they say, not because it is a crime, but rather because it is a sin. The Supreme Court, in its rulings, appears to have accepted the argument that pornography is offensive, rather than harmful, and that obscenity is in the nature of "fighting words" that could excite instinctive outrage and thus lead to a breach of the peace.

On the second question, it is best to give the answers of the Supreme Court justices themselves, from the landmark *Roth* case of 1957. First, the minority opinion of Justice William O. Douglas:

---

*This question is considered in some detail in Chapter 10.

... if the First Amendment guarantee of freedom of speech and press is to mean anything in this field, it must allow protests even against the moral code that the standard of the day sets for the community. In other words, literature should not be suppressed merely because it offends the moral code of the censor ... the test that suppresses a cheap tract today can suppress a literary gem tomorrow. All it needs is to incite a lascivious thought or arouse a lustful desire. The list of books that judges or juries can place in that category is endless.

I would give the broad sweep of the First Amendment full support. I have the same confidence in the ability of our people to reject noxious literature as I have in their capacity to sort out the true from the false in theology, economics, politics, or any other field.

But Justice Brennan, delivering the majority opinion, wrote that the Supreme Court had always assumed that obscenity is not within the area of constitutionally protected speech and press. He added:

All ideas having even the slightest redeeming social importance—unorthodox ideas, controversial ideas, even ideas hateful to the prevailing climate of opinion—have the full protection of the guaranties, unless excludable because they encroach upon the limited area of more important interests. But implicit in the history of the First Amendment is the rejection of obscenity as utterly without redeeming social importance.

If obscenity was not protected by the First Amendment, it remained for the Supreme Court to set down guidelines for identifying obscene material. Anything not fitting the description would then be "protected." In a series of rulings, beginning with the *Roth* decision, the Court established these major tests:

1. Whether the material is *utterly* without redeeming social importance.
2. Whether to the average person, applying contemporary (national) community standards, the dominant theme of the material appeals to the prurient interest of the average adult, or to the prurient interest of a clearly defined deviant group for which it was designed.

3. Whether the material is patently offensive (hard-core pornography).

A publication, to be found obscene, must fail all three tests independently. In other words, if the material can pass only one test, it cannot be judged obscene, even if it fails the other two. In addition, the Court has established three other special situations in which "borderline" obscenity could bring convictions: 1. sale of smut to minors, 2. obtrusive presentation of titillating material—"publication in a manner so obtrusive as to make it impossible for an unwilling individual to avoid exposure to it," and 3. pandering promotion—advertising that emphasizes the sexually provocative aspects of the material.

Out of the Supreme Court rulings have come several qualifications to the identification of obscene material. These can all be placed under the heading *variable obscenity*, which means simply that what is obscene for one group may not be obscene for another, and what is obscene in one place may not be obscene in another place. For example, material not obscene for adults may be obscene for minors; material not obscene to the average person may be obscene for homosexuals—and would be adjudged obscene if it is directed at that group. Also, material that is obscene if offered for "public distribution" may not be obscene if it remains in the privacy of one's home. It is this latter principle of variable obscenity that is most likely to open the door to more liberal interpretation of obscenity laws in the years ahead.

Regulations Preventing Access

By law and by tradition, many public meetings are out of bounds for all or part of the press. These include all levels of government, ranging from municipal bodies to the United States Congress. Although "open meetings" laws exist in a number of states, the laws provide for exceptions. In any case, committees and legislative bodies can avoid the technicality by moving into closed executive sessions or by simply holding informal premeeting conferences. A wide variety of reasons can be given for holding closed meetings, some of them legitimate. Congressional committees, for example, may contend that they are discussing national security or foreign policy secrets. Municipal bodies may argue that newspaper reports may be embarrassing to personnel whose records are being discussed, or that the city may be put to greater expense if plans for new roads are publicized before right-of-way can be purchased. Even so, information which the public has a right to know is often withheld under such camouflage. It is a problem for which there is no solution other than the establishment of strict guidelines for closed meetings, and the prodding by newsmen to see that they are kept.

Motion picture, television, and still cameras are barred from the general sessions of most state legislatures and the two houses of Congress. The argument is made that many legislators would be tempted to "perform" for the cameras, lengthening the legislative sessions. Some state legislatures have not only permitted television cameras, but set up special booths for them in the main galleries, without noticeable ill effects. The United States Congress, however, permits television cameras into regular sessions only on special (usually ceremonial) occasions. The Senate gives committee chairmen the prerogative of allowing television cameras into open sessions; the House of Representatives bars TV from all committee meetings (although members of the House are now moving to liberalize this rule).

Many of the same reasons given for closing meetings are also given for closing public records to the public and the press. Newsmen have been more successful in getting "open records" laws established in the various states. The most ambitious "open records" law ever passed was the Freedom of Information Act of 1966, which made it mandatory for all federal agencies to make records available. The law gave citizens immediate recourse to the courts if they were denied access to records. However, the possible loopholes in such a carefully drawn act as this one are apparent when one considers that there are nine major categories of information exempted from the provisions of the law. These include categories such as national defense and foreign policy secrets, inter agency and intra agency memorandums, personnel and medical files, and investigatory files compiled for law enforcement purposes.

The courts—local, state, and federal—have increasingly placed obstacles in the path of media coverage of the judicial processes. Restrictions on the press were intensified as a result of the Supreme Court's *Sheppard* ruling of 1966, but other shackles on the press had been put into effect well before that date. Cameras had been barred from the courtroom, and juvenile cases in many states had been closed completely to the press. In 1965 Attorney General Nicholas Katzenbach had set forth guidelines limiting the amount of pretrial information that could be released by personnel of the Department of Justice, and these rules were quickly adopted by state and local jurists and law enforcement officials. Justification for all these restrictions was concern for the rights of the defendant, to assure that he would receive a "speedy and public trial, by an impartial jury," as provided by the Sixth Amendment.

But the contradiction that exists between barring the press and assuring the defendant a fair trial has been lost on many members of the legal profession. There is no doubt that a few individuals, involved in sensational trials, have not received justice, partly as a result of press irresponsibility. Even in such cases, however, the defendant has always had certain safeguards against negative press influence. These include legal processes such as change of venue, challenge of jurors, request for mistrial, and appeal.

But for every case of "trial by newspaper," there are dozens where the functions of a free press vis-a-vis the judicial system have been a boon to defendants and society. In a modern society, where few members of the concerned population can attend the trial itself, press coverage of pretrial, trial, and posttrial procedures fulfills the "public" trial provision of the Sixth Amendment by bringing the trials and their processes to the people. This has assured a "speedy" and "fair" trial to the defendant in the following ways: the press is able to expose abuses of police power, jurists are more likely to perform properly under scrutiny of the press, witnesses are more inclined to tell the truth, and pretrial publicity is likely to bring forth witnesses who did not know about the case. Pretrial and trial publicity benefits society by acquainting citizens with their rights under law, while the publicity attendant to a trial serves as a deterrent to further crime.

The subpoena and contempt powers of the courts have also indirectly served to bar the reporter from access to his sources. Reporters or their notes have been subpoenaed for law enforcement purposes or actual trial testimony. The reporter is held in contempt if he does not reveal the names of his sources, the information he may have been told in confidence, or his notes from specific stories. Though unintended, the effect of such legal action is to cut the reporter off from his sources of information.

The answer to this problem might appear to be the establishment of "shield laws" granting reporters the same right of professional secrecy sometimes accorded to doctors, lawyers, and religious ministers. However, it must be pointed out that the reporter, in his relationship to his source of information, is in an entirely different position from the doctor or priest. These other professionals normally keep to themselves the information given to them by patients, clients, and parishioners; the reporter gathers his information in order to make it public. In such cases, innocent individuals are often hurt by the resulting publicity. If "shield laws" absolved reporters from accountability for this damage, society as a whole could suffer. In addition, many attorneys and public officials argue that members of the press, like other citizens, have an obligation to disclose information that would further the cause of justice. Therefore, fewer than one-third of the states have enacted "shield laws" that would grant reporters an exemption from compulsory testimony. And the courts have also been reluctant to extend this privilege.

Higher courts seem to be moving in the direction of a compromise solution to this problem. Without relinquishing the legal right to compel reporters to testify, they have indicated that the subpoena power should be highly restricted where the press is concerned, and only utilized when government can demonstrate a compelling need for testimony that could not be obtained by any other investigatory process.

Where press freedom has been an issue, the Supreme Court at one time accorded First Amendment rights a *preferred position*. This meant that when the First Amendment seemed to be in conflict with other constitutional or human rights (especially rights protected by the Sixth Amendment), the Court ruled in favor of press freedom.* During the last few decades, however, the Supreme Court appears to have been applying a *balancing doctrine*, weighing carefully the rights in conflict with the First Amendment, and no longer according it a preferred position in the struggle. Thus, where the press seems to have interfered with an individual's right to obtain a fair trial, the Court has ruled in favor of the Sixth Amendment (the *Sheppard* decision is one example).

Pressures Against "Harmless" Publication

In addition to laws punishing the press for harmful publication, and laws and regulations limiting press access to the news, a number of subtle pressures exist in the United States to discourage the press from printing news that is legally harmless, but discomforting or embarrassing to governments, businesses, or individuals. Sources of some of these pressures have been mentioned in other chapters, but briefly mentioned below are factors—not always so obvious—that facilitate these pressures:

Government ownership of media. The federal government is involved in media ownership to a greater extent than the

---

*See the majority decision in the 1941 *Bridges* v. *California* case for an example of a *preferred position* ruling.

average person realizes. Through the Government Printing Office, the U.S. is one of the major book publishers in the country. It owns two wire services (an agricultural and a weather wire), produces hundreds of magazines through its federal agencies, publishes numerous military camp and service-wide newspapers, produces motion pictures for the United States Information Agency, and broadcasts throughout the world over armed forces radio and television networks and the Voice of America. Quite obviously, the government is a gatekeeper in each one of these wholly owned enterprises. For example, congressmen may alter so-called verbatim accounts of their speeches before they are published in the *Congressional Record*. There are recurrent charges of censorship in the armed forces broadcasting networks and *Stars and Stripes*. The Voice of America tells the truth in its news reports, but not necessarily certain aspects of the truth that one would hear on a commercial network news program.

Licensing. The power to license electronic media enabled the government to exert more pressure on broadcasting than it has ever been able to exert on print media. For example, it has always been understood that the First Amendment gave publishers a right to be one sided, opinionated, and highly critical, without giving opponents a chance to reply. Broadcasters, under the theory that they are accountable to all of the people in return for the loan of an exclusive frequency or channel, have no such right. And the licensing authority, the Federal Communications Commission, holds each station accountable for violations.

Government advertising. Advertising from state, county, and township governments is an important source of livelihood to weekly newspapers. Such advertising may well determine profit or loss for many of them. Therefore, the ability of governments to withhold these legal notices, or perhaps give them to one favored newspaper, discourages papers in some areas from being too critical of their local government. In most states, adequate safeguards against this form of pressure have been written into statute. But the statutes are subject to change.

Tax powers. Although few newspapers and broadcasting stations are cowed by this hidden threat, the power to tax can be a potent weapon in the hands of county and municipal governments. This threat takes the form, primarily, of assessed valuation of plant and equipment, rather than tax on the product (newspaper, advertisements). If press units are given favored treatment (that is, assessed at a lower level than equivalent business plants), then they already operate under the knowledge that they "owe" a return favor to the taxing authority.

Marginal press units. The American tradition holds that competition is a good thing. In the case of newspapers and broadcasting stations, too much competition may be a bad thing. Press units that are not economically strong are subject to all sorts of pressures—from subscribers, from advertisers, and even from themselves. The threat of a canceled subscription or canceled advertisement is more dangerous when one is on the borderline of profit than when one is well into the black. And the temptation not to antagonize, not to be too critical—in short, to exercise more "self-censorship"—accompanies economic insecurity.

Press councils. Experiments with local press councils were conducted in Oregon, California, Colorado, and Illinois in the late 1960s. More recently, there have been suggestions by foundations and journalism educators that a national press council be formed in the United States.

A national press council can take one of two forms. It could be a commission that observes and reports on the performance of the press each year, or a council that hears individual complaints about press units and passes down specific judgments. Those who argue in favor of a press council have emphasized that it does more to extend press freedom than to abridge it. The press council can improve the image of the press by clearing up false accusations against the press in general and by placing its weights against restrictive legislation. At the same time, it can improve society by using its moral pressure to improve press responsibility.

Even if the motives are good and the results beneficial, however, the press council is a potential control on the press. Although it would be "self-regulation," its function would be similar to that of libel laws. Few people would like to live in a country that had no libel laws, but most newsmen would agree that libel laws restrict the press, even though the restrictions may be necessary. There has been concern by many newsmen that the press council concept, even if completely shorn of enforcement provisions, would result in gradual erosion of press freedom. In the words of J. Russell Wiggins, former editor of the *Washington Post*, "It is one of the virtues of a good newspaper that it does not have to give way to every transient majority. It does not have to please or persuade a jury every day."

Pressures to Encourage Publication

We have mentioned in this chapter three broad areas of press restrictions. But it must be noted that there are those who believe government should interfere in a *positive* way to encourage publication of certain information.

This is not a new attitude in the United States. The early mail acts prior to 1800 set ridiculously cheap rates for newspapers in order to promote the diffusion of political information to those living on farms, as well as in towns. But whereas the old attitude favored government intervention to bring the press to the people, the latest plea is for government intervention to bring the people into the press. Certainly the "equal time" and "fairness" doctrines of the Federal Communications Commission support this idea. And Dr. Jerome A. Barron would extend these doctrines to the print media as well, giving citizens a "right of access" and "right of reply."* Barron has contended

---

*"Access to the Press—A New First Amendment Right," *Harvard Law Review* (June 1967), pp. 1641-78.

that "protecting" the right of free expression is not "providing" the right of free expression, because the press practices its own repression of ideas and opinions.

According to those who generally support the Barron thesis, the monopolistic nature of mass media and their dependence on advertising have meant that they reflect the opinions, and exist to serve, only the mainstream majority. This means that intellectual minorities, ethnic minorities, political minorities, and nonconsumer minorities (i.e., pre-school-age children) are left out in the cold. The government can alter this situation in one of two ways: 1. by using its coercive powers to force publication or transmission of minority information and opinion in the mass media, or 2. by using government funds to subsidize or wholly sponsor publications and programming that commercial enterprises would find unprofitable.

In a sense, the government is already utilizing both alternatives in its dealings with the electronic media. It insists on public service programming to justify license renewals, and enforces the "equal time" and "fairness" doctrines in controversial matters. It subsidizes special interest programming through money made available to the Corporation for Public Broadcasting. The government is also involved in other media operations that commercial media would find unprofitable—the *Congressional Record*, military publications, and Voice of America, to name only a few. Even so, *Stars and Stripes* is a direct competitor to commercial, military-oriented newspapers such as the *Army Times* and *Overseas Weekly*. The government can justify this on the grounds that *Stars and Stripes* is intended for its own employees, no one else.

But when government delves more deeply into publishing or broadcasting in a way that would bring it into open competition with commercial media, certain First Amendment conflicts are bound to appear. State and other governmental bodies that established and still subsidize educational television stations are already grappling with this problem.

What happens, for example, if the programming is so good

that the educational station attracts a majority, instead of a minority, audience? Can such a broadcasting station remain part of the "fourth branch" of government when it is essentially married to the other three? What, in short, happens to freedom of the press, including the right—even the obligation—to criticize government? And every question posed about government involvement in electronic media remains just as relevant to government involvement in print media.

The Hutchins Commission of 1947 spoke of direct government competition with the mass media as a last resort, "when the stakes are high and the risks are great." Zechariah Chafee, who served as a staff adviser to the Commission, implied that government should attempt to alter the content of mass media only when the need was "desperate," because of the threat of such interference to press freedom. This remains the crux of the problem today, whether the need outweighs the potential threat to press freedom, or whether press freedom is more important than fulfilling the need.

14.

Propaganda

SOME PERSONS MAY WONDER IF A DISCUSSION OF PROPA-
ganda is appropriate to a book such as this. Probably the best
justification for the inclusion of this subject is that propaganda
is tied very closely to the mass media: it is transmitted largely
by them, and in many cases is created by them. In fact, it is
almost impossible to think about mass media in the modern
world without considering propaganda. We contend, then, that
the mass media are: 1. filled with a wide assortment of propaganda, and 2. filled with a wide assortment of propagandists.
Media are both transmitters of, and formulators of, propaganda.

Propaganda loses any kind of meaningful significance if it
is defined too broadly, if it (as some writers propose) becomes
synonymous with organized dissemination of messages. Then,
of course, every kind of communication effort would be propaganda, depending admittedly on the connotation of the word
"organized." Propaganda in the context of journalism, or in the
context of the mass media, must be understood to be something
more limited, more specific. Otherwise, we might as well scrap
the word altogether. It has been said that the term *propaganda*
has a negative or evil connotation in a journalistic context. This

is undoubtedly true, especially in that part of journalism that purports to be objective, reliable, balanced, thorough, and credible—the *news* aspects.

On the other hand, many journalists and other toilers in the vineyards of the mass media embrace propaganda as a very necessary part of the media output. Propaganda has, even in its most negative meanings, chiseled out a niche for itself in the most highly respected of the mass media. Columnists and news commentators accept it as a valid aspect of their journalistic endeavors. Editorial writers could not operate without it. Even many so-called "interpretive" or "analytical" writers and speakers call on propaganda techniques to explain, interpret, analyze, discuss, and persuade.

The "straight" newscast on radio and television or the news story in the press is about the only mass media sector still holding out against the inroads of propaganda. At least this is the case in theory. In practice, however, many students of propaganda recognize that the very best propaganda vehicle is the so-called objective, neutral, dispassionate news report. Journalism today is spilling over with propaganda, not only in advertising where one would expect it, but in voice inflections, facial expressions, headlines, photographs, captions—everywhere. In fact, many cynics suggest that *journalism is propaganda*. Although we also feel that propaganda manifests itself in journalism to a very great degree, we do not want to go so far as to propose that there is no journalism that cannot be considered free of propaganda. The distinction between propaganda and nonpropaganda must be preserved in journalism if the credibility gap we hear so much about does not become so broad as to be total disbelief.

Toward a Definition of Propaganda

One of the main problems, of course, in talking about propaganda is that so many concepts or definitions of the term exist. And it might be said that the definers of the term are propagandizing when they submit their definitions. What is the core meaning of propaganda? Are there any common denominators of meaning associated with the term? We believe there are. And, although the semantic tangle which has grown up around the term is sticky and dense, we believe that the whole subject of propaganda is important to the journalist and should be considered seriously. Why? Because any extended definition of, or talk about, propaganda brings the concerned person into an area of discourse where certain basic issues of journalism have their roots. When one considers propaganda in the context of journalism he forces himself to look directly at many of the "first principles" or foundation stones of journalistic endeavor.

Regardless of which of the many definitions one is examining, he finds certain core ideas about propaganda: "manipulation," "purposeful management," "preconceived plan," "creation of desires," "reinforcement of biases," "arousal of preexisting attitudes," "irrational appeal," "specific objective," "arousal to action," "predetermined end," "suggestion," and "creation of dispositions."

Out of all these terms one may gather a certain impression about propaganda. It seems that propaganda is related to an attempt (implies *intent*) on the part of somebody to manipulate somebody else. By manipulate we mean *to control*—to control not only the attitudes of others but also their actions. Somebody (or some group)—the *propagandist*—is predisposed to cause others to think a certain way, so that they may, in some cases, take a certain action. Propaganda, then, is the effort or the activity by which an initiating communicator intends to manage the attitudes and actions of others through playing on their preexisting biases with messages designed largely to appeal to their emotions and/or irrationality.

The propagandist does not want his audience to analyze or to think seriously about his message. He does not want to be questioned about his remarks. He does not want to be forced to deal in specifics or to present evidence. He has what Harold Lasswell has referred to as a noneducational orientation; by this he meant that the ends or solutions had already been determined before the search for truth began. Contrasted to this is what in Lasswellian terms may be the "deliberative" attitude, the nonpropagandistic orientation that implies an unprejudiced and open search for the truth.* Lasswell uses the term "deliberative attitude" to refer to education as distinct from propaganda. Propaganda is not an invitation to the audience to deliberate, to contemplate, to analyze, to think, to question. It is an invitation to come to rather quick conclusions or to reinforce existing conclusions. It is an invitation to change or strengthen one's attitude and to involve oneself in an action of some type.

Another way to say this might be: Propaganda is dependent on the *intention* of the communicator to use his message to affect the attitude of his audience so as to achieve an end or goal in keeping with the communicator's desires. This emphasizes the *deliberate* nature of propaganda, the *desire* of the communicator to achieve a preconceived purpose.

Before looking more specifically at propaganda in journalism, perhaps it would be well to make these points about the propagandist: 1. He is *not* disinterested, 2. he is *not* neutral, 3. he *has* a plan, a purpose, a goal, 4. he *wants* to influence, to persuade, to affect attitudes and action, and 5. he is not interested in his audience members making up their own minds on the basis of a fair and balanced presentation of information.

Journalism and Propaganda

The journalist may well ask: Am I a propagandist? Quite likely he will have to answer that he *is* more often than he

---

*H. D. Lasswell, "The Theory of Political Propaganda," *American Political Science Review*, XXI (1927); for other good discussions of propaganda, see Hadley Cantril, *The Psychology of Social Movements* (New York: John Wiley & Sons, 1941); L. W. Doob, *Propaganda: Its Psychology and Technique* (New York: Henry Holt, 1935); A. M. and E. B. Lee, *The Fine Art of Propaganda* (New York: Harcourt, Brace & Co., 1939); P. M. Linebarger, *Psychological Warfare* (New York: Duell, Sloan & Pearce, 1954); F. E. Lumley, *The Propaganda Menace* (New York: Century, 1933); William McDougall, *The Group Mind* (New York: G. P. Putnam's Sons, 1920), and Graham Wallas, *The Great Society* (New York: Macmillan, 1914).

might like to admit. At least he is probably propagandistic at many times and in many circumstances as he indulges in various aspects of his work. Some journalists, of course, are almost pure propagandists. Others have very little of the propagandist in them. It depends on many factors, but two stand out as most significant:

1. the type of journalistic work the particular journalist performs, and
2. the basic ethical, ideological, and psychological "character" of the particular journalist

Editorial writers, for example, deal in propaganda far more often than does the writer of sports stories or obituaries. And, generally speaking, a by-lined columnist is more of a propagandist than is the anonymous "straight" news writer. The television "analyst" or "commentator" is more likely to propagandize than is the reporter in London or the "anchorman" in Washington. However, as we have already pointed out, there are exceptions to these generalizations. In fact, *news* writers are potentially in a more favored spot to propagandize than are the editorial writers. For the editorial writers are *expected* by their readers to propagandize (to try to affect attitudes and action), while the news writers are expected to simply present the facts. The *facts*, of course, may be carefully selected, juggled and twisted; certain facts may be played up or down, or omitted altogether. And the reader will never know it. So the idea that propaganda is only on the editorial page is a "myth"; propaganda is on every page of a newspaper, and on every radio or television news show.

The fundamental journalistic orientation of the person engaged in disseminating information and interpretation has much to do with the amount of propaganda contained in his effort. What is his basic ethical inclination? (We will go into this further in Chapter 16.) What are his ideological and political commitments? In other words, is he *inclined* by personality, political commitment, ethical standards, etc., to want to be *informational* (dispassionate, neutral, balanced) rather than *persuasive* (involved, passionate, concerned, subjective)?

If a journalist is inclined to be persuasive, even if he writes only anonymous news stories, he *will* be as a general rule. On the other hand, there are editorial writers who are inclined to be balanced, dispassionate, and neutral; their editorials reflect this orientation. Therefore, it may well be that audiences of the mass media need to revise their old stereotypes concerning propaganda, and subscribe to a new one: Don't analyze the particular *article* to determine the presence of propaganda; rather analyze *the writer* of the article for the presence of propaganda.

The question arises, of course, as to how a reader, listener, or viewer can detect propaganda in the mass media. For certainly every member of the audience cannot analyze the communicator even if every audience member were a trained psychiatrist. If he gets a clue as to propaganda in a message, he must depend largely on getting it from the message itself. Of course, in the case of television, the viewer may suspect the propagandistic nature of a message by watching the facial expressions of the speaker or speakers very carefully. But inferences drawn from smiles, raised eyebrows, voice inflections, and general demeanor can be quite misleading.

The only way, really, to check on propaganda or the lack of it in a newspaper or some other medium is to be in a position to verify the information, the quotations, and the total context of the communication being considered.* By and large, this is impossible. Audience members must accept most of what they get from the media on faith—or, of course, disregard it or suspect it. Certainly most of us are not well enough informed about all of the complex events reported to us, and analyzed for us, every day to know when we are being misled. In some cases—especially when a story relates to us or to some event we

---

*By the same token, the communicator himself is often unable to determine whether his facts are "propaganda products" if he and his staff are barred by government from the sources of news.

witnessed—we are able to detect bias in a story. But this does not happen very often.

If we know a great deal about a particular writer or commentator, we may be able to detect propaganda in his message —*especially if we are not in the same ideological "camp."* We are more critical of, more suspicious of, the reporter or commentator who is known to be of a different political persuasion than ourselves. We either "tune him out" altogether or we constantly look for flaws and weaknesses, contradictions and irrationality, in his message. On the other hand, when we are listening to an ideological or political "colleague," we are prone to accept most of what he says as rational and truthful.

We are also more prone to have faith in a message if it is compatible with our own culture and national interests. Egyptians believe *Al Ahram* because it reinforces their own beliefs —what they want to believe. *Ma'ariv* has the same credibility value for the Israelis for the same reason. Accepting this basic proclivity to believe what one wants to believe, what kind of credibility can an *outside*, supposedly disinterested, voice have on a specific country or on persons in it? Undoubtedly, the more a citizen is convinced of the disinterest (fairness) of the outside voice, the more credible the message is likely to be. The BBC, for instance, is likely to be considered far more credible in Southeast Asia because it is *disinterested* politically in the area and because it has a tradition of objectivity. The South Vietnamese radio perhaps *reinforces* opinions in that country, but BBC is *believed*. It is quite possible that reinforcement and belief are two entirely different "news" objectives.*

Propaganda in a closed society (dictatorship) obviously serves a fundamentally different purpose than does propaganda in an open society (democracy). In a closed society it serves mainly to confirm and reinforce attitudes created by the restrictive environment so as to keep down social disharmony and

---

*For a good discussion of the importance of communicator credibility see Ch. 2 ("Credibility of the Communicator") in Carl Hovland, Irving Janis, and Harold Kelley, *Communication and Persuasion* (New Haven: Yale University Press, 1953).

friction; on the other hand, in a democracy or open society propaganda is pluralistic and competitive and provides the information and ideas for political argument and for the formation of public opinion.

Some Techniques of Propaganda

Techniques of propaganda abound. The skilled propagandist is an artist with the techniques; he blends them, changes them, obscures them, and generally uses them carefully depending on the particular audience and the specific occasion. He generally subscribes to the belief that the end justifies *any kind of propaganda technique*. If he needs to lie, he lies; if he needs simply to distort, he distorts; if he needs to generalize, he generalizes. The propagandist is a pragmatist; he uses what will work. Therefore, he must constantly study himself, people, techniques, and results. He is a practicing psychologist. He uses everything at his command to manipulate, to persuade, to cause action. Technique—tactic and strategy—is his weapon. Therefore, he takes it very seriously.

A main strategical technique is a constant concern with passionate rhetoric and advocacy. The propagandist has little or no use for traditional and dispassionate argument. He tries to avoid open discussion, questions. The whole Socratic method is out of the question; the propagandist *already* has his answers determined. So his main technique is *avoidance of rational dialogue*.

In line with this overriding strategical objective is a wide variety of tactical techniques. These are used singly or in clusters to achieve specific objectives in differing situations with varying audiences. Many persons are led to believe that if they can only learn these tactical techniques and condition themselves to recognize them, they can defend themselves against them. Often propaganda devices are taught for this reason: so that people can defend themselves against them. The only thing wrong with this is that people may know something of the nature of these techniques—they can recognize them and label them—but still be unable to effectively become immune to their effects. The propagandist knows this. He is aware that some of his propaganda will get through and accomplish its purpose.

Some techniques of propaganda are wasted on some people in some situations. The propagandist is aware of this. He simply makes his propaganda campaign broad enough, flexible enough, to catch all the fish, but he really does not need to catch them all. He constantly revamps his techniques; he blends one with another to make a new one. He keeps a step ahead of the general level of propaganda sophistication in his audience. He keeps his audience guessing, off-balance, and uncertain.

Seven basic propaganda devices, defined by the Institute for Propaganda Analysis during World War II, are usually presented in textbooks and discussions of propaganda. Since they are found in so many source materials and are generally well known, we shall only name them here, without discussing them. They are: name-calling, testimonial, glittering generalities, bandwagon, transfer, plain folks, and card-stacking.* Although these seven are important, and are used regularly by propagandists of all kinds, they are by no means all the techniques. For example, repetition is a basic one. And another type is *faulty analogy* and its first cousin, *unfair association.*†

The Journalist as Propagandist

Few people like to think of journalists as propagandists. Journalism is to be believed, trusted, respected: this is the traditional concept. Even though opinion has always been accepted as an important part of journalism, the basic "image" of journalism is one of reliability, factualness, and trust. At any rate, it does not seem quite right to go around referring to journalists as "propagandists." For if the image changes and journalists are looked upon as propagandists, what would hap-

---

*See Alfred McClung Lee, "The Analysis of Propaganda: A Clinical Summary," *American Journal of Sociology* (September 1945).

†This is not simply "guilt by association" but also "virtue by association." The association tactic is perhaps the most useful of all propaganda techniques.

pen to the libertarian idea that a free people must remain free by being informed by the press so that they might make *rational* decisions? Do we really want to take our important political information, with which we make our "popular sovereignty" work, from a propagandistic press?

It would be rather presumptuous to say that all journalists are propagandists, but it is probably safe to say that most of them are. We may not like to think of them in this way, but a careful observation and analysis of journalists will indicate that they at least have the traits and characteristics of propagandists—at least in many of their activities.

We are not talking here about journalists as propagandists in that they "propagate" or spread information. We are talking about journalists as propagandists in that they "propagate" or spread their own prejudices, biases, and opinions—*trying* to affect the attitudes of their audiences. Without a doubt, there are journalists who are "machinelike" in their work or who have the kinds of duties not involving them in potentially propagandistic situations, but these are probably a minority. Large numbers of journalists—even among those involved in "straight" news reporting—are propagandists in that they purposely intend to mislead or influence their audiences in specific ways.

What are some of the techniques used by journalists who participate in such propaganda efforts? There are, of course, dozens of them, but the following are a few of the most notable:

Use of stereotypes. The mass media, in their news and interpretation aspects, simplify the reality of events with regularity. They present men and events as one dimensional and static. They not only create stereotypes but they perpetuate and spread them through repetition and emphasis. The journalist who wants to propagandize finds this an easy and effective tactic.

Opinion as fact. Even a casual analysis of the mass media will show that a favorite technique is to present opinion disguised as fact. "The audience gave the speaker an enthusiastic welcome." "There was no doubt in anyone's mind that Mr. X was criticizing the President out of a desire for revenge." So much reporting of this type exists in the mass media—in almost every story—that a whole book could be written on this technique.

Biased attribution. How does the mass medium attribute information to a source? What kind of language is used? An attribution verb such as "said" is neutral (not opinionated and evokes no emotional response); an attribution verb such as "snapped" (negatively affective) is a word designed to appeal to the reader's emotions, to give a judgmental stimulus. A verb such as "smiled" is a "favorable" term, for it is positively affective. The journalist's bias for or against some person in the news can be ascertained by analyzing his method of attributing statements to the person.

Information selection. What will the journalist choose to say about a person or an event? Is there a pattern in his choices? Does he stack his message by presenting only *bad* or only *good* information? What is the nature of what he ignored as contrasted with what he chose to communicate? Of course, every reporter must select, but the message becomes propagandistic when a pattern of selection becomes evident. Quoting out of context is, of course, a form of this technique. And it is really impossible for an audience member of the mass medium to recognize or detect this type of propaganda. He has no standard for comparison.

Misleading headlines. The headline writer can propagandize effectively because he knows that, by and large, people come away from stories with the substance of the headline—not the story—in their minds. In fact, many see the headline, but do not read the story under it. So many headlines are twisted, biased, distorted, and otherwise rigged, that one is led to believe that headlines bear about as much resemblance to their stories as the stories bear to the reality they purport to report.

Biased photographs. Present your heroes from the best perspective, smiling, positive, calm. Show your enemies from the worst possible perspective, frowning, negative, nervous. Photographs may not lie, but they can mislead. They, like facts and quotations in a story, can be selected for a purpose. Anyone who has ever taken news photographs or shot television film knows that the potential for propaganda is extremely great. And, anyone who analyzes photographs in newspapers and magazines and film on television can observe the practical tactics of photographic propaganda.

Censorship. Usually we do not think of the mass media indulging in censorship; that is something for government officials to do. But the media do censor, even if they might call it exercising their editorial or news prerogatives. They leave this story or this picture out; they delete part of this quotation; they throw that entire story into the wastebasket; they chop away two-thirds of this story. They censor, all right, and anyone who thinks it is all perfectly innocent and that journalists restrict information only out of the purest of motives simply has not faced the realities of a journalistic medium. Those who would say that the journalist or the medium has the right under press freedom to censor may well be right; here we are only stating that censorship *by the media themselves* is a very real propagandistic tactic. Two main forms of censorship exist and the mass media use them both. They are: 1. selective control of information to favor a particular viewpoint or editorial position, and 2. deliberate doctoring of information in order to create a certain impression.

Repetition. Look at a newspaper which you know to have a particular bias—political or otherwise. You will see that certain themes, persons, ideas, and slogans appear again and again, day to day, week to week, on its pages. A reader of a "liberal" newspaper such as the *Washington Post* or the *St. Louis Post-Dispatch* gets caught up in the newspaper's repetitive pattern of news presentation, editorial stand, etc., until he can predict exactly what "line" the paper will take on almost any event or issue that arises. A reader of the "conservative" *Chicago Tribune* can do the same. Television network documentaries and newscasts, with certain rather obvious biases also, are predictable as to their repetitive positions, themes, and issues.

Negativism. This is a very potent (and observable) tactic of propaganda in journalism. In its news and interpretation, a mass medium should not just be *for* something or somebody. It should emphasize the negative; it should spotlight the "enemy"; it should be *against* something or somebody. Mass media appear to find it much more exciting, for example, to be against an American President than to be *for* him. They likewise seem to relish the idea of blasting away at established institutions, and lending support to the forces in society that are violent, emotional, irrational, atypical, and destructive. Emphasize the negative: this is an important journalistic propaganda tactic. Focus on an enemy, selecting targets in line with preexisting dispositions of the audience.

Appeal to Authority. This tactic is closely related to the common "testimonial" technique in that it relies heavily on support from well-known and reputable sources and persons. The journalist may attribute a statement to a veiled or vague authority or he may quote selectively a prominent person.* In many news stories there are "leading educators" or "prominent theologians" who say or believe this or that. There is some Pentagon spokesman saying something, or some "source close to the President" who is taking a certain stand. If a commentator wants to make a point for his television audience on a controversial subject, he may well find it advantageous to quote some prominent person (who agrees with him) relative to the subject rather than present his own position directly.

Fictionalizing. The mass medium may present mere fic-

---

*A journalist may quote a suspicious or discredited source, also, depending on the effect he wishes to achieve.

tion, camouflaging it, of course, as fact. Most often, the journalist does not totally fictionalize; he simply mixes some fiction (or conjecture) into his fact skeleton. He does not have everything he needs to make a good, complete, impelling story, so he splices in a little fiction—what he thinks might well have happened. He fills "creatively" the gaps in his story, even dreams up certain direct quotations to put in the mouth of his source. Nobody, after all, will ever know any better—except perhaps his source, and what will that matter in the long run? For, after all, has not he maintained a "core of truth" in the story—and, as the old saying goes, you cannot be completely objective in a story, anyway.

Journalists undoubtedly use many other techniques than those mentioned above. They propagandize every time they slant the news, and, as Tamotsu Shibutani correctly points out, slanting the news is a very old and extremely widespread practice.* Most journalists will admit to using many of these techniques, such as misrepresentation of facts, censorship of certain items tending to favor an ideological "foe," giving undue prominence to one side of an issue, selectively quoting from a speech or interview to make a person look good or bad, and arousing strong negative feelings against scapegoats to take attention away from main issues. The propagandistic journalist does not simply tell lies; whenever possible he tells the truth (or at least a portion of it), but this "truthful" slice-of-reality reporting can be propaganda. Shibutani talks of true or factual propaganda, and it is very difficult to distinguish it from news.

What does all of this mean? Does it imply that consumers of mass media messages should look upon these messages as basically propagandistic? It is difficult to answer such a question, for different persons would respond variously, depending on their sophistication, knowledge, experience with the media, and their cynicism. But it is probably safe to say that the mass media and their functionaries generate propaganda and spread

---

Improvised News (Indianapolis: The Bobbs-Merrill Co., 1966), pp. 188-89.

the propaganda of others to a far greater extent than most citizens believe.

Is it possible for the receiver of the mass media messages to detect bias and propaganda in them? Probably not, in most cases. The audience member, seldom in a position to check on the factual accuracy, balance, and thoroughness of press reports, is largely at the mercy of the media reporters and editors. He is also in a "detached" position from the communicator so that he has no real knowledge of the intent and motivation—or standard of ethics—of the person designing the message. He can assume, of course, that most media messages are misleading or biased; he can be skeptical and even cynical. He can disbelieve *everything* he reads in the newspapers or sees on television; then he will, of course, be safe from journalistic propaganda. But, if he takes such a drastic position, he will also be ignorant of major events and trends going on in his world.

So what must the sensible audience member do? He must accept some information and opinion and reject some. He must expose himself to as diverse a sample of media matter as he possibly can. He will still be frustrated (if he is intellectually alert) because he will find discrepancies among his sources as to factual statements and contradictions among the opinions and observations of columnists and commentators. He will never know just which source is most reliable, but he will develop some ways to make decisions and preserve his sanity in the frustrating welter of information. He will build up his own complex "safety" mechanism for screening incoming information; he will see less and less that does not agree with his dominant dispositions (selective exposure); he will then select from these selected media only those messages that are compatible with his own biases (selective perception) and, finally, he will remember or be affected by only those parts of the message that give him comfort or mental pleasure (selective retention). This whole selectivity process permits the audience member to protect himself largely against hostile propaganda; at any rate, he uses propaganda to simply reinforce—not challenge—his basic attitudes and predispositions. If he did not do this, he would quickly fly into a million emotional pieces in the face of unverifiable and disharmonic information and opinion that surround him every day.

It may well be, then, that propaganda is really not very potent after all. At least it does not seem extremely powerful in changing opinions; a study of newspaper support of candidates and election outcomes in American history would indicate this is the case. But undoubtedly journalistic propaganda provides comfort and reinforcement for the receiver if it is compatible with his basic needs. In a pluralistic media system this function of propaganda may work very well; the danger arises when the press begins to contract in its pluralism and the propaganda becomes more and more standardized, causing increasing numbers of persons to become unable to find self-supporting and satisfying propaganda.

Strange as it may seem, then, one of the principal reasons for maintaining a pluralistic press is so that we can minimize frustration among the populace through providing a wide variety of propaganda, suitable for a multitude of needs.

15.

Objectivity: An Attitude

WHENEVER ANYONE BEGINS DISCUSSING JOURNALISTIC OBJEC-
tivity, he can be assured that he will be misunderstood. No
subject, with the possible exception of press freedom and responsibility, has garnered as much journalistic attention in recent years as objective reporting. Everyone has an opinion on it
and is willing and able to discuss it at a moment's notice. One
thing is certain: opinions are many and varied. However, for the
sake of simplification and discussion in this chapter, we propose
that there are two main ways of looking at journalistic objectivity:

1. As a "myth" purely and simply; an impossible goal to achieve;
   mere rhetoric, a holdover from an earlier "nonscientific" two-
   valued (subjective/objective) orientation.
2. An ideal, a goal or desire, largely reachable, on the part of the
   journalist which forces him to *try* to be fair, accurate, balanced,
   dispassionate, uninvolved, unbiased, and unprejudiced.

The first of these two perspectives or ways of looking at
objectivity—the *myth* approach—is interesting to contemplate,
but it ultimately relegates the whole concept of objectivity to
the trash can; it concludes that really there is no distinction

between objectivity and nonobjectivity. However sophisticated this may be from the viewpoint of the general semanticist, it begs a realistic issue: that there really is a *difference* between a story which can be considered "objective" and one which can be considered "subjective."

The second of these perspectives is the more traditional one; it is based on the assumption that a reporter can *to a significant extent* "objectify" his story in that he *demands* of himself that he be as factual, balanced, fair, and unbiased as it is humanly possible to be. It is his *attitude* toward reporting that makes him an objective reporter.

It may be said that the first perspective (objectivity as a "myth") is growing in popularity—especially among younger journalists in this country. Existentialism and its first cousin in the pragmatic media world—"advocacy journalism"—appears to be "in" today and gaining converts with each passing year. The traditional idea that a reporter *can be objective* tends to be losing ground; certainly it is being challenged with increasing vigor from many directions.

There is a certain danger, of course, in being tied too tightly to either one of these basic perspectives or viewpoints. The person who says that objectivity is impossible when one considers reality and abstraction (selection) is the person who may be simply building a rationale for his own forays into biased, polemic, propagandistic journalism. On the other hand, the traditionalist who is so tied to the idea that he can, most assuredly, be objective, is living in a fool's paradise and may well get to the point where he believes he has told the story —the whole story, the true story, and nothing but the story.

To be quite realistic and truthful, one must admit that actually a reporter—wrapped as he is in the constricting net of language, reality, and his own psychological and ideological conditioning—cannot be perfectly objective in his writing. He strains reality through himself and it comes out distorted. So, in a sense, the *anti*-objectivists are correct. But those who contend that a reporter *can* be objective are not thinking in absolutes;

they say that the reporter with a proper *attitude* toward objectivity can be *very far along* the objectivity continuum. These persons are talking about objective reporting as an objective (however impossible) toward which to strive continually; they are proposing that a reporter with the attitude of sincerely trying to achieve objectivity (an attitude of dedicated neutrality) can at least come rather close to objectivity.

It might be worthwhile to consider these two basic perspectives or ways of looking at objectivity in journalism more closely. Undoubtedly each journalist is inclined toward one or the other of these two positions: the anti-objectivity position (the subjectivists or advocates) and the pro-objectivity position (the neutralists or observers).

The Subjectivist or Advocacy Position

Those subscribing to this position believe basically that objectivity in journalism is no more than a myth. There is simply no such thing as objective reporting. It is possible, as many readers will point out, that a person who is convinced that objectivity is impossible to achieve *may not be* in favor of advocacy journalism. However, generally those who would toss out the concept of objectivity because it is nothing but a "myth," are also those who have nothing against advocacy journalism—at least in the sense of *advocating* a particular position or idea through consciously or purposely subjectivizing his journalism. We believe that subjectivism and advocacy are extremely closely correlated in a journalist. The journalist who has little concern for, or faith in, objective reporting is quite likely to be a person who is anxious to involve himself in his journalism, to take sides, to want to persuade, to slant stories, and to advocate what is to him the proper course for others to take.

Objectivity: a myth? The subjectivist feels that objectivists cling unrealistically to a myth. It is time, he says, for these believers in objective reporting to be intellectually honest and admit that it is impossible to be objective. Let us look for a moment at the concept of "objective reporting" from the point of view of the subjectivist. Just what is objective reporting?

The objective report would be detached, unprejudiced, balanced, fair, dispassionate, unopinionated, uninvolved, unbiased, and omniscient. It would, in effect, match reality: it would tell the truth, the whole truth, and nothing but the truth. Where, the subjectivist asks, do we find this kind of report in the mass media? No reporter knows the truth; no reporter can write a story that can match reality, for as the general semanticists point out, the "map is not the territory." The story is never what it purports to report.

Perhaps truly objective reporting might be called "sponge reporting"—soaking up everything, with the reporter more as a *thing* instead of a *person*, a spongelike something that is unfeeling, unbiased, completely neutral, soaking up reality. Of course, this is not really the way it is with reporters, the subjectivists point out; reporters of *persons* and as persons cannot be objective. So the whole idea of journalistic objectivity is no more than a myth, something to hold on to—and nothing more.

A few assumptions. When one talks of objective reporting, he must make several assumptions. One is that he is a "free" agent to be objective. This is not really true, however, for the reporter is *conditioned*—by experiences, by intelligence, by circumstances, by environment, by education, and by a host of other factors. This conditioning, often completely unconscious, makes it impossible for the reporter to be objective. He is in a sense a trapped person, destined to bring to his reporting his own perspectives, slants, and emphases. He is, in effect, conditioned to be nonobjective; he can be nothing else.

Another assumption is that the reporter can be objective in the sense that he can present the *whole* story. This, too, is false. Every reporter *must* be selective. He cannot, even if he wishes, report everything. How does he select? Here are a few ways: by what is most easily obtainable; by what appears to him to be the most interesting; by what is "pushed" most forcefully and

cleverly upon him; by what reinforces his concepts of importance; by what reinforces his already existing ideological values;
by what he is exposed to personally; by what he is "led to"
purposefully; by what is "obvious"; by what is "colorful"; and
by what he has been taught is the essence of "news." At any
rate, he selects, and this selection of what to put in his story
automatically *subjectivizes* his story—in a sense biases and distorts the reality that he is claiming to *objectify* in his report.

Another assumption is that the reporter can be *detached*.
This is really impossible, say the subjectivists. Any reporter
must, in order to try to get at the meaning of a story, become
involved in the story; he must become concerned; he must make
judgments; he must take positions in regard to persons and
viewpoints related to the story—even if these positions are
overtly expressed. There are many meanings of "detachment,"
of course, but it would seem that in *any* case a stance of detachment will not assure any degree of objectivity. In fact, many
subjectivists insist that the degree to which a person is detached
indicates the degree to which he is *subjective*, not objective.

Another assumption is that a reporter can be unprejudiced.
Prejudice is usually understood to mean an opinion for or
against anything without adequate basis, or sometimes it is used
to mean a bias. The key word in the preceding sentence is, of
course, "adequate." One wonders if the basis for almost any
opinion (or against any opinion) is *adequate*—total, satisfactory
in the sense of being valid, complete, or true. Is not all reporting, ask the subjectivists, based on at least some degree of prejudice—or inconclusive evidence? Try to imagine a reporter operating in a context where he would have no prejudices. Of
course, the more complex and controversial the reportorial context becomes the more prejudice becomes operative. Is not every reporter, then, a victim of his prejudices?

A final assumption is that a reporter can keep his opinion
out of his story. The subjectivists deny that he can. They raise
these questions: How can he select certain things to include in
his story, or make determinations as to their order and empha-

sis, without exercising his *opinion*? How, indeed, can he even *decide to report a certain* event or personal action in the first place without exercising his opinion? How can he select, reject, structure his story, giving emphasis to certain aspects without being led to his particular decisions by his *opinions*? The reporter's *opinions* determine his entire reportorial activity, say the subjectivists; it is impossible to report without opining, and when one opines he is subjective.

Is it not reasonable, then, say the subjectivists, to state categorically that a reporter *must* be subjective, that objective reporting is really nothing more than a myth?

The Objectivist or Neutralist Position

Those subscribing to this position believe that it is possible to be "objective" in reporting; of course, they have (as do the subjectivists) their own definition or concept of "objective reporting." Not being so semantically oriented as the subjectivists and recognizing that we must *force* words and terms to mean something in a pragmatic way, the objectivists do not find it impossible to conceive of objective reporting. Perhaps they would admit that as the subjectivist defines "objectivity" there is no such thing; but they say that the concept should not be considered as *pure* or perfect, but pragmatic. They say that objectivity is a goal—an approachable goal—that a reporter should constantly strive for; and although he may never reach it in the perfection that the subjectivist talks about, he can attain it to such a degree that it is a meaningful term—no "myth" at all.

It's the attitude that counts. The objectivist believes that the way to achieve pragmatic objectivity in a story is to *desire* to achieve it. If a reporter sincerely *wants* to be fair, unbiased, balanced, and factual in his story, he can be—at least to the extent that the term "objectivity" is meaningful and valid. A key question, then, is this: What is the reporter's attitude toward his story and toward his audience? Does he have a *neu-*

tralist attitude, or does he want to have an attitude of *engagé*, of participation, of involvement or of advocacy? Objectivity, if built on an attitude of neutralism, is a realistic concept in journalism.

Objectivity is related to an attitude (a bias toward) accuracy, completeness, balance, truth, verifiability, and on and on. Objectivity is a show of good faith. It is the *conscious attempt* on the part of the reporter *to be objective*; it indicates a desire, an *ideal* on the part of the reporter. And, the objectivists insist, if the reporter does not keep trying to be objective he will slip quickly and deeply into the slough of pure opinion, carelessness, and polemic.

Obstacles to Surmount. Although the objectivist sees reportorial objectivity as a realistic and valuable concept in journalism, he recognizes that there are many obstacles in his path. He *knows* just as well as does the subjectivist that language restricts his full and accurate reporting; he knows that he has biases and prejudices; he knows that he must make value judgments in selecting facts and writing his stories; he knows that he has been conditioned by his experiences, education, etc.; he knows that he cannot be completely detached from his story. He knows all these things.

He looks upon these facts of language and existence as obstacles to be overcome. This is one of the greatest challenges of journalism to him. Just because he cannot be *fully* objective (as the subjectivist would define objectivity) does not mean that he is to despair of the battle to surmount the obstacles. His recognition of his humanness and weaknesses does not mean that he must forsake the goal or ideal of objectivity in reporting; this only imposes an even greater and more challenging demand upon him. He at least knows that he wants to be objective, that he desires to present a full, unbiased, balanced, reliable account. And, he believes that this *desire* will make it possible for him to achieve objectivity to a far greater degree than the person who scoffs at the concept of objectivity and plunges headlong into opinionated, subjective, or advocacy journalism.

So, the objectivist, for all practical purposes, believes he *can* be "objective"—certainly objective in his reporting as compared to the subjectivist or advocacy journalist who makes no special effort to be objective. Trying is better than not trying, say the objectivists, and the reporter who *tries* will in the long run be more credible and more objective than will the reporter who does not try. In other words, the objectivist believes the attitude of the reporter—the *attitude toward objectivity*—will determine how objective his stories will be.

General Semantics and Objectivity

Alfred Korzybski* and the many general semanticists who have followed him have been, and are, vitally interested in the matter of objectivity—in trying to develop an orientation in language users that will make their writing and talking more scientific, more precise, more balanced, more accurate. The general semanticists have much to say to journalists about how to become more objective, how to make the language "map" resemble better the "territory" it describes.

No attempt will be made in this chapter to go into all (or most of) the teachings of general semantics. There is ample literature available for the person who desires to hear the "fine tunings" of the discipline—or orientation. We shall deal here with a few of the most important of the principles that relate to objective reporting. And we shall discard some of the traditional labels common in the writings of Korzybskian disciples, using only those that we feel are the most useful. Let us now consider a few of the basic principles, as adapted specifically to the journalist:

---

*Korzybski, a Polish immigrant to the U.S. who died in 1950, is known as the "father of general semantics." His classic work in this area was *Science and Sanity* (Lancaster, Pa.: Science Press Printing Co., 1933). Many writers have translated his ideas into lay terminology; among the best known of these writers have been Stuart Chase, S. I. Hayakawa, Wendell Johnson, Irving J. Lee, and Bess Selzer Sondel.

1. Need for a multivalued orientation. The journalist must realize that people and events are multifaceted and extremely complex. Simple descriptive "tags" will not do; a person is far more than a "liberal" or a "conservative," than a "professor" or a "legislator." The journalist must break his good-bad, black-white, this side-that side orientation; he must get in the habit of thinking on a continuum, avoiding hard-and-fast classification. Describing in detail what a person thinks is better than simply labeling him a "fundamentalist" or a "progressive." The journalist with a multivalued orientation will avoid talking about *big* crowds, *tall* men, and *rich* widows. Such words are on a continuum and are meaningless in a report.

2. Events and persons have unlimited characteristics. A habit of thinking about this principle is a good first step in the direction of becoming more objective. The journalist who recognizes this will consciously attempt to give *as many of these characteristics as he possibly can.* Of course, much of his story will be cut away by editors and printers, but he can at least feel that he has done all he can do to make the story more objective.

3. Members of the same class or group are quite different. The recognition of this basic principle will help the reporter to avoid stereotypes. He will become ever more careful about using generalized "tags" and "labels" by which he depicts a whole group of people as being virtually the same. $Democrat_1$ is not $Democrat_2$ and student $activist_1$ is not student $activist_2$, as the general semanticists say. The journalist may say he knows this —that such a principle is only "common sense," but a continuing analysis of journalism indicates that in practice many reporters do not write or speak as if they gave much thought to the principle. Individual differences must be stressed by the reporter.

4. Every person and everything constantly changes. Reporters often treat persons, institutions, etc. as if they are what they have been and as if they will be what they seem to be at

With the Compliments

of

JIM ANDERSON

-:-

DAVID McKAY COMPANY, INC.

750 Third Avenue

New York, N. Y. 10017

present. President X_{1972} is not President X_{1974}. He is, in effect, a new person. Reporters should not assume that persons do not change. There is a natural tendency to dredge up old descriptive phrases from the past to tie to a person in the news today; very much of this is unfair and biasing, for it ties the man to old actions, thoughts, and places and causes the reader, listener, or viewer to think in static terms, in old images. Harvard$_{1900}$ is certainly not Harvard$_{1971}$, nor will it be Harvard$_{1980}$; the good reporter will not treat *Harvard as Harvard,* but as an institution in flux.

5. Highly abstract terms are subjective. The reporter should realize that abstract terms like "patriotism," "radical," "reactionary," "liberal," "socialist," "democracy," are subjective in that they are colored by the reporter's own *meaning* for them and *feeling* toward them. He should also realize that they are very nearly meaningless so far as having any kind of general or agreed-upon signification. Therefore, the objective reporter —or the one who wishes to be as objective as possible—will be careful to use such terms sparingly. If he must use them, then he should make every attempt to *show* what the word implies by associating the person's *actions* and *thought* with them. In other words: Don't say the man is a "liberal"; tell us what he believes, how he acts, how he votes, what he says. Then we may come a little closer to understanding him.

6. Descriptive adjectives are often subjective. Many journalists will describe persons, places, and things with adjectives that they feel add to the "objectivity" of their story. However, many adjectives—probably *most* adjectives—really tell far more about the reporter (the user of the adjectives), than about what is being described. For example, the reporter refers to Mrs. John Jones as "lovely" or "elegantly dressed"; he thinks he is telling his reader something about Mrs. Jones. Actually, he is simply talking about himself—telling us something about *his concepts* of feminine loveliness and clothing preferences. The reporter must even be careful of using phrases such as "enthusiastic audience," for often he projects his feeling about a speech or concert to the audience. How does a reporter measure enthusiasm?

7. *A natural tendency exists to bias through selection.* The journalist should recognize his tendency to select (or abstract) from reality those portions that appeal to him, coincide with his biases, and give him pleasure. The reporter, seeking to be objective, must constantly be on guard against this proclivity. He must *force* himself to include information that is unpleasant to him, with which he disagrees—information that he is normally disposed to leave out. If he gets into the habit (difficult as it is to form) of doing this, he will find that his stories will be better balanced and fairer.

There are many other principles of general semantics that could be adapted to reportorial objectivity, but those above are felt to be especially important. Of course, a reporter (or anyone else) can take general semantics *too* seriously; if one becomes a "true believer" in the orientation or discipline or whatever it is, he will tend to become frustrated in his language usage. In fact, he may well develop some psychosis as well as several unpleasant social habits such as always asking, "What do you mean by that term?" or sitting in silent speculation when he is expected to answer a question or respond to a statement.

The journalist can greatly profit from having a general-semantics orientation if he does not take it too far. If he becomes too preoccupied with the subject, he will become bogged down in his own language sophistication and will harm his ability to communicate. In addition, he is likely to become a linguistic eccentric and a real social boor. A little general-semantics orientation, then, is a healthy and helpful thing; too much emphasis on the subject is a dangerous thing. Taking a small dose of general semantics should help make the journalist more tolerant, less dogmatic, and better able to see the many sides of what is going on around him and the complex, dynamic personalities who take their places in his stories. He should be able to examine himself to a great extent, to recognize that he often projects himself into his report in a multitude of ways. And, finally, a general-semantics orientation should make the reporter more *scientific* (objective) in that he becomes more and more an *observer*, a neutralist, a careful selector, and arranger of data. He does, in fact, tend to increasingly disengage himself from that which he is reporting. He becomes, in effect, more flexible and tolerant while at the same time more self-disciplined, dispassionate, and precise.

Objective Reporting: Its Future?

We have discussed two principal ways of looking at objective reporting and have considered a general-semantics orientation as a way of achieving a great degree of objectivity. It might be well, in conclusion, to speculate briefly on what promises to be the status of journalistic objectivity in the future.

Most of the signs point to a continuing deemphasis of reportorial objectivity and further advances made by the "analytical" or interpretive school of journalists. And, without a doubt the *advocacy journalists* will break out of their underground world of ghetto and campus and thrust themselves more deeply into the mainstream of modern journalism. More and more "Establishment" newspapers and magazines and even network television will quite likely, in the remaining years of this century, have staffs heavily larded with dedicated polemicists, analysts, editorialists, and other assorted subjectivists. Increasingly the mass media will, more than likely, turn into specialized outlets for certain "lines"—ideological and others. With the freedom-loving existentialists flooding from campuses into journalism (and into audiences of journalism) with their strong feelings, political attachments, and dedication to involvement, there is little doubt but that they will affect journalism greatly.

Young people of today are growing up accustomed to frank and open discussion, to hearing others make value judgments, to observing others involving themselves. They are the audience members of the mass media of tomorrow, and it is doubtful that they will tolerate the dull, lifeless, "but on the other hand" neutralism in journalism that characterized the journalism of their fathers. And, if history is to be any kind of guide, the media will adapt themselves to the wishes of the potential audience members. Therefore, during the next several decades at least, we may expect to see far more polemic and opinion media appealing to specialized audiences than ever before; in addition, there will probably be a more drastic shift toward subjectivism even in the general mainstream or "Establishment" media.

As James Reston and others have suggested, the whole trend in *objective* reporting in the United States started with the establishment of the wire services—back when the Associated Press and the United Press had to deal with large numbers of newspapers with widely different political and regional interests. The news had to be "objective" (or neutralist) in order to be accepted by such a heterogeneous group. And, it is quite likely that the tradition of objectivity was further strengthened by the trend toward monopolization of dailies. Homogeneous newspaper audiences became heterogeneous audiences—and even local news had to become more objective in order to satisfy total audience demands (wire service news was already by this time objective). Has this trend ended? We believe it has.

One reason why the new "advocacy" journalism and the whole new trend toward subjectivity has become as popular as it has (and will become more popular) is that it has become a salable item. The general mass audience has become fragmented by a proliferation of new media, and in a sense has broken into specialized homogeneous groups that will not be upset by subjective journalism. Leading the way in this trend have been the cheap-to-produce underground papers, the increasing number of AM and FM radio stations, specialized magazines, and cheap paperback books.

What will probably be the result of the new subjectivist trend? It is hard to say, of course, but one result will quite likely be that *opinions* will become far more important than *factual information*. Who said something will carry more weight than what he said—at least with audience members who like the source. Nobody, or few persons, will seek information from the media—simply entertainment and opinions that give them pleasure. Few audience members will actually *believe* news they get from the media; in fact, they may well not get any such thing. The whole concept of *news* as we know it today may be unknown by the end of the century. The "credibility gap" that we hear so much about today will probably not exist much longer. Why? Because nobody can believe *anything* in tomorrow's new world of subjective journalism; there will be no "gap"—only a credibility *vacuum*, a fuzzy kind of opinion world of journalistic dialectic with no solid foundation stones of verifiable fact.

Many people have come to believe that information in the mass media, by the year 2000, will be monolithic, and carefully controlled from a central source. As we watch the trend toward big government, monopolization, and other forms of collectivization taking place, we may see reason to accept such a premise. But, on the other hand, when one examines the media system a little more carefully and sees the very substantial increase in pluralism, he may be led to believe otherwise. For there is an obvious trend toward "many voice" advocacy journalism spurred on by the existential spirit nurtured largely in our high schools and universities. So, more than likely—unless a large-scale reaction sets in against press freedom and advocacy journalism—the traditional objective journalism will give way to a clash-of-opinion journalism the likes of which this country has never seen, even in the heyday of the polemic pamphleteering of the Colonial period.

Objective reporting is slowly being eased out; it has become too staid, dull, pallid, and noncommitted for the new generations of audience members being raised in a climate of instant confrontation, dissent, and permissiveness. It will be interesting to see if the truth will emerge (win out) from the cacophony of clashing *opinions* to any greater degree than it emerged from the clashing of many *factual or objective* stories in the past.

16.

Journalistic Ethics

IN A SENSE THIS ENTIRE BOOK HAS DEALT WITH THE ETHICS OF mass communication and the mass media. For there is really no way to divorce the problems and basic issues of journalism that have been discussed on these pages from the ethics of journalism. Stemming from these basic issues are questions such as these: What ought journalism to do for its practitioners, its audiences, and its society? What standards (if any) should journalists adhere to in the practice of their journalism? What is good journalism, and what is bad journalism? What should the journalist do in a particular situation?

Journalistic ethics may be defined as the branch of philosophy that helps journalists determine what is right to do. It is, in a sense, *moral* philosophy—a normative science of conduct— with conduct considered as *voluntary* actions. Journalistic ethics should set forth guidelines, rules, norms, codes, principles that will lead—*not force*—the journalist to make certain moral decisions. Ethics should give the journalist standards by which he can judge actions to be right or wrong, good or bad, responsible or irresponsible.

Although it has always been difficult to discuss ethics, it is especially so today, for the entire intellectual atmosphere is filled with voices—often unrestrained, arrogant, and undisciplined—crying to be heard, insisting to be taken seriously when discoursing on ethical matters. This is indeed the day of egalitarianism, freedom, intuition, and relativity, and these emphases have projected themselves into the field of ethics.

Listen to the voice of the young university graduate, especially if he has a liberal-arts education, as he articulates his concept of ethics before stepping into journalism. His independent spirit, his suspicion of external standards, his egoistic arrogance, and his cynicism about tradition are manifest in his typical liturgy, which goes something like this:

> What I do, I do freely, naturally and instinctively, and therefore what I do is the right thing for me to do. I do today what I may not do tomorrow; I am unpredictable in my ethical behavior; I am natural and uninhibited, freely involving myself, committing myself to the issue and event of the moment, and accepting for myself the responsibilities which I feel I need for my commitment. I am the existential man, the unimprisoned journalist, the master of my own committed self. My ethics is my own; I can never project it to anyone else or to myself at any other moment. I am responsible only to myself for my own action *now*, in this situation, in this place. I cannot be concerned about your morality or the ethical standards of my "profession"; I must do my ethical "thing" in my own way; you are free to do yours.

The foregoing words might well come from the lips of thousands of new existential journalists who are pouring from academe into the media of mass communication. And these words probably express about all they have to say about morality, for they look upon ethics and moral codes as restricting their freedom and imprisoning them in the value systems of others. This "guidance," which they see ethical "codes" imposing upon them, therefore, must be repelled; they must be guided only by their own existential whims, instincts, and fancies—not by externally "imposed" values. So, here they come: the "new journalists," armed with a freedom, individualism, dedication, and commitment seldom found in the history of journalism. Here they come onto the stage of modern journalism, assuredly—even arrogantly—jousting with windmills of a society they view as corrupt, and what is more interesting, jousting with ethical lances fashioned in their own individual shops and tipped with points of untried metal.

It is difficult to speak of ethics with persons such as these; they are too self-assured, too certain of their relativistic value systems, too flamboyant and scornful of anything that smacks of established ways of doing things and judging things. These are the journalists who are currently manning the underground (misnomer!) newspapers; they who are championing "advocacy" journalism; they are the ones who are the *subjectivists* discussed in the preceding chapter. It is our contention that they are growing rapidly in number and vitality, and that the older, traditionally oriented journalists are either dying out or adapting themselves to many of the ideas of the new existential journalists. It would be wrong, certainly, to imply that *all* young journalists have this antagonism toward ethical standards. For there are, indeed, many young journalists of a more conservative bent, who respect standards, need them, defend them, and seek to belong to groups and associations that take them seriously and try to inculcate them in all their members.

Two Basic Journalistic Orientations

Before getting into a discussion of ethics *per se,* let us consider two main tendencies or orientations. These, undoubtedly, lead to the kind of ethical outlook the journalist adopts, and it is well that we consider them before dealing specifically with ethics.

1. The 'people-oriented'' journalist. This person makes most of his journalistic decisions on the basis of the way he thinks they will affect *people:* others and/or himself. He is either an egoist or an altruist—and sometimes a little of both. His concern is with people, and he takes their feelings and areas of sensitivity into consideration before he writes a story. His news determinations and decisions are made largely on the basis of the way he thinks they will affect himself and others connected with the story. It might be called a "personal consequence" journalistic orientation; certainly it is very much a *subjective* one.

The "people-oriented" journalist, therefore, places people always at the center of his journalism—not in the traditional sense of "names make news," but in a more subjective sense whereby he considers the *impact* of his journalistic actions on these people. A certain story may be slanted one way because of the journalist's concern for a particular person, because he has a certain bias for or against a participant in the story or on the periphery of the story. The journalist's sensitivity to, or bias toward, certain people will determine to a large degree *what* will be considered news in the first place; it will also determine the *emphasis* or the *slant* provided it—what really will be omitted, selected, or played up or down.

In other words the "people-oriented" journalist will be largely controlled (have his journalism determined) by his sensitivity to people—himself included—connected with the story. *People* are constantly having an impact on news determination, emphasis, and writing. The journalist's main concern is with the way the story will affect people. This is very much the "involved," subjective orientation, and it is vastly different from the second orientation that we now come to consider—the orientation of dispassionate neutralism.

2. The "event-oriented" journalist. This journalist is concerned with facts, with events, with circumstances *per se.* Of course, he knows that people are important in news stories, but he is little concerned about the *consequences to people related to the news stories.* He cares only about the event. He stands as aloof as possible, ever the "neutralist," telling the story and letting the proverbial chips "fall where they may." He is fundamentally the reportorial objectivist described in the preceding chapter.

He makes a constant attempt not to become involved with people, and he tries to keep his own feelings out of the story. He tries to detach himself from all personal opinions, attitudes or biases for self or for others so that these "feelings" about people will not determine what he considers news or how he will treat this news. He seeks to be dispassionate and objective in his news presentation. The important thing for him is to get the facts; if they are connected with persons (and they almost always are), then so be it. Facts, to the "event-oriented" journalist, are indeed sacred; they are essential to a report of the total event, the account of what happened.

Ethics: A Matter of Concern

The two orientations just discussed, without a doubt, largely determine the kind of ethics a journalist adopts. The person who is an egoist or an altruist, or both, will find that his ethics follows or supports his basic psychological orientation. And his concern with ethics will be quite different from that of the person who is basically an objectivist or neutralist, who tries to keep himself aloof from his journalism, and who focuses on the event or facts rather than on the way his journalism may affect people.

In fact, we might say that these two orientations are really *a part of* a journalist's ethics, at least to the degree that they are deterministic. If the journalist is worried about the *consequences to people* in his news story, for example, he is going to march to a different ethical drum than is the journalist who seeks to relate the story as accurately as possible and is not very sensitive to the consequences of his story.

Ethics is truly a personal matter, personal in the sense that it arises from a personal *concern* for one's conduct. It is also personal in the sense that one's conduct is self-directed and self-enforced; the person voluntarily follows a code of conduct because he feels it is the thing to do. There are those who wish that ethical standards could be externally imposed and *enforced*, that people could be made to be ethical. This, of course, is contradictory to the concept of ethics, for ethics is unenforceable. When a person's conduct is enforced, he is then under legalism, with free will taken away. Ethics, then, is a code of conduct that is self-enforced and, in general, is considered to be *rationally arrived at*. Reason enforces one's ethics. It might be said that a person's ethics is: 1. personal, 2. directive or predictive, and 3. rational. It is personal in the sense discussed above; it is predictive in that it serves as a guide for conduct and indicates pretty well what one can be expected to do in a certain situation, and it is rational in that *reason* dictates its acceptance.

Regardless of the particular form of ethical decisions made, the important thing for journalists is that they have a *concern* for ethics. They should care about ethics; they should not be amoral or nonethical in their activities. The person in journalism (like any person) needs to have values and standards for himself—rationally arrived at and rationally enforced.* Having these at least indicates that the person is trying, is thinking about proper conduct, and is interested in being a moral person. Ethics or moral philosophy, then, must be a "concern" of the journalist, regardless of what code of ethics (written or unwritten) he subscribes to. Personal codes are, of course, always changing to some degree, evolving, becoming refined. But they should always be becoming more *demanding*—not less demanding—on the individual journalist. Demanding in what respect? Demanding in the sense that the standards become ever more difficult to achieve and that they become increasingly more rational. Ethics—at least a concern for ethics—instills in the journalist a continuing sensitivity to his every action, to his every decision; it integrates or blends with his total search for truth, and it gives him greater awareness of himself, of others, of the consequences of interpersonal relations. A concern with ethics is the key plank in any journalistic platform; it is the "alpha and omega" of public communication.

---

*There are many *existential* persons, of course, who will not agree that rationality is essential to "moral" journalistic conduct.

Ethical Theories or Systems

Like so many other important and complex subjects, ethics is looked at from a number of perspectives. There are numerous ways of classifying and analyzing ethical theories and systems; names and labels have proliferated as philosophers have ranged the frontiers of moral philosophy down through the years, seeking new insights and forming new "schools." Consequently we have a multitude of labels for the various ethical theories and concepts. There is no need here to confuse the reader with all of these; it is enough to say that there is a system of ethics that must surely be agreeable to almost every person. If not, then one is free to combine ethical theories into a personalized composite system compatible with his own philosophical position at a particular time.

It would seem that *all* systems of ethics are based on the concept of man's freedom, for man is truly free to accept (or devise) for himself his ethical position. But what about the person who uses his freedom *not* to accept an ethical position? Then, we must say that he is beyond the scope of this discussion; he is, *as man* involved in society and civilization, expected by others to be ethical, *i.e.*, to have a concern for ethics. If he is not so concerned, then he must be classified as *immoral*—or to be kinder, as *amoral.* Ethics implies self-established and enforced rules, and if a person has no such rules, then he is simply playing semantic games with the concept of freedom. Immanuel Kant, the eighteenth-century German Idealist who is usually considered the "philosopher's philosopher," said that man is free only by setting up rules for himself, and that no person's conduct can be moral if there is any outside compulsion such as reward or punishment.

Kant, then, put his finger on the key aspect of ethics: *self*-enforcement or *self*-legislation. And he expressed this idea in his famous "Categorical Imperative," which enthroned *duty* and which said in effect that we are required to (duty bound to) act in such a way that we would be willing to see our conduct become a universal law.* Kant was stressing the socialization of ethics; he was saying that, although ethics is indeed personal, a person only acts ethically or morally when he relates or identifies himself in principle to all mankind. Kant's theory also implies rationality, for a person must use reason to determine his own duty. Thus rational deliberation is basic to an ethics—at least in Kant's view.

As we have said, there are many ways to classify ethical theories and although we shall not attempt to catalogue all of them, we will mention briefly a few of the most prominent typologies.†

Absolute/relative. The ethical absolutist believes that there is one universal and eternal ethical code that basically applies to everyone in all ages. He contends that changing opinions, traditions, and conditions make no significant difference in this absolute moral code. There are actions that are "right" and actions that are "wrong"—regardless of the place, time, or special circumstance.

The ethical relativist, on the other hand, has his morality tied more closely to emotions. He puts considerable faith in intuitions, inclinations, and feelings. He says, in effect, that we have no right to make judgments about the ethics of others, for these judgments only indicate a bias—a prejudice—on our part. He sees no moral superiority of one code over another, an idea that would—if carried very far—indicate that no action (or man) is any better than another. The relativist also holds that the moral standard varies with different circumstances, at different times, in different cultures.

Objective/subjective. The ethical objectivist might be considered an advocate of absolute ethics; he sees all absolute stan-

---

*See H. J. Paton, *The Categorical Imperative: A Study of Kant's Moral Philosophy* (London: Hutchinson & Co., 1947; New York: Harper & Row, 1967).

†The terminology and typology used here is adapted from several sources, but largely from William Lillie, *An Introduction to Ethics* (London: Methuen, University Paperbacks, 1961).

dards in ethics as necessarily objective. Ethical standards are objective in the sense of being formed *outside the person*; they are rational, based on something other than feelings or opinions. Something is "right" or "wrong," then, independent of the way the person might subjectively *feel* about it.

The ethical subjectivist, taking the contrary view, looks at ethics as simply the opinion or preference of a person; ethics to him is a form of relative morality that views the variability in moral judgments as caused purely and simply by the *mental state* of a particular person. For example, a "good" action for me is one which I myself like.

Attitudinal/consequence. An attitudinal ethical theory, a variety of subjectivism, is one defining a right action as one which a person feels disposed toward. In other words, conduct is "right" if it is harmonious with one's "attitude." A consequence theory is quite different: it is closer to the objectivist position in that it places standards of value *outside* the person— specifically *in the consequences* of the action. So it is a kind of "hindsight" theory, determining the goodness or badness of an action only after the consequences have been noted. Utilitarian ethics, as espoused by such men as Jeremy Bentham and J. S. Mill, in which the benefits to the greatest number of persons would be taken as the moral yardstick, would be an example of *consequence ethics.*

Deontological/teleological. The deontological ethical theory states that the rightness or wrongness of an action is dependent on the action itself and not on the results or consequences it produces. The intuitionist or existential journalist described earlier in this chapter would be an example of a person with a deontological orientation; he feels that he has a natural and spontaneous "sense" of what is right and wrong, and this sense or "conscience" will be a reliable guide.

The teleological ethical theory is the same as the consequence theory discussed above. For example, the journalistic *hedonist,* teleologically oriented, would say that the rightness or wrongness of a particular journalistic action would depend on the pleasure or displeasure it brings to him. Theoretically, then, if he received pleasure from lying or misrepresenting in a news story, he would have done the right thing. So we see that the bringing of pleasure, for example, either to the person acting or to others, is one aspect of the consequence theory.

Ethical Dialectic: Another Typology

In addition to the several ways of classifying ethical theories mentioned above, another might well be discussed briefly. It is a ternary typology that seemingly has developed by a Hegelian dialectical process through which a kind of compromise (or *synthesis*) has grown out of a clash between two extreme theories (*thesis* and *antithesis*). There is reason to believe that all the many theories and systems of ethics can be accommodated in this concept of the ethical dialectic with its three basic systems. In this typology, the thesis can be called *legalistic* (or code) ethics; the conflicting extreme or antithesis can be called *antinomian* ethics, and the synthesis or compromise theory may be called *situation* ethics.* Let us look briefly at these three:

Legalistic ethics. This is, of course, an absolute or objective ethical system based largely on tradition, on social agreement or on a firm religious moral code. It is partly—perhaps largely—rational, although many persons insist that any kind of reliance on a rigid code of conduct cannot really be rational. The rationality of legalistic ethics stems from the fact that adherents to this morality have good *reason* to follow it; they have found through the years that there have emerged certain basic, objective, absolute principles of conduct that serve the society best and bring the greatest amount of pleasure to the most people. So, although it is traditional ethics—and quite rigid in

---

*These three ethical theories have the best and fullest exposition in Joseph Fletcher, *Situation Ethics: The New Morality* (Philadelphia: The Westminster Press, 1966). As far as we know, however, we are the first to view this trinary classification in the light of Hegelian dialectics.

most respects—the legalistic theory is rational in that it is pragmatic, socially beneficial and personally comforting. It is also, we might add, very much *consequence oriented*.

When a person breaks the code, goes against the ethical law, he is considered *unethical* in his action by the members of his society; morality, then, is defined by the vast majority of a person's contemporaries. This kind of *consensus ethics* says that a person is ethical or unethical to the degree that he conforms to, or deviates from, the norms or codes of his society. If, for example, American journalism had *a* code of ethics that was adopted by journalists throughout the country, and if a practitioner "broke" a part of the code, his action would (or could) be considered *unethical*, at least in the context of his own "profession." Legalistic or code ethics implies a general agreement (at least in a context) on basic ethical or moral precepts; if this agreement is lacking—as it seems to be in libertarian press systems—then there is little chance of legalistic ethics having any great impact.

So we see that the legalistic ethical system is an absolute one in which wrong is wrong and right is right, and judgments can be passed rather easily on personal conduct. It is basically an absolute system, a rigid system, not permitting for very much permissiveness and rationalizing. It is only natural that a reaction should set in against it; and, as is true with most reactions, the reactionaries (or rebels) quickly equal, or outdistance, the advocates of the old system in their extremism and rigidity. This is what has happened in the case of those who despise code ethics to such a degree that they, in effect, have repudiated all ethics and have rebelled against any kind of standard or law.

Antinomian ethics. These rebels, reacting negatively to the constrictions and absolutes of code ethics, have accepted what has been called antinomian (against laws) ethics. The antinomians have desired to toss out all basic principles, precepts, standards, and laws. Whereas the legalists tend toward absolutist or autocratic ethics, the antinomians gravitate toward anarchy or nihilism in ethics.

The antinomian is against standards; he thinks he needs no directions, no rules. He "plays it all by ear," making decisions in the area of morality "as the spirit moves him," intuitively, spontaneously, irrationally. He is, in a sense, the existentialist* who has lost faith in reason so far as ethical decisions are concerned. He wants no guide other than his senses, his existential intuitions and instincts. In many ways, this person does not really subscribe to an ethical theory, for antinomianism is a kind of *un*ethics or *non*ethics that leads to behavior that is quite unpredictable, erratic, and spontaneous. Although the antinomian claims to be the real *humanist*, his irrational and sensory inclinations resemble more those of lower animal orders, for instinctivism is hardly compatible with humanism.

The antinomian in journalism will be found most often in the freedom-loving world of the advocacy journalist, in the world of the existential journalist who fights against the traditional rigidity of the mainstream establishment media. He makes his ethical decisions as he goes, not even realizing that he is making them—not even really considering them ethical decisions. Rather they are just feelings, instincts, inclinations, intuitions. This ethical (or nonethical) system might simply be referred to as "whim ethics."

Situation ethics. Now we come to the "synthesis" theory of ethics, the in-between ethics, the compromise ethics that is generally known as situation ethics. This is the middle ground between code and antinomian ethics, although it must be admitted that it is very often confused with the "nonethics" of antinomianism just discussed. This confusion is unfortunate for situation ethics is *rational*, while antinomian ethics is *irrational*. The two have very little in common.

As we have said, however, situation ethics is a synthesis, a compromise between code and antinomian ethics. Therefore,

---

*Of the many excellent books on existentialism, two we feel are especially good discussions: William Barrett, *Irrational Man: A Study in Existential Philosophy* (New York: Doubleday & Co., 1958), and F. H. Heinemann, *Existentialism and the Modern Predicament* (New York: Harper Torchbook paperback, 1958).

situation ethics does have *something* in common with each of the other two. It resembles antinomian ethics in that it is not tied tightly to absolute principles. It resembles legalistic or code ethics in that it is rational and not intuitive, and it has not entirely forsaken traditional legalistic or absolutist moral principles. In fact, situation ethics begins with traditional code ethics.

But there the resemblance ends. The situationist is guided generally by the traditional code ethics having universal appeal and relevance; but he is not tied tightly to any ethical rules. He breaks them when he thinks there is a need to do so. He takes special *situations* or circumstances into consideration; in this sense he is a relativist, but a rational relativist—one who *thinks* before he departs from a basic ethical principle. He is rational because he has a *reason* for departing from an ethical principle.

The journalistic situationist may well be the person who believes it is all right to distort a particular story, or even to lie, if he foresees the harm done to his newspaper or his country to be very great if he "plays it straight" and tells the truth. There are times when it is *right* to play down—or leave out completely—certain stories or pictures; there are other times when it would be *wrong*. But the important thing here is that the journalist *thinks* before taking a certain action; he has a reason for doing what he does. He is not acting on instinct or intuition.

It appears to us that today the majority of American journalists subscribe to the situation ethical position. There are some rigid legalists or code moralists in journalism, to be sure, but they do not seem to exert very much influence. Increasingly one finds the antinomian in the mass media or in journalism schools, scorning rationalism and flaunting his existential instinctivism, but the mass media—rather rigid institutions that they are—have not yet fallen under the spell of these ethical nihilists.

Marshall McLuhan with his "retribalization" (decivilization?) theory and his psychedelic multimessage appeal to all the senses (the total person) has either been a stimulant to, or result of, the growing influence of the antinomians. What happens in journalism—and in society generally—in the next few years should give us a much clearer insight into which of these three ethical positions will dominate by the end of this century. We believe that it will be the *situation* ethical position, the "synthesis" in the dialectic, but it is presently too early to tell.

Journalistic Ethics: Final Comments

Having presented a number of possible ethical systems or theories in survey fashion, we have not been very specific about journalistic ethics. We have used broad strokes instead of relating these concepts and theories to particular journalistic problems. This has been done purposely, for if we were to begin discussing specific ethical situations related to the mass media, we could well launch into an entirely new book.

Rather than going into great detail about journalistic ethics in a specific way, we have tried to present ethical concepts into which any journalist or journalism student can meld his individual problems and questions. Naturally the journalist is interested in such ethical questions as these: Should a newsman honor "off-the-record" statements? Should the names of juvenile offenders be published if it is legal to do so? Should a newsman ever create a "pseudo-event" or pose a pseudo-picture? Should a newsman form a preconceived or idealized story and select material to fit it? What about the ethics of quoting out of context? Is failure to print something you have in hand unethical? What about the ethics of invading privacy in order to get a news story? What about the ethics of a newspaper writing a letter to itself, ostensibly from a reader? And on and on.

There are hundreds of such specific ethical questions that could be dealt with in this chapter. But it would, in fact, be useless and senseless to try to give ethical answers to such questions. The journalist must, on the basis of the ethical theory to which he subscribes, make these decisions *on his own*, by himself. We would hope that he would make them rationally, but at any rate, they are questions that only the individual journalist can answer—in his own time, in his own way. And it would be presumptuous of us to try to answer such questions.

However, in conclusion and as a kind of bonus for those readers who feel that we should make a judgment, take a position and commit ourselves to something, we will say that we believe: 1. the only kind of moral judgments that have any lasting validity are *absolute* ethical standards, however much their application is modified in various contexts and in varying circumstances (situation ethics), and 2. no *subjective* theory of ethics, which in reality washes away the whole concept of objective standards, can ever be taken very seriously by rational men. Now, with these two judgments about ethics in general (relate them to journalism as you will), made with what we believe to be appropriate modesty and ethical insight, we end our discussion of this extremely complex subject.

17.

The Future of Mass Media

THE SPECTER OF THE HUTCHINS COMMISSION REPORT STANDS before anyone preparing to foretell the future of mass communication. The report, issued in 1947, predicted that FM would soon supplant AM radio and implied that transmission of facsimile newspapers into the home was right around the corner. Members of the Commission noted only briefly the possible impact of television and could not foresee at all the transistor radio, cable television, and communication satellites.

It may well be that remarkable new inventions, as yet undreamed of, will revolutionize some aspects of journalism in the next decade. But in the authors' opinion, the revolution in mass media technology has already moved into high gear, although there is a distinct lag in some quarters in admitting it and preparing for the future. During the past few decades, the electronic revolution has existed side by side with the print media "establishment." In many ways, the print media have adopted new roles as electronic media moved in to take over some of their old functions. During the next few decades, the electronic media are likely to take over even more functions of the print media, leaving the older media in a completely subordinate position.

This prophecy may frighten employees in the print media. It need not. The evolution from print to electronic media will be gradual; in fact, it has been underway for more than a half-century already. A characteristic of this evolutionary process is an expansion in the number of print and electronic channels, not a contraction. Accordingly, there must be an expansion in the number of persons employed in the new channels, as well.

We can say, then, that the media revolution of the immediate and foreseeable future will be *electronic* in form and *specialized* in nature. The change from print to electronics will proceed in two stages, which we can call the "open channels stage" and the "personal retrieval stage."

The Open Channels Stage

The *open channels stage* will be dominated by CATV (cable television) and cassette TV (taped video recordings playable on individual television sets). CATV operators will be able to offer customers more than fifty channels. In addition to the programming of the three major networks, an educational network, and time and temperature signals, the CATV spectrum will also feature:

small-audience networks with emphases such as ethnic, all news, farming, stock market, etc.

pay television: live theater, operas, new movies, sporting events, and the circus.

local programming: local news (updated and presented live every hour for fifteen minutes, then replayed in tape form three complete times until the next updating); local events of interest (city council, school board, special meetings and speeches); political programming over one channel every night, featuring partisan political views and debate.

music channels, with and without pictures, offering FM reception and stereophonic sound.

previews of the total programming day; one channel will be set aside as a preview channel, offering a continual listing of title, subject, and time of all individual programs scheduled on all channels that day.

Cassette TV will supplement CATV programming by offering thousands of tapes appealing to specialized tastes. The tapes, which can be rented or purchased, will include musical recordings (with motion pictures of the recording group), movies, old television programs, sporting events, and educational films of infinite variety. The availability of these tapes will lend to television a quality of "reviewability" and highly selective choice missing in even the greatly expanded CATV channels.

Print media will not change radically during the *open channels stage*, but certain trends, already apparent, will be accelerated. The expanded channels on CATV will mean that many in-depth features of general interest will be accommodated there instead of in magazines. Magazines will cater even more to specialized interest groups, and will even add and subtract whole segments of an individual issue to appeal to the different regional and ethnic interests of subscribers.

With increasing percentages of the population attending universities, book publishers will find larger markets for hardbacks and paperbacks. But newspapers will face greater competition from CATV. The most important local news will get a full play on CATV, and its news programs will even have a quality of "reviewability," since the programs can be rerun every fifteen minutes. It is quite possible that newspaper staffs will be under contract to provide this news programming for CATV. (Some newspapers, of course, are already CATV operators.) Newspapers will emphasize aspects of journalism that CATV does least well. For example, papers will present local and national news in depth, featuring a wide array of political and social columnists, and they will begin to emphasize "internal specialization" more than they have in the past—offering daily television, science, medical, foreign news, and leisure-time sections, in addition to sports and business news sections already in existence.

Ironically, the present "electronic" media will suffer most. The *open channels stage* will see the decline of local television stations. This will not be as great a loss as some people would immediately assume. Most local stations are now little more than transmitters of network signals. Confined by license to one channel, they must fit snippets of the local news scene into the network programming day. CATV operators will be able to do everything that local stations now do, and they will do it more thoroughly. They can offer a continuous local news channel, and allot additional channels to live or filmed local events of interest.

Radio will also suffer, since CATV can offer more channels for specialized music programming than are now available in most areas. Since CATV receivers will still depend upon an umbilical cable, radio's strength will rest solely upon its "portability," its ability to send its signal through the air to transistor receivers and car radios.*

It is difficult to predict how advertising will be affected by the first stage of this media revolution. The "subscription" nature of CATV would indicate that viewers will have a greater say in the degree of commercial intrusion into this medium. At least in the United States, however, the history of broadcasting would indicate otherwise, and—unless there is government interference to prevent it—one could expect CATV operators to sell their time and messages to advertisers as assiduously as did the radio and television stations of the country. In any case, the established commercial networks will undoubtedly maintain the highest viewership since advertising income will enable them to produce the most professional general interest programs. Network educational television, with massive government subsidies in place of advertising, will be of a similar professional caliber, although appealing to a smaller audience.

Although this first stage of the new media era will cause

---

*However, new technology is already being developed to eliminate this "umbilical" weakness of CATV. Available in prototype even now is laser beam transmission of multiple television signals over short distances.

dislocations in existing media, it will also open up enough new channels of mass communication to evaporate the twentieth-century threat of press monopoly. With so many channels available to all the pluralistic views and tastes of society, the free countries will have a new opportunity to establish a "libertarian" press system. Authoritarian societies, of course, will use this new technology as just another tool in their arsenals of control.

Personal Retrieval Stage

CATV and cassette television are only intermediate steps to an ultimate technology that will allow each viewer to select his own programming at his own convenience from central computers. This technology is available now, but its implementation awaits a progressive evolution in affluence, and perhaps in politics.

In order to understand the impact of this "personal retrieval" stage upon society, try to picture its effect upon a single home. Each room of the home has a television screen, and a fingerboard full of numbered keys at some convenient or inconspicuous place in the room. If the mother of the family wants a recipe, she taps out the proper number on her kitchen keyboard, and a film showing how to prepare the dish comes up on her kitchen screen. Children do their homework by "retrieving" educational film or specific pages of the latest encyclopedia on their desk screens in their rooms. They may even plug in to a computer via television to do their math homework.

Each television receiver will be capable of printing out onto paper any picture or message appearing on the television screen, whether it is a diagram from an educational film or a page from the encyclopedia. Each person, in the McLuhanesque sense, will become his own publisher.

In the same manner that his children read the encyclopedia—electronically—the father of the house reads his newspaper, a favorite magazine, or a recently published book. For example, he "retrieves" the magazine table of contents with his keyboard, and then reads the magazine page by page, in order, each successive page appearing at a touch of one key; or he can skip swiftly to an article of particular interest. Retrieval TV, it would seem, will even make turning pages a thing of the past.

In fact, the only books one is likely to find in this home will be books of indexes that list the cost per minute and call numbers of books, films, television programs, Broadway plays, etc. Every bit of filmed, taped, or published knowledge will be at the instant call of the average family. All such information will be stored in giant central computers in each country, ready to be fed on personal call into any room of the home at a moment's notice. Each family will be billed according to the value of the material used, and a computer-totaled accounting will arrive each month, much as utility bills do now. A Broadway play or new movie may be much more costly than, say, fourteen pages from the *Encyclopaedia Britannica*; the latest novel (not yet in the public domain) will be more costly than Plato.

Commercial television networks will still be with us, and certainly all the programming described above for the *open channels stage* will still be available. But everything will be repeatable at the convenience of the viewer. The viewer will see the news—local or national—at the moment *he* wants to see it.

Computerized, personal retrieval TV will give television reviewability and true single sales independence. Communication satellites will also offer the possibility of direct transmission to portable, transistorized screens at any spot on earth, relieving this multichannel personal television system of any dependence on a fixed cable.

Newspapers, magazines, and books will be designed much as they are now—except that writers and editors need only produce a single copy, and this for storage on computer tape. Once print media are relieved of the age-old necessity of reproducing duplicate messages for each member of the audience, they will have achieved the same possibilities for *message saturation* as the electronic media.

Each book or publication distributed via retrieval TV will be sold through a computerized royalty system, with the publisher receiving a fixed sum for each copy or portion of a copy that appears on a viewer's television screen. The possibilities in this sort of system can hardly be imagined, but these are a few: Publications could reach circulations impossible to achieve within the confines of newsprint; *The New York Times*, for example, would immediately become a national newspaper in every sense. Publications will eliminate the costliest part of their operations—all personnel and equipment involved in the mechanical reproduction and distribution processes, including the expense of newsprint. Society will benefit in these ways: Almost anyone with something to say and/or a unique way of saying it can become a publisher with minimal capital investment. And the problems of ravaging forests for wood pulp, polluting water supplies to manufacture newsprint, burdening sanitation departments to collect old publications, and dirtying the atmosphere to dispose of waste paper will be greatly diminished.

If the individual can take advantage of this personal retrieval system in his own home, as we have described above, then we must also consider the advantages that will accrue to all institutions in society—schools, businesses, governmental bodies—when all knowledge is instantly retrievable at very little cost. These same advantages will be available, also, for every nation in the world that can afford to install this sophisticated personal retrieval system. Communication satellites will enable the individual in one country to tap into the stored knowledge in another country by an act no more complicated than direct distance dialing with an ordinary phone.

If one must consider the advantages, he must also consider the possible disadvantages of this new era in mass communication. There is something to be said for true "mass" communication that exposes a large number of people to a limited number of channels, because individuals are thereby exposed to a wide spectrum of cultures, ideas, and opinions, even those that he would normally reject. Personal retrieval TV will offer a vast number of sources and channels, permitting any individual to build a political, social, and educational cocoon around himself. To the extent that this occurs, society will suffer since it is likely to be divided into highly polarized, and probably unempathic, segments.

Also, there are obvious dangers in centralizing the storage and transmission facilities for all information and knowledge. Who will determine what material is excluded from the computer banks, and how will this determination be made? Ironically, there are two vastly different consequences implicit in the development of the personal retrieval system. With proper safeguards, the new system would fulfill the hopes of the libertarian philosophers; without proper safeguards, it would extend the scope of authoritarian control over the minds of men.

However, even this potential disadvantage will not hold back the tide of the future. All the equipment for the first, or *open channels*, stage is available now. It need only be popularized, and undoubtedly will be during this decade.

Technology for the second, or *personal retrieval*, stage has been developed. Whether it becomes a reality in twenty years instead of fifty will depend upon the ability of communicators and politicians to recognize that this is the development that can fulfill media's role of multiplying education and democracy, two commodities now in short supply throughout the world.

Selected Annotated Bibliography

Aronson, James. *The Press and the Cold War.* Indianapolis: Bobbs-Merrill Co., 1970.

Aronson's basic theme is as follows: the American press misunderstood and misreported political phenomena such as Joe McCarthy and Vietnam not because of a devotion to "objectivity," but rather because of a devotion to the conservative Establishment. In pursuing his thesis, Aronson fails to provide objective balance, but he does provide a catalyst for reconsidering the role of the press in American society.

Bagdikian, Ben H. *The Information Machines: Their Impact on Men and the Media.* New York: Harper & Row, 1971.

Basing his insights on data gathered by Rand Corporation studies, Bagdikian surveys the nature of the news media and their audiences. This is an up-to-date survey throughout, but the most interesting portions are those dealing with the technological developments that will determine the media's future.

Baker, Robert K., and Ball, Sandra J. *Violence and the Media.* Washington: U.S. Government Printing Office, 1969.

A staff report to the National Commission on the Causes and Prevention of Violence—but this book contains much more than the title indicates. Included are a history of journalism, a review of the functions of mass media, and a survey of a wide range of research involving mass media and society.

Barrett, William. *Irrational Man: A Study in Existential Philosophy.* New York: Doubleday & Co., 1958 (paperback edition, Doubleday Anchor, 1962).

Probably the finest definition of existentialism ever written. The heart of the book is composed of four long chapters explaining the views of existentialism's foremost spokesmen—Kierkegaard, Nietzsche, Heidegger, and Sartre.

Berns, Walter F. *Freedom, Virtue and the First Amendment.* Baton Rouge: Louisiana State University Press, 1957 (paperback edition, Chicago: Henry Regnery Co., 1965).

An interesting book that contends that freedom is not justice and that some limitation on freedom is required for the maintenance of the common good. One of the best defenses of limited censorship and restraint in the name of "virtue" written in this country.

Blumler, Jay G., and McQuail, Denis. *Television in Politics.* Chicago: University of Chicago Press, 1969.

An investigation into the use of television by political parties in England, and the effect of political broadcasts on the voter.

Boorstin, Daniel J. *The Image: A Guide to Pseudo-Events in America.* New York: Harper & Row, Harper Colophon Books, 1964.

A fascinating discussion of the growing art of self-deception, of how we hide reality from ourselves. Chapter 1 ("From News Gathering to News Making: A Flood of Pseudo-Events") is certainly the most interesting for the journalist, but the entire book is easily adapted to the concerns and problems of mass communication.

Brown, J. A. C. *Techniques of Persuasion: From Propaganda to Brainwashing.* Baltimore: Penguin Books, 1963.

A clear and concise discussion of the process of persuasion and the related concept of personality itself. This survey ranges from political propaganda, religious conversion, and advertising, through an appraisal of the mass media of communication and their roles in indoctrination and persuasion.

Brucker, Herbert. *Freedom of Information.* New York: Macmillan Co., 1949.

This book provides an excellent discussion of the entire problem of government-press relations as they revolve around freedom and censorship. Especially insightful are the chapters on the concept of the press as the "fourth estate" (Chapters 5 and 6), the chapter on objective reporting (Chapter 18), and the final chapter (Chapter 19) on freedom of information.

Bryson, Lyman, ed. *The Communication of Ideas.* New York: Harper, 1948.

An excellent anthology of lectures on communication, including those dealing with interpersonal (small group) communication and those dealing with inter-cultural communication. Probably the best available book of readings related to the total communication process.

Carr, Edward H. *The New Society.* New York: Macmillan Co., 1951.

Although somewhat dated, this highly readable and provocative book provides one of the most valuable analyses of the transition of American society from an individualistic to a highly organized, institutionalized society.

Cater, Douglass, *The Fourth Branch of Government.* New York: Random House, Vintage Books, 1959.

A lively portrait of reporting in the nation's capital, with the underlying thesis that the reporter has a crucial role in helping a democratic government to function effectively. Beyond the value of "government by publicity," as he calls it, he describes the press as a "quasi-official fourth branch of government" in spite of the fact that there is a basic conflict between government and the press.

Cherry, Colin. *On Human Communication.* Boston: M.I.T. Press, 1959.

A book of lectures by an outstanding British communication scholar at the University of London, exploring the extent to which relationships exist among such "communication sciences" as linguistics, mathematics, cybernetics, psychology, semantics, and phonetics. A classic work of references, citations and definitions in the broad area of communication.

Cirino, Robert. *Don't Blame the People.* Los Angeles: Diversity Press, 1971.

Another in the genre of Aronson's *The Press and the Cold War,* this book is an angry denunciation of an Establishment, status-quo press. Supporting his polemic with data, Cirino contends that media bias is pro-conservative; he proposes that all viewpoints be allowed equal access to the media.

College of Journalism, Marquette University. *Social Responsibility of the Newspress.* Marquette, 1962.

A book of lectures given at Marquette comprising five speeches on various aspects of "social responsibility" of the press. Probably the most relevant of the lectures to the subject of the emerging theory of Social Responsibility is the last, by Professor Jay W. Jensen of the School of Journalism, University of Illinois, entitled "Freedom of the Press: A Concept in Search of a Philosophy." Other lectures in the book are by Alan Barth, John B. Oakes, Mark Ethridge, and Marya Mannes.

Commission on Freedom of the Press. *A Free and Responsible Press.* Chicago: University of Chicago Press, 1947.

A basic criticism of the U.S. press by a self-appointed "commission" headed by Robert Hutchins. Criteria for a responsible press are set up and the American press is held up to these criteria—and it is found deficient. One of the most controversial and catalytic books published in this century in the field of journalism, it is probably the main stimulant to the current concern about "social responsibility" of the press.

Commission on Obscenity and Pornography. *The Report of the Commission on Obscenity and Pornography.* New York: Bantam Books, 1970.

The complete recommendations of the special commission established by Congress to investigate this problem. Included are the minority opinions and summaries of specific research on the effects of pornography.

Cone, Fairfax M. *With All Its Faults.* Boston: Little, Brown & Co., 1969.

An advertising executive combines biography and criticism in one volume. He finds all is not well with the advertising industry and its messages. But he does not think all is wrong, either.

Cooper, Kent. *The Right to Know*. New York: Farrar, Straus and Cudahy, 1956.

A former chief executive of the Associated Press exposes the evils of government news suppression and propaganda and contends that press freedom in this country is the same as the right of the people to know.

De Fleur, Melvin L. *Theories of Mass Communication*. New York: David McKay Co., 1970.

A study of the processes and phenomena of mass communication within a sociological perspective. De Fleur's chapters on the development of newspapers, motion pictures, radio, and television provide a particularly good background for the Elite-Popular-Specialized (EPS) curve of media progression discussed in this text.

DeGeorge, Richard T. *Soviet Ethics and Morality*. Ann Arbor: University of Michigan Press, 1969.

Although this book deals primarily with the basis, structure, and content of Soviet ethical theory, the curious and adaptive reader can glean from its pages a wealth of general information and ideas relative to morality that is extremely timely and pertinent to the morality—and to the ethics of the journalist.

Dewey, John. *Theory of the Moral Life*. New York: Holt, Rinehart and Winston, 1908 (paperback edition, 1960).

A concise, highly readable general discussion of ethics with six chapters that give helpful insights into the moral philosophy, not only of Dewey, but of Aristotle, Augustine, Hobbes, Butler, Hume, Kant, Bentham, Sidgwick, and Moore—among others.

Ellul, Jacques. *Propaganda*. New York: Knopf, 1965.

In this seminal book (translated by Konrad Kellen and Jean Lerner), a Frenchman who does not like propaganda decries the inescapable necessity of propaganda in the modern world and curses its effects on mankind. The book is a fresh discussion of the mechanisms, categories, and effects of propaganda. Especially interesting is the discussion of how propaganda tends to splinter or partition society and how it is necessary to a democratic society.

Ewing, A. C. *Ethics.* New York: Macmillan Co., 1953 (A Free Press Paperback, 1965).

A leading British philosopher presents what is one of the clearest, most readable general discussions of ethics in which he focuses on the two main considerations of ethics (What is good? What is one's duty?). The book provides especially good analyses of egoistic hedonism, utilitarianism, and Kant's ethics of "duty for duty's sake."

Fagen, Richard R. *Politics and Communication.* Boston: Little, Brown & Co., 1966.

An excellent little book, not only giving valuable insights into the essence of communication, but showing how communication affects the performance of the political system.

Fisher, Paul L., and Lowenstein, Ralph L., eds. *Race and the News Media.* New York: Frederick A. Praeger, 1967 (paperback edition, New York: Anti-Defamation League of B'nai B'rith, 1967).

Newspapermen, broadcasters, advertising executives, and black leaders offer comments on the performance of the press in racial coverage, with recommendations for improvement. Among the contributors are representatives of *The New York Times*, New York *Post*, Los Angeles *Times*, Chicago *Daily News*, St. Louis *Post-Dispatch*, *Life*, ABC, CBS, NBC, the U.S. Community Relations Service, and the National Association for the Advancement of Colored People.

Fletcher, Joseph. *Situation Ethics: The New Morality.* Philadelphia: The Westminster Press, 1966.

This little paperback by a professor of social ethics at Episcopal Theological School, Cambridge, Mass., deals mainly with the love ethic of *agape* and is oriented specifically to the Christian context, but its principles are easily applicable to human morality and conduct generally. The author contends that any act—even lying, adultery, and murder—may be right, depending on the circumstances.

Friedrich, Carl J., and Brzezinski, Z. K. *Totalitarian Dictatorship and Autocracy.* 2nd ed., revised by C. J. Friedrich. New York: Frederick A. Praeger, 1965.

An excellent general discussion of the historical roots of totalitarian ideology, the general characteristics of totalitarian dictatorship, and a look at the future of totalitarianism—both Left and Right. Especially interesting to the journalism student and journalist are Chapters 11 and 12 dealing with propaganda and the monopoly of mass communications, and with education as indoctrination and training.

Friedrich, Otto. *Decline and Fall.* New York: Harper & Row, 1970.

The human and financial agony of a mass magazine in its death throes is recorded by the last managing editor of the *Saturday Evening Post.* Friedrich considers the reasons why the *Post* could not adjust to changing times and a changing audience.

Friendly, Fred W. *Due to Circumstances Beyond Our Control . . .* New York: Random House, Vintage Books, 1967.

A readable and compelling analysis of how commercial television works, what is wrong with it and how it got that way. An "outsider" now who was an important "insider" at CBS offers important and constructive criticism of perhaps the most influential news and opinion medium in modern society.

Fromm, Erich. *Escape from Freedom.* New York: Holt, Rinehart & Winston, 1941. (paperback edition, Avon Library, 1965).

Using the insights of psychoanalysis, Dr. Fromm discusses the inclinations of people to "escape from freedom" to some kind of institutionalized situation where they will not feel so isolated, anxious and powerless. The flight from individuality and freedom to some form of authoritarianism and control is analyzed in a very interesting and readable manner.

Glessing, Robert J. *The Underground Press in America.* Bloomington: Indiana University Press, 1970.

Glessing examines operations and trends in the underground press by studying thirty of its papers. He cites examples to support his contention that the underground press is leading a graphic, as well as a cultural and political, revolution.

Gross, Gerald, ed. *The Responsibility of the Press.* New York: Simon and Schuster, Clarion paperback, 1966.

Some thirty articles, encompassing a wide range of ethical issues relating to the press' struggle to attain higher standards of responsibility, are found in this useful book. Various journalists and other mass media personalities discuss their concepts of press responsibility to society.

Hall, Edward T. *The Silent Language.* New York: Doubleday & Co., 1959.

An exciting look at nonverbal communication—our manners, behavior, customs, etc—and how they often communicate more plainly than our words. The important part that culture patterns play in international communication is discussed.

Haselden, Kyle. *Morality and the Mass Media.* Nashville: Broadman Press, 1968.

This book, out in a paperback edition, is one of the very few books in recent years that has dealt with the ethics of the mass media in a systematic way. Lucid in style and provocative throughout, it approaches journalistic ethics mainly from a Christian perspective.

Hayakawa, S. I. *Language in Thought and Action.* New York: Harcourt, Brace & World, 1964.

An excellent survey book pointing out the relationship among language, thinking, and acting, and showing how we might improve our communication and our emotional stability through a more sophisticated orientation (general semantics) to language. One of the most readable "translations" of the ideas of Alfred Korzybski into layman's terminology by one of the foremost contemporary proponents of a more scientific use of language.

Heinemann, F. H. *Existentialism and the Modern Predicament.* New York: Harper & Row, 1953. (paperback edition, Harper Torchbook, 1958).

A definitive survey of the origins, achievements, and prospects of existentialism by the German philosopher who coined the term *Existenzphilosophie* in 1929.

Hiebert, Ray E. and Spitzer, Carlton E., eds. *The Voice of Government.* New York: John Wiley & Sons, 1968.

As government, and all of society, becomes more complex and increasingly institutionalized, communication between the various parts of the social mechanism is undergoing extreme strain. This book describes the ways the American government communicates with the public; it shows very clearly in the articles, written by 24 top public information men in Washington, how the government's public information apparatus is institutionalized.

Hocking, William Ernest. *Freedom of the Press: A Framework of Principle.* Chicago: University of Chicago Press, 1947.

This book, by one of the members of the Commission on Freedom of the Press (Hutchins Commission), is one of the best philosophic discussions of press freedom to be found anywhere. It discusses the problems of press freedom, the development of the concept, the conflicting interests of those concerned with press freedom, and the various impediments to such freedom.

Hoffer, Eric. *The True Believer.* New York: Harper, 1951.

This little paperback provides one of the most readable discussions of mass movements and the people who lead them and make them up that has been written. In memorable epigrammatic language, Hoffer reports on the psychology behind mass movements and analyzes the motives and responses, and the potential power, of the true believer, and shows how propaganda is used in the process.

Hoffman, Arthur S., ed. *International Communication and the New Diplomacy.* Bloomington: Indiana University Press, 1968.

A dozen thoughtful essays on the role of communication in international relations, with Margaret Mead, Karl Deutsch, and Daniel Lerner among the contributors.

Hughes, Frank. *Prejudice and the Press.* New York: The Devin-Adair Co., 1950.

A Chicago journalist, obviously disgusted with the 1947 report on the American press by the Commission on Freedom of the Press, presents a well-documented albeit somewhat emotional and biased criticism of the Commission chaired by Robert Hutchins and of its main report, *A Free and Responsible Press.* Undoubtedly the most thorough of the many criticisms of the Hutchins Commission.

Hulteng, John L., and Nelson, Roy P. *The Fourth Estate: An Informal Appraisal of the News and Opinion Media.* New York: Harper & Row, 1971.

This survey book, designed specifically as a text, runs the entire gamut of traditional journalism books with a whole basketful of interesting contemporary issues thrown in for good measure. Mainly a fact-oriented book, but with a few fresh insights and ideas interspliced.

Jaspers, Karl. *Nietzsche: An Introduction to the Understanding of His Philosophical Activity.* Chicago: Henry Regnery Co., 1965.

The leading German existentialist philosopher, in this seminal work on Nietzsche, interprets with deep insights the controversial nineteenth-century thinker. Jaspers analyzes the total philosophic thinking of Nietzsche and shows how he was one of the leaders in existentialist thought. This book was first published in 1935, and this paperback Gateway Edition came out in 1965.

Johnson, Nicholas. *How to Talk Back to Your Television Set.* Boston: Little, Brown & Co., 1970 (paperback edition, Bantam Books, 1970).

An outspoken FCC Commissioner criticizes content and ownership patterns of commercial television. He makes a number of proposals for reforming the medium.

Jung, C. G. *The Undiscovered Self.* Boston: Little, Brown & Co., 1957). Translated from German by F. F. C. Hull. (paperback edition, Mentor, 1958).

One of the greatest of modern psychiatrists pleads that we abandon the concept of the organization man, which he sees as leading to loss of individual freedom. He urges that we bring to light the true nature of the individual human being—"the undiscovered self," and points out the dangers in mass thinking and conformity.

Kendrick, Alexander. *Prime Time: The Life of Edward R. Murrow.* Boston: Little, Brown & Co., 1969.

A biography of a man whose life was inextricably bound up with the early history of news and public affairs broadcasting in both radio and television. In the first chapter, the author reviews the strengths and weaknesses of commercial broadcasting.

Klapper, Joseph T. *The Effects of Mass Communication.* Glencoe, Ill.: The Free Press, 1960.

A basic book for those who are interested in the research that has been done (or had been done up until 1960) on the effects of the mass media on society. Although the book leaves much to be desired so far as coming up with definite "conclusions," it does shed much light on many of the most significant effects of mass communication and points out many areas needing further study.

LeBon, Gustave. *The Crowd: A Study of the Popular Mind.* New York: Ballantine Books, 1969.

This is a paperback edition of LeBon's long-out-of-print classic work on crowd behavior written in 1895. Although dated in some respects, this book still provides one of the clearest and most perceptive discussions available of the nature of crowds and the psychological dispositions of those who compose them.

Levy, H. Phillip. *The Press Council: History, Procedure and Cases.* New York: St. Martin's Press, 1968.

Everybody talks about a press council. England did something about it. This is the most thorough chronicle yet published about the history and attainments of the British Press Council. When reading this book, an American should consider whether this British machinery for encouraging press responsibility is adaptable to the American concept and structure of the press.

Levy, Leonard W. *Legacy of Suppression.* Cambridge: Harvard University Press, 1960.

One of the most original investigations into the evolution of press freedom in America, supported by solid scholarship. Levy reveals that the founding fathers had a concept of press freedom far more restrictive than the one now associated with the First Amendment. Passage of the Alien and Sedition Acts was a trauma that caused press law to move in a more liberal direction.

Liebling, A. J. *The Press.* New York: Ballantine Books, 1961.

Liebling is dead, but the insights of this newspaper reporter live on—although a number of the newspapers he mentions do not. Surprisingly, publishers generally accepted with good humor Liebling's barbs, many of which originally appeared in the columns of the *New Yorker.*

MacNeil, Robert. *The People Machine.* New York: Harper & Row, 1968.

A critical view of the processes of television network news, and the medium's influence on American political life. MacNeil, a former NBC correspondent, now works for the BBC in England.

McGinniss, Joe. *The Selling of the President, 1968.* New York: Trident Press, 1969.

An irreverent diary of an outsider allowed inside to watch the marketing of Richard M. Nixon by his media consultants during the 1968 campaign. The reader must keep in mind that McGinniss was not allowed near the inner sanctum of the Humphrey camp, where similar activities undoubtedly took place.

McLuhan, Marshall. *Understanding Media: The Extensions of Man.* New York: McGraw-Hill, 1965.

Those who like to quote McLuhan should plow through this source book first. Hot, cool, and "the medium is the message" are all here. McLuhan shoots forth several hundred communication ideas in this book, now a classic, although most of the ideas are open to differing interpretations.

Merrill, John C. *The Elite Press: Great Newspapers of the World.* New York: Pitman Publishing Corp., 1968.

Lists and discusses the criteria used to determine "elite" or quality newspapers in both open and closed societies. On the basis of many surveys, the author determines the top one hundred daily newspapers of the world, and rounds out this extended essay on quality journalism by presenting historical and analytical profiles of forty representative "elite" newspapers from every continent.

Mill, John Stuart. *On Liberty.* Chicago: Henry Regnery Co., 1955.

First published in 1859, *On Liberty* is one of the most important tracts on which the libertarian press system is based. This paperback edition, with an introduction by Russell Kirk, is perhaps the best known defense of liberty versus authority, of the individual versus the community.

Miller, Arthur R. *The Assault on Privacy.* Ann Arbor: University of Michigan Press, 1971.

Although this book does not focus on the press as such, it outlines in scholarly and frightening detail the dangers of centralized-computerized information. This book is "must" reading for those interested in the legal and political ramifications of the "personal retrieval" stage of media future discussed in Chapter 17.

Minor, Dale, *The Information War*. New York: Hawthorn Books, 1970 (paperback edition, New York: Tower Publication, 1970).

A forceful survey of news controls exerted by sources such as the military, governmental licensing agencies, monopolistic media, and the networks. Minor frequently writes from his own experience as a newsman in both the print and electronic media.

Moore, G. E. *Principia Ethica*. London: Cambridge University Press, 1966.

This paperback edition of Moore's classic (1903) book on ethics is essential reading for those interested in the basic principles of ethical reasoning. It is concerned basically with these two questions: what kinds of things are intrinsically good; and what kinds of actions ought we to perform?

Ortega y Gasset, José. *The Revolt of the Masses*. New York: W. W. Norton & Co., 1932.

This classic book by one of the greatest of Spanish philosophers is perhaps one of the truly relevant for twentieth-century man. In the last one hundred years in Europe and America the population has more than tripled, and out of this has risen the mass man. Ortega poses, among others, these questions: Can Western culture survive the encroachments of the mass man? Can republican institutions survive this chaotic democracy?

Phelan, John, ed. *Communications Control: Readings in the Motives and Structures of Censorship*. New York: Sheed and Ward, 1969.

A readable book of ten essays dealing with the problems of censorship and the mass media in modern society, with emphasis on censorship and social structure, censorship and aesthetics, and censorship and conflict.

Qualter, Terence H. *Propaganda and Psychological Warfare*. New York: Random House, 1962.

A small paperback with an excellent bibliography, this discussion of propaganda by a Canadian professor is one of the most useful available to the person interested in propaganda. It takes up the theory of propaganda, its development, how it is used in war, and provides a stimulating discussion of the techniques of propaganda.

Rand, Ayn. *For the New Intellectual.* New York: Random House, Signet Books, 1961.

This book, as well as the author's *The Virtue of Selfishness* and *Capitalism: The Unknown Ideal* (by the same publisher), presents Ayn Rand's "objectivist ethics" of rational self-interest. These are excellent books for the journalism student or journalist who would like to divorce his activities from the ethics of altruism and self-sacrifice.

Reardon, Paul C., and Daniel, Clifton. *Fair Trial and Free Press.* Washington: American Enterprise Institute for Public Policy Research, 1968.

A series of lectures, presented as a debate, between Justice Paul C. Reardon of the Supreme Court of Massachusetts and Clifton Daniel, an executive of *The New York Times.* Justice Reardon presents arguments in favor of restrictions on crime and trial coverage that were adopted by the Bar's House of Delegates in February 1968, and Mr. Daniel clearly presents the arguments against such restrictions and points out the danger the "Reardon Report" poses for the free press of the country.

Reston, James. *The Artillery of the Press.* New York: Harper & Row, 1966.

Observations by a veteran *New York Times* news executive and former Washington bureau chief on the difficulties of reporting all the news emanating from a powerful and complex governmental bureaucracy. He also proposes some solutions.

Riesman, David. *The Lonely Crowd.* New Haven: Yale University Press, 1950.

An interesting analysis of the growth of a mass society with the concomitant deemphasis of the individual person. This discussion of depersonalization of society is well worth reading, in spite of its heavy dose of sociological jargon.

Rissover, Fredric, and Birch, David C. (eds.). *Mass Media and the Popular Arts.* New York: McGraw-Hill Book Co., 1971.

An anthology of short but interesting articles by a wide variety of writers on advertising, journalism, cartoons, radio and television, motion pictures, popular music and literature, and public education.

Rivers, William L. *The Adversaries: Politics and the Press.* Boston: Beacon Press, 1970.

A fascinating discussion of press-government relationships, analyzing how officials, elected and appointed, at all government levels deal with the media of mass communication. An excellent discussion of the problem of objective reporting and many other basic issues of journalism. See also, Rivers's *The Opinionmakers* (Beacon Press, 1965) in which the author throws light on some of the most influential journalists in Washington, D.C. and analyzes their impact in the political arena.

Rivers, William L., Peterson, Theodore, and Jensen, Jay W. *The Mass Media and Modern Society.* San Francisco: Rinehart Press, 1971 (2nd ed.).

This book by three journalism professors deals with various aspects of mass media in contemporary society, stressing the various roles of the media and their relationship to government.

Rourke, Francis E. *Secrecy and Publicity: Dilemmas of Democracy.* Baltimore: The Johns Hopkins Press, 1961.

Government information activity is discussed in this excellent little volume, and the issues and problems arising out of this activity are considered in terms of their impact on individual freedom as well as on national security. Rourke contends that twin threats to democracy in the United States are secrecy in government and publicity in government.

Rucker, Bryce W. *The First Freedom.* Carbondale: Southern Illinois University Press, 1968.

An updated version of the 1946 book by the same title by Morris Ernst; it traces the development of newspaper monopolies in the U.S. and pushes the thesis that there is an abandonment of the competition of ideas. A controversial book attempting to make a case for the proposition that press pluralism is disappearing in this country.

Ruesch, Jurgen, and Bateson, Gregory. *Communication: The Social Matrix of Psychiatry.* New York: W. W. Norton & Co., 1951.

A general look at communication largely from a psychiatric perspective, illustrating how communication has become the social matrix of modern life. Discusses communication related to culture, human relations, mental illness, and values, bringing to bear on the subject psychological, anthropological, and philosophical insights.

Russell, Bertrand. *Human Society in Ethics and Politics.* New York: Simon & Schuster, Mentor Books, 1962.

A noted philosopher redefines some traditional ethical terms as he subjects a whole series of conventional assumptions about moral codes, authority, and politics to vigorous rational investigation. Many ideas are easily adaptable to journalistic ethics in the modern world.

Russell, Bertrand. *Power.* New York: W. W. Norton & Co., 1938. (paperback edition, New York: The Norton Library, 1969).

An excellent general discussion of the impulse to power, the types of persons involved in a power struggle, and the different forms of power. Chapter 11 ("The Biology of Organizations") is of particular interest to the student of mass media of communication as institutions and their potential as power wielders. Here is presented an analysis of the trend toward organizing, toward institutionalizing—a process to which the "average man submits because much more can be achieved co-operatively than singly."

Schramm, Wilbur, ed. *The Process and Effects of Mass Communication.* Urbana: University of Illinois Press, 1954.

A very valuable anthology on communication, with a wide variety of readings by leading scholars in the field, dealing with the process of communication, the audiences, channels, and effects. See especially the first article in the volume by Schramm ("How Communication Works") for an excellent survey of the communication process illustrated with helpful diagrams. See also these other books edited by Schramm: *Communication in Modern Society*, Urbana: University of Illinois Press, 1948, and *Mass Communications*, Urbana: University of Illinois Press, 1960.

Shannon, Claude E., and Weaver, Warren. *The Mathematical Theory of Communication.* Urbana: University of Illinois Press, 1949.

Shannon deals with the communication process in mathematical terms, while Weaver discusses many of the theoretical implications in layman's language.

Shibutani, Tamotsu. *Improvised News: A Sociological Study of Rumor.* Indianapolis: The Bobbs-Merrill Co., 1966.

An interesting look at rumor and its relationship to news, with some insights into the nature of news. The paperback also provides the person interested in journalism pertinent observations about news story "objectivity" and documents some of the principal ways of biasing and slanting news (See especially Chapter 2 "The Failure of Formal News Channels.") '

Siebert, Fred S.; Peterson, Theodore; and Schramm, Wilbur. *Four Theories of the Press.* Urbana: University of Illinois Press, 1956 (paperback edition, Illini, 1963).

The four "theories"—authoritarian, libertarian, social responsibility, and Soviet Communist—are analyzed and interpreted by three journalism professors. One of the most widely used, and useful, books available in the area of press systems and concepts.

Skornia, Harry J. *Television and Society: An Inquest and Agenda for Improvement.* New York: McGraw-Hill, 1965.

A book critical of the television industry in America, an industry which the author believes has been carefully shaped, controlled, and corrupted by a handful of greedy, selfish men in top management positions. Broadcasting takes one of its heaviest blows in recent years from this professor of Radio-TV at the University of Illinois. See also: Skornia's *Television and the News* (Palo Alto: Pacific Books, 1968) which elaborates on his earlier book and dips into new areas of concern (e.g. the selection by TV newsmen of the visual over the significant).

Small, William. *To Kill a Messenger: Television News and the Real World.* New York: Hastings House, 1970.

The news director of CBS News in Washington examines the role of television in our society, presenting the inside, factual problems of the everyday decision-making process of news selection and presentation. Small contends that the public does not like having bad news brought into their homes and has turned its anger on the messenger—television—that is bearing bad tidings.

Smith, Alfred G., ed. *Communication and Culture*. New York: Holt, Rinehart and Winston, 1966.

This excellent book of readings, broad in scope, first deals with the theory of human communication (from three approaches: mathematics, social psychology, and linguistic anthropology), and then in the following three main parts it uses this theory to analyze the three dimensions of human communication (syntactics, semantics, and pragmatics).

Sorensen, Thomas C. *The Word War: The Story of American Propaganda*. New York: Harper & Row, 1968.

An even history of the United States Information Agency by one of its former deputy directors. The book considers all aspects of a central dilemma of the USIA: Is it possible to present information truthfully while efficiently fulfilling a propaganda function?

Spinoza, Baruch. *The Ethics: The Road to Inner Freedom*. New York: The Philosophical Library, 1957.

This paperback edition of Spinoza's influential work on "the road to inner freedom" is a valuable guide to the person who wishes to be master of his passions and emotions. It is probably one of the most profound and basic works in all philosophical literature.

Steinberg, Charles S., ed. *Mass Media and Communication*. New York: Hastings House, 1966.

Book of readings covering most aspects of communication by more than twenty writers. See especially articles in Part I ("The Structure and Development of Mass Communication").

Steiner, Gary A. *The People Look at Television*. New York: Knopf, 1963.

A report of perhaps the most thorough television viewing survey ever made in the United States. In essence, it is still not dated, because the same patterns of viewing among economic and educational levels of the population undoubtedly exist today. Intellectuals will be disappointed in Steiner's finding that they tend to avoid "cultural" programming almost as much as the less educated.

Stephenson, William. *The Play Theory of Mass Communication*. Chicago: University of Chicago Press, 1967.

What is most characteristic of mass communication, the author contends, is the entertainment it affords, and this book isolates the neglected play element in newspaper reading, television and movie watching, and radio listening. The theme of the book is that mass communication makes it possible for persons to converge freely upon their own selections, thereby enhancing and developing their private, subjective selves.

Stevenson, Charles L. *Ethics and Language*. New Haven: Yale University Press, 1944.

An American philosopher relates ethics to a sound scientific attitude, and presents an analysis of the meaning of ethical judgments and the methods by which these judgments can be supported. One of the very best ethical discussions from the perspective afforded by studies of language and its impact on morality.

Tebbel, John. *Open Letter to Newspaper Readers*. New York: James H. Heineman Inc., 1968.

A short, concise explanation (and sometimes a lament) for the disappearing and changing traditions in newspaper content. Tebbel, a regular contributor to the communications section of the *Saturday Review*, devotes sections of the book to the editorial page, the comics, the women's section, sports, and cultural news.

Toulmin, Stephen. *The Place of Reason in Ethics*. London: Cambridge University Press, 1968.

This paperback edition of Toulmin's book, first published in 1950, is designed to answer questions such as: How can we decide which ethical arguments are to be accepted, and which denied? What kinds of reasons for moral decisions constitute *good* reasons? And, how far—if at all—can we rely on *reason* in making moral decisions?

Turner, E. S. *The Shocking History of Advertising*. London: Michael Joseph Ltd., 1952.

An amusing, and frequently pointed, commentary on the history of advertising in England and America. The author is an Englishman, so the British perspective prevails. Turner has a lot to say about the ethics of the profession; he also recounts the efforts of advertising to dominate broadcasting in America (successful) and England (unsuccessful).

Whale, John. *The Half-Shut Eye: Television and Politics in Britain and America.* New York: St. Martin's Press, 1969.

By comparing the British and American experiences, this book places in better perspective the problems of both countries in achieving television fairness during political campaigns.

Whitaker, Urban G., Jr., ed. *Propaganda and International Relations.* San Francisco: Howard Chandler, Publisher, 1960.

A fascinating little paperback of readings relative to propaganda and psychological warfare. It looks at the nature of propaganda, discusses propaganda agencies of the leading nations, and presents proposals for government action in psychological warfare.

Whyte, William H., Jr. *The Organization Man.* New York: Simon and Schuster, 1956.

One of the most widely read and discussed books dealing with the change American society is undergoing—from one emphasizing the individual to one that is group oriented. Certainly what Mr. Whyte says about business organizations in general can be related to the mass media of communication as institutions. He gives interesting insights into the group-related person, and sees mass education as a stimulator toward organizing as it increasingly trains people for group activity.

Wiener, Norbert. *The Human Use of Human Beings: Cybernetics and Society.* Boston: Houghton Mifflin Co., 1950 (paperback edition, Avon Books, 1967).

The founder of the science of cybernetics discusses important principles of communication in layman's language, and provides a fascinating case for the need for better communicators (helped by man-made machines) to fight against the powerful, disintegrating forces at work on our world.

Wright, Charles R. *Mass Communication: A Sociological Perspective.* New York: Random House, 1959.

A well-organized, readable little book about the sociology of mass communication, exploring the characteristics that distinguish mass communication from other forms. Considers mass communication as to aims and functions, giving attention to the communicator, the audiences, and the effects.

Index

285